Private Funds: Where and How?

Private Funds: Where and How?

Dechert LLP
www.dechert.com

Bloomsbury Professional

Bloomsbury Professional
An imprint of Bloomsbury Publishing Plc

Bloomsbury Professional Ltd
41–43 Boltro Road
Haywards Heath
RH16 1BJ
UK

Bloomsbury Publishing Plc
50 Bedford Square
London
WC1B 3DP
UK

www.bloomsbury.com

British Library Cataloguing-in-Publication Data

A catalogue record for this book is available from the British Library.

ISBN:	HB	978 1 52650 300 8
	Epub	978 1 52650 301 5
	Epdf	978 1 52650 302 2

Typeset by Phoenix Photosetting, Chatham, Kent
Printed and bound by CPI Group (UK) Ltd, Croydon, CRO 4YY

To find out more about our authors and books visit www.bloomsburyprofessional.com. Here you will find extracts, author information, details of forthcoming events and the option to sign up for our newsletters

Contents

CHAPTER 1

INTRODUCTION

PRIVATE FUNDS: WHERE AND HOW?

A COMPARATIVE ANALYSIS OF THE MAJOR PRIVATE FUND JURISDICTIONS

1.01 Our global private funds practice typically launches several funds every week, on average. This book summarises the key features of some of the fund domiciles that we see in most common use: Bermuda, British Virgin Islands, Cayman Islands, France, Germany, Guernsey, Hong Kong, Ireland, Italy, Jersey, Luxembourg, Malta, Singapore, UAE, UK and USA (Delaware).

1.02 As fund counsel, one of our initial tasks on a fund-raise is usually to help the sponsor select the optimal place to establish a fund's component vehicles. In the case of a master/feeder or parallel fund structure, this may involve multiple jurisdictions. A wide range of factors have a bearing on whether a particular jurisdiction would be appropriate, some of which will be much more relevant than others in any particular case. These include:

- Likely preferences of the target investors, including their familiarity with the jurisdiction and perceptions of it.
- Marketability of funds in that jurisdiction (from a regulatory perspective), including the availability of a 'marketing passport' (for example, funds domiciled outside the EU are currently not able to obtain the Alternative Investment Fund Managers Directive (AIFMD) marketing passport).
- Target investor tax and/or regulatory issues with the jurisdiction.
- Familiarity of the regulator and service providers in the jurisdiction with the investment strategy or asset class.
- Degree of local regulation; accessibility and approach of local regulator.
- Laws on confidentiality, commercial lending, banking, bankruptcy, enforcement, foreign exchange controls or other matters relevant to the strategy of the fund.
- Local tax treatment of the fund and, if relevant, ease of access to double tax treaties relevant to the fund's investment strategy.
- The choice, quality and cost of required local service providers.

- Convenience for holding board meetings.
- Organisation for Economic Co-operation and Development (OECD) status of the jurisdiction, which can be important for some investors and marketing regimes.
- Availability of, and ability to obtain, a listing on a stock exchange, if desired (not necessarily in the place of establishment).
- The speed and cost of local incorporation, licensing and approval processes.
- Stability and predictability of the political system, currency and local infrastructure.
- Whether the choice of fund jurisdiction will enhance the sponsor's ability to pursue its investment program (for example, in the context of private lending strategies, certain European jurisdictions are much more accommodating towards loans made by EU domiciled funds than funds from non-EU domiciles).
- Any existing links between the sponsor and the jurisdiction, including any existing substance or employees that the sponsor has in the jurisdiction; any existing relationships with service providers, directors, etc (this can be helpful in terms of both efficiency and tax planning).
- The availability of, and preferences as to, directors to sit on the fund board, or the board of a general partner or investment holding entities.
- The choice of legal vehicles available in the jurisdiction and their suitability for the asset class and the desired fund-raise.
- The popularity of the jurisdiction relative to others (in general, sponsors will want to follow a well-trodden path rather than blaze a trail; preferring to distinguish themselves on factors other than fund domicile).
- The legal system of the jurisdiction, including the familiarity of the commercial courts with private funds matters and the speed, accessibility and ease of access to the courts or enforcement (which can vary considerably among jurisdictions).

1.03 As it is unlikely that any single jurisdiction will fully satisfy all determining criteria, the process usually involves weighing the most relevant factors in the balance, and either selecting a single fund jurisdiction or creating a parallel or master/feeder structure that allows different jurisdictions to be offered.

1.04 It may be necessary, or otherwise appropriate, to establish a local management company to operate the fund structure. That local company may take investment decisions locally, or may delegate investment decisions back to an investment manager or sub-adviser based elsewhere. Each chapter gives some consideration to this aspect.

1.05 This publication comprises chapters on each fund domicile which have been written in conjunction with numerous partners in our fund formation practice, as well as expert local law firms. However, as is invariably the case with publications of this nature, the information contained herein is provided for general information only. It is not legal advice and should not be relied upon as such. We hope you find it useful.

Dechert LLP

December 2017

CHAPTER 2

BERMUDA

GENERAL DESCRIPTION OF THE JURISDICTION

Geographical, political and legal

2.01 Bermuda is one of the most prominent financial centres in the world. Conveniently located 650 miles east-southeast of North Carolina and less than a seven-hour flight to London, Bermuda is ideally situated to serve as a hub between global markets. Its business community includes a network of fund service professionals with extensive experience in alternative investment products including hedge funds, fund-of-funds, private equity, venture capital, real estate, infrastructure funds, hybrid funds and insurance-linked securities (**ILS**) funds.

2.02 Bermuda takes great pride in its financial regulators and their sensible yet robust approach to regulation and is globally recognised as being a business friendly, pragmatic jurisdiction that is committed to compliance, transparency and regulatory cooperation.

2.03 Bermuda, being the oldest self-governing British Overseas Territory, has developed a diverse and stable political makeup. It employs a multi-party and bicameral parliamentary system, with a premier as head of government and a governor appointed by the Queen as her representative.

2.04 Bermuda's legal system is based on English common law, doctrines of equity and Bermuda statute dating from 1612. Its practices and procedures have seen it respected and recognised for providing effective and fair enforcement of property and contractual rights. The Judicial Committee of the Privy Council in London is the final court of appeal on all matters. As an alternate form of dispute resolution, Bermuda has arbitration legislation which provides that the United Nations Commission on International Trade Law (UNCITRAL) can apply to all international commercial arbitrations held in Bermuda.

Currency and, if appropriate, exchange control measures

2.05 The Bermuda Dollar (**BMD**) is pegged to the US Dollar (**USD**).

Exchange control measures

2.06 Exchange control in Bermuda exists under the Exchange Control Act 1972 and related regulations and is administered by the Bermuda

Monetary Authority (BMA). Generally, exempted companies, permit companies, limited liability companies, exempted partnerships and permit partnerships are able to conduct their day-to-day operations free of exchange control formalities. Such undertakings are able to pay dividends, distribute capital, open and maintain bank accounts in any currency other than resident Bermuda dollars and to acquire assets and meet all liabilities without reference to the BMA.

2.07 Prior approval from the Controller of Foreign Exchange is required regarding (i) the issue or transfer of securities in an exempted company, and (ii) the issue or transfer of securities in a local company to or from non-residents of Bermuda, except where a general permission has been granted as set out in the Notice to the Public of June 2005. Securities issued to investors in a Bermuda fund that is an exempted company are usually within the scope of the general permission.

Membership of relevant international organisations

2.08 Bermuda ensures it complies with the highest regulatory standards through its co-operation with the Organisation for Economic Co-operation and Development (OECD) and the Financial Action Task Force (FATF). The Bermuda Stock Exchange (BSX) enjoys membership of the World Federation of Exchanges and is also an affiliate member of the International Organization of Securities Commissions. There is also a Bermuda network of the Alternative Investment Management Association.

KEY MANDATORY REQUIREMENTS

2.09 Bermuda has not adopted a 'one size fits all' approach. Accordingly, there should not be any issues that would discourage a promoter of a specific fund as the jurisdiction is very solution focused. In terms of advance planning, a promoter will want to factor in the timelines for formation of the vehicles as same day formations are not available. However, any potential issue is easily addressed by forming the vehicles whilst the offering documentation is being finalised with a view to amending constitutional documentation as required once terms are in agreed form.

Although it is possible to launch Bermuda funds on a same-day basis in Bermuda, this is contingent upon any appropriate anti-money laundering (**AML**) registrations having been completed. Again, if these are front loaded alongside the formation process, they are unlikely to cause an issue.

RECENT DEVELOPMENTS

2.10 Below are some notable recent developments in the Bermuda funds industry:

Common Reporting Standard

2.11 Bermuda has adopted the OECD's standards for Base Erosion and Profit Shifting (**BEPS**) compliance for the automatic exchange of financial account information via Common Reporting Standard (**CRS**) and Country-by-Country reports. The OECD has introduced the CRS initiative to improve the exchange of information on financial institutions between jurisdictions. Countries outside the European Union may enter into the Multilateral Competent Authority Agreement, in which they agree to exchange information with participating jurisdictions. Similar to the Foreign Account Tax Compliance Act (**FATCA**) introduced by the US, CRS requires financial institutions which are subject to the rules to report certain information in respect of account holders. Any financial institutions (including custodial institutions, depositary institutions, investment entities and specified insurance companies) resident in Bermuda are now required to establish, implement and comply with procedures to fulfil their obligations under CRS.

Alternative Investment Fund Managers Directive (AIFMD)

2.12 The BMA has signed agreements with most European Union member states on the AIFMD. Bermuda is awaiting a decision by the EU authorities on whether passporting rights will be granted to alternative investment fund managers (AIFMs) operating in non-EU jurisdictions. If permitted, Bermuda-based AIFMs could market funds to European investors.

Data Protection

2.13 Bermuda, as have other comparable jurisdictions, recently enacted legislation which will take effect in 2018 to protect individuals' personal information. In due course, funds will need to take advice to ensure compliance with this new standard.

Limited Liability Companies

2.14 Given the popularity amongst primarily US advisors of the limited liability company (**LLC**), Bermuda has introduced its own LLC product which has been closely modelled on the laws of Delaware. The funds legislation in Bermuda has been amended so as to enable the funds industry to utilise this new vehicle.

THE REGULATION OF INVESTMENT BUSINESS

The local financial regulator

Registrar of Companies (ROC) and Ministry of Finance

2.15 The ROC in conjunction with the Ministry of Finance regulates the ability of overseas companies to engage in or carry on any trade or business in Bermuda.

2.16 Pursuant to the Companies Act 1981, as amended (**Companies Act**), an overseas company is restricted from engaging in or carrying on any trade or business in Bermuda without a permit from the Minister of Economic Development (**Minister**). Overseas companies are deemed to be engaging in or carrying on any trade or business in Bermuda when they establish a physical presence (eg, a branch office), or otherwise occupy premises in Bermuda, or make it known by way of advertisement, or by an insertion in a directory, or by means of letterheads that they may be contacted at a particular address in Bermuda, or are otherwise seen to be engaging in or carrying on any trade or business in Bermuda or from within Bermuda on a continuing basis. That said, an overseas company will not be deemed to engage in or carry on any trade or business in Bermuda where (i) a travelling salesman representing the overseas company who has been permitted to land in Bermuda as such establishes a temporary place of business in Bermuda; (ii) meetings of the overseas company's officers or members are held in Bermuda; or (iii) the overseas company is buying or selling or otherwise dealing in shares, bonds, debenture stock obligations, mortgages or other securities issued or created by an exempted undertaking, a local company or any Bermuda partnership which is not an exempted undertaking.

Bermuda Monetary Authority (BMA)

2.17 Established under the Bermuda Monetary Authority Act 1969, the BMA supervises and regulates financial institutions which it deems to be operating in or from within Bermuda. Under the Bermuda Investment Business Act 2003, as amended (**IBA**), a person cannot carry on or purport to carry on investment business 'in or from' Bermuda without a licence or an exemption from the BMA. The promotion, marketing, offer and sale of investment services or products to Bermuda residents in Bermuda may constitute 'carrying on business'. The term 'investment business' for the purposes of the IBA essentially includes dealing, arranging, managing and advising with respect to investments.

INVESTORS

2.18 Increasingly, investors are shying away from secretive jurisdictions and looking for jurisdictions that have an excellent reputation for transparency and compliance with the highest international standards. Bermuda is recognised as a gold standard in this regard, included on the OECD 'white list' and an early adopter of the 'common reporting standard' for the automatic exchange of tax information.

2.19 The BMA is an independent regulatory body that works closely with industry to create an environment that is conducive for the operation of funds. Legislation is constantly under review to ensure that it is fit for purpose and feedback has been and continues to be solicited from onshore counsel and industry.

2.20 Bermuda's legislative and regulatory framework has been developed in such a way that options are available which allow funds to effectively set the level of regulation that its investor base requires and, in that, is able to appeal to a wide range of investor types, not only a small targeted segment.

2.21 To service the needs of funds and its investors, a deep pool of experienced and qualified professionals work for a range of service providers to provide a one-stop shop if required. However, as there are relatively few requirements for a Bermuda fund's service providers and personnel to be located on island, there is flexibility for a fund to receive Bermuda-based services in combination with those based in other jurisdictions if there is a preference to do so.

2.22 As noted, Bermuda is a common law jurisdiction derived from, and familiar to those with experience of, English law. The court system is recognised for delivering sound judgments with the ultimate court of appeal being the Privy Council in the UK. This gives investors comfort that, in the event of a dispute, there is a mechanism for appropriate resolution.

SETTING UP A FUND

2.23 The primary piece of legislation that regulates funds in Bermuda is the Investment Funds Act 2006, as amended (**IFA**). In order to be within scope of the IFA, the definition of 'investment fund' must be satisfied.

2.24 For there to be an 'investment fund', there must be arrangements whereby persons are essentially able, or intend to be able, to participate in or receive profits or income arising from the acquisition, holding, management or disposition of property.

2.25 Those persons who are to participate cannot have day-to-day control over the management of the property but must have a right to have their units redeemed in accordance with the fund's constitution and prospectus which must include how the redemption price is determined. In a non-Bermuda specific context, this is commonly referred to as being an 'open ended' fund.

2.26 Finally, there is a requirement that the contributions made by the participants together with the profits or income from which payments are to be made to them are pooled and/or that the property is managed as a whole by, or on behalf of, the operator of the fund. In the context of a company and an LLC, the operator is the company or LLC itself. The operator of a limited partnership is the general partner and a unit trust's operator is its trustee.

2.27 In terms of documentation needed to establish the fund, each fund will typically have an offering document or prospectus, documentation between the fund and its service providers and a form of subscription agreement. The constitutional documentation of the fund will depend upon the vehicle used. Typically, the documentation tends to be generic and drafted to defer and be subject to the terms of the offering document or prospectus. If more tailored drafting is preferred, that can of course be accommodated.

2.28 Whether a fund meets the definition of an 'investment fund', and is therefore subject to the provisions of the IFA, often comes down in practice to whether the participants have the right to redeem their units. Where no such right exists, the fund, again in a non-Bermuda specific context, would often be referred to as being 'closed ended'. Where a fund does not satisfy the definition of an 'investment fund', there is no need for the fund to comply with the provisions of the IFA.

2.29 Bermuda offers a range of options for structuring a fund that can be registered under the IFA if it is formed as a company limited by shares, limited partnership, unit trust or the recently introduced LLC. With respect to a company, limited partnership or LLC, the vehicle would be established as an 'exempted' vehicle – this means that the requirement that it is at least 60% owned and controlled by Bermudians does not apply.

2.30 Provisions exist for the creation of segregated account companies so that if there is a desire to effect a separation of liability amongst classes of investor, it is not necessary to incorporate separate entities. The IFA also recognises the possibility of achieving segregation in a unit trust context by the creation of sub-trusts.

2.31 To come within the scope of the IFA, a company limited by shares must qualify as a 'mutual fund company' as defined in the Companies Act. A mutual fund company is a company that has been incorporated for the purpose of investing the moneys of its members for their mutual benefit and has the power to redeem or purchase for cancellation its shares without reducing its authorised share capital. It is a requirement that the memorandum of association of the company states that it is a mutual fund.

2.32 The IFA prohibits investment funds from being operated in or from Bermuda unless they are either authorised, exempted or are deemed to be private funds. An investment fund is a private (otherwise known as excluded) fund if the number of its participants is 20 or less and if the promotion, communication and offer to participate in the investment fund is restricted and not made to the general public.

2.33 Bermuda offers the opportunity to launch a fund on a same day basis without requiring the approval of the BMA. This is known as a Class A exempt fund and, in order to be eligible, a fund must (i) only be offered to qualified participants (essentially high value/experienced natural and legal persons), (ii) have an investment manager in Bermuda or a jurisdiction recognised by the BMA that is either authorised/licensed or has assets under management singly or on a consolidated basis of not less than $100 million, (iii) have an officer, trustee, or representative that is resident in Bermuda with access to the books and records of the fund, (iv) have an auditor, fund administrator, registrar and a custodian (or prime broker) and (v) prepare financial statements in accordance with International Financial Reporting Standards (IFRS) or Generally Accepted Accounting Principles (GAAP).

2.34 If a fund does not meet the Class A exempt criteria, it may qualify as a Class B exempt. The requirements are fundamentally the same save that the BMA need only be satisfied that the investment manager is a fit and proper person. It is also possible to request that the BMA waive one or more of the requirements that would otherwise need to be met for a fund to be granted status as a Class B exempt fund if the BMA is satisfied that appropriate arrangements are in place to safeguard the interests of investors in the fund.

2.35 There are four categories of authorised investment funds under the IFA:

(a) 'institutional fund' – only open to either qualified participants or requires each participant to invest a minimum of $100,000 in the investment fund and must also have an officer, trustee, or representative resident in Bermuda with access to its books and records;

(b) 'administered fund' – the investment fund must have an administrator licensed under the IFA and require each participant to invest a minimum of $50,000 in the investment fund or be listed on a stock exchange recognised by the BMA for this purpose;

(c) 'specified jurisdiction funds' – the appropriate Minister has the ability to recognise that a law or set of laws of a jurisdiction outside of Bermuda in which a fund operates are applicable to such fund (this is particularly popular in the context of unit trusts and Japan);

(d) 'standard funds' – any investment fund that does not otherwise meet the criteria needed to qualify under any of the other categories.

AUTHORISATION PROCEDURE

2.36 The time taken to set up an investment fund will depend upon the form of vehicle used. To form a company, LLC or limited partnership, the timeframe is typically two-three business days. That clock starts when certain forms and applications have been prepared and submitted to the BMA and ROC. This process is typically co-ordinated by a corporate services provider on the island together with a law firm that would work together to guide a prospective operator of a fund through the specific documentation required given the proposed structure of the fund. A unit trust need only have its trust deed executed in order for it to be formed; although the permission of the BMA would be required before units could be issued and transferred.

2.37 The BMA does not need to give its approval of the launch of a Class A exempt fund, instead the operator of a Class A exempt fund simply certifies to the BMA that it meets the criteria for the Class A exemption. The certification form includes certain details surrounding the fund, its offering, investment programme and service providers and a copy of the fund's prospectus must be filed as part of the online process. Once filed, the fund is able to launch that day provided it has been registered as a non-licensed person under the IBA or is otherwise licensed thereunder.

2.38 Similarly, an excluded fund need only file a notification to the BMA that it constitutes an excluded fund. The only requirement is that the fund provides such notification as soon as reasonably practicable following the establishment of the fund.

2.39 The process for a Class B exempt fund and authorised fund is broadly the same as that which applies to a Class A exempt fund except that neither can be launched on a same-day basis as the BMA must first approve the application. With an authorised fund, the time taken to obtain the BMA's approval is typically five-ten business days. In the case of a Class B exempt fund, the BMA actually has a longstop date of ten business days from receipt of the application (subject to a right to request further information) otherwise the application will be deemed to have been approved.

SUPERVISION

2.40 The BMA is responsible for supervision of an authorised fund. In order to be authorised and operate as an authorised fund, an investment fund must (i) prepare annual financial statements that are audited, (ii) have appointed or on authorisation appoint an investment manager, an auditor and a suitably independent administrator to the fund, (iii) ensure that the property of the investment fund is entrusted to an independent custodian licensed or regulated in accordance with the IFA or under the laws of an equivalent jurisdiction, (iv) have operators of the fund who, together with its officers and service providers, are 'fit and proper persons;, (v) satisfy the BMA that the combined experience and expertise of the operator and service provider is suitable for the purposes of the fund, (vi) comply with the requirements of the fund rules and the fund prospectus rules and (vii) ensure that certain provisions are included in the constitutional documents of the fund (largely surrounding the rights and restrictions attaching to the shares, valuation terms and provisions relating to issue and transfer). As the regulator, whether these requirements have been met is for the BMA to determine. In its discretion, the BMA is able to waive some of these requirements.

2.41 Where a fund is not required to file its prospectus with the BMA, consideration should be given as to whether it may be required to be filed with the ROC. Such a determination will turn on its facts and specific legal advice should be sought at that time.

2.42 The BMA has wide powers to regulate the operation of an authorised fund which includes sanctions that may stop short of revocation of a fund's authorisation but which can extend to revocation and can even seek to have a fund wound up. In order to exercise its supervisory role effectively, the BMA also has broad information gathering and investigatory powers.

2.43 Once a fund has launched, changes to the fund, its offering and its service providers will often require notification to, and in certain instances, the consent of the BMA. The BMA is also entitled to receive reports of activities and performance at such times or at such intervals as the BMA may require. No later than six months from the end of a fund's financial year, an authorised investment fund is required to submit a statement to the BMA confirming that the fund has been in compliance with the provisions of the IFA, fund rules and prospectus rules that are applicable to it during that financial year or, alternatively, identify the breaches. In the event that a service provider becomes aware that the assets of an authorised fund have not been invested materially in accordance with its prospectus or offering memorandum or that the general management of an authorised fund is not materially in accordance with the fund's constitution, they must notify the BMA within 14 days of becoming aware and make a written report to the operator of the fund which must be included in the next annual report and, if earlier, the next periodic report.

2.44 Class A and Class B exempt funds are subject to minimal supervision by the BMA. Each year, on or before 30 June, a Class A and Class B exempt fund must make an annual certification to the BMA stating that the fund both satisfies the requirements for exemption and will continue to satisfy them. Together with the certification, such exempt funds must file a copy of its audited financial statements for the preceding year and provide a statement of any material changes to its prospectus or offering memorandum. In addition, a Class B exempt fund must include a schedule to show the changes made to its directors and service providers and is required to obtain the permission of the BMA before changing any of its directors or service providers. The operator of an exempt fund is also required to provide notification in the event that a fund fails to continue to satisfy the qualifying criteria of the Class A or Class B exemption (as applicable) within 14 days of becoming aware.

INVESTMENT RESTRICTIONS

2.45 Bermuda does not impose any investment restrictions on Bermuda funds, however, an authorised fund is required to include any investment restrictions in its constitutional documents and its offering documents are required to disclose any limitations on the fund's investment policy. As part of submissions made to the BMA for both exempt funds (whether Class A or B) or authorised funds, the BMA requires details of any investment restrictions (a cross reference to the relevant page in the offering memorandum will suffice).

FEES

2.46 An exempted company is required to pay an annual fee charged at a variable rate calculated by reference to its 'assessable capital'. The assessable capital of an exempted company is its authorised share capital together with any premium paid for the shares. Share premium is disregarded if the exempted company is a mutual fund company and therefore fund companies in Bermuda typically qualify for the lowest variable rate.

2.47 An LLC and an exempted limited partnership are each required to pay a flat annual fee. A unit trust is not liable to pay any annual fee, although if its manager is a company to which the Companies Act applies, fees would be payable by that company calculated by reference to the number of unit trusts for which it acts as manager.

2.48 Where a company is a Class A or Class B exempt fund, an authorised fund or an excluded fund, an initial fee is payable to the BMA. Class A and B exempt funds and authorised funds (other than specified jurisdiction funds) are also liable to a fee payable on an annual basis.

ACCOUNTS/AUDIT REQUIREMENTS

2.49 A Bermuda company is generally required to prepare annual audited accounts unless waived in accordance with the Companies Act. However, as noted earlier, all investment funds authorised or exempted under the IFA are required to audit their annual financial statements. However, as further noted earlier, there is scope for the BMA to waive that requirement other than in respect of a Class A exempt fund.

SETTING UP A LOCAL MANAGEMENT COMPANY/INVESTMENT MANAGER

2.50 A local investment management company is not required under Bermuda law to manage a Bermuda fund. However, any person who carries on or purports to carry on investment business 'in or from' Bermuda will be required to be licensed unless there is an exemption available to be claimed. To be deemed to be carrying on investment business 'in or from' Bermuda, a person must carry on investment business from a place of business maintained by such person in Bermuda, employing staff and paying salaries and other expenses in connection with that business. This means that an investment manager that has a registered office in Bermuda but not a physical office will not fall within the ambit of the IBA and will not required to be licensed.

2.51 An application for a licence under the IBA may be made by a natural or legal person. Where an applicant is a legal person, it must have the objects and powers in its memorandum of association, articles of incorporation or similar document that enable it to carry on investment business of the type proposed by the applicant.

2.52 The IBA Application Form must be submitted and completed by a senior executive and must be accompanied by certain supporting documents.

Minimum Criteria

2.53 In giving consideration to whether a licence should be granted, the BMA is required to be satisfied that certain minimum criteria as stipulated within the IBA are met. The BMA has published a Statement of Principles which provides guidance on the BMA's approach to interpreting the minimum criteria and in exercising its power to grant, revoke or restrict a licence and in exercising its power to obtain information, reports and to require production of documents.

2.54 The BMA will not grant a licence unless it is satisfied that the minimum criteria are met or are capable of being met by the applicant. However, even when so satisfied, the BMA always retains discretion not to grant a licence – notably if it sees reason to doubt that the criteria will be met on a continuing basis or if it considers that for any reason there might be significant threats to the interests of clients or potential clients.

Continuing Obligations

2.55 An investment provider who carries on investment business and who holds a licence under the IBA has a duty with respect to their ongoing operations including the preparation and filing of financial statements and reports, disclosure of the fact that they are in possession of an IBA licence, compliance with a code of conduct and the obligation to seek permission with respect to changes to the investment provider and its controllers. The BMA has the power to carry out onsite inspections to ensure that the licensed entity is in compliance with the IBA. If a licensed entity is not fulfilling the minimum criteria for licensing, or does not comply with any obligation imposed on it by the BMA under the IBA, then the BMA may revoke the licence. There are also offences and penalties that can be imposed under the IBA for non-compliance.

Annual Licence Fee

2.56 Each successful applicant company is required to pay an annual licence fee based on the business activity it undertakes. The annual fees must be paid on or before 31 March of each calendar year. As of 1 April 2015 (and which remain unchanged), the annual fees are as follows:

Advising or arranging deals – collective investment schemes	BMD$2,163.00
Dealing, arranging deals, or managing investments (not holding them)	BMD$5,408.00
Dealing, arranging deals, or managing investments (holding client investments)	BMD$10,815.00

Where an investment provider is part of a group which is subject to consolidated supervision by the BMA as home regulator under the IBA and that group has consolidated net assets not exceeding $500 million	BMD$62,470.00
Where an investment provider is part of a group which is subject to consolidated supervision by the BMA as home regulator under the IBA and that group has consolidated net assets exceeding $500 million	BMD$249,827.00

OTHER KEY SERVICE PROVIDERS

2.57 Given Bermuda's longstanding position in the market, it should be no surprise that there is a wealth of service providers available on the island with a deep bench of talent which frequently is able to boast of international experience. Any residency requirements are generally satisfied by engaging a Bermuda resident company secretary and/or directors and officers and there is no requirement to have local third-party service providers although, as shown from the preceding paragraphs where certain criteria has been outlined, they do offer one way of evidencing suitably qualified service providers.

2.58 Where any service provider does not have a demonstrable authorisation, exclusion, exemption or license and purports to be based in Bermuda, an increased level of diligence should be applied to ensure compliance with local laws.

TAX REGIME

2.59 Bermuda is fiscally neutral in the sense of having no tax applicable to the establishment and operation of investment funds. Bermuda investment funds are not subject to any tax, as there are no Bermuda corporation, profit, withholding, capital gains or income taxes applicable to an investment fund or to its share or unit holders or partners which are not resident in Bermuda.

2.60 Upon application, usually made just after incorporation of a mutual fund company or formation of a unit trust fund or partnership fund, the Minister will issue a certificate confirming the exemption of the investment fund from such taxes, which is presently expressed to operate until 31 March 2035. This assurance is given as a matter of course to any investment fund with exempted status.

2.61 In addition to the above, instruments executed by or in relation to an investment fund are exempt from stamp duties. Thus, stamp duties are not payable upon, for example, an instrument that affects the transfer or assignment of a share, unit or interest in an investment fund.

Foreign Account Tax Compliance Act and the Common Reporting Standard

2.62 Bermuda may become subject to US withholding tax under certain US tax provisions commonly known as the Foreign Account Tax Compliance Act (FATCA) which imposes a reporting regime and a 30% withholding tax on certain payments of US source income and the proceeds from the disposition after 31 December 2018 of property of a type that can produce US source interest or dividends. This is directed at (i) any non-US financial institution (a 'foreign financial institution', or 'FFI' (as defined by FATCA)) that does not become a 'Participating FFI by entering into an agreement with the Internal Revenue Service (**IRS**) to provide the IRS with certain information in respect of its account holders and investors or is not otherwise exempt from or in deemed compliance with FATCA and (ii) any investor (unless otherwise exempt from FATCA) that does not provide information sufficient to determine whether the investor is a US person or should otherwise be treated as holding a 'United States account' of the relevant FFI.

2.63 Bermuda has signed an intergovernmental agreement with the US government to facilitate the implementation of FATCA in Bermuda (**Bermuda IGA**). The Bermuda IGA directs and enables any 'Bermuda Financial Institution' (**BFI**) to register with the IRS and comply with the terms of an FFI Agreement, as modified by the Bermuda IGA. Under the Bermuda IGA, a BFI generally includes a 'Financial Institution' (**FI**) organised under the laws of Bermuda, but excluding any branch of such FI that is located outside Bermuda.

2.64 There is still the risk that Bermuda tax laws may change and that exempted companies may become subject to new Bermuda taxes following the expiration of the current exemption after 2035.

2.65 In an effort to minimise the damaging effects of tax competition, the OECD took measures to establish open communication between members and non-members alike. The mandate for the published reports was to reduce or eliminate the effects of income tax havens and preferential income tax regimes. The OECD, noticing Bermuda's commitment to a high standard of regulation, transparency, and open reporting, has placed the island on the OECD 'white list.'

BEPS and Country by Country Reporting

2.66 As mentioned in the Recent Developments section above, the OECD, together with the G20 countries, has committed to reducing perceived abusive global tax avoidance, referred to as BEPS. As part of this commitment, an action plan has been developed to address BEPS with the aim of securing revenue by realigning taxation with economic activities and value creation by creating a single set of consensus-based international tax rules. As part of the BEPS project, new rules dealing with the operation of double tax treaties, the definition of permanent establishments, interest deductibility and how hybrid instruments and hybrid entities are taxed have already been introduced, or their introduction is anticipated.

LOCAL STOCK EXCHANGE

2.67 The Bermuda Stock Exchange (BSX), established in 1971, is the local securities market specialising in offshore securities. With over 700 listed issuers, it is a fully electronic listing program that offers domestic and international options.

2.68 As a full member of the World Federation of Exchanges, the BSX has been acknowledged by its peers as meeting the highest regulatory and operational standards. The BSX is bound neither by the US Securities Exchange Commission (SEC) regulations nor European Union Listings Directive. Internationally recognised as an appealing venue for the listing of ILS products, fixed income structures and investment fund structures, the BSX also operates a Mezzanine Market for early stage companies. The BSX has a light but effective regulatory environment which makes it both nimble and innovative when it comes to new listings.

2.69 The BSX enjoys the recognition, designation and/or authorisation by a significant number of foreign regulators/international organisations including being a full member of the World Federation of Exchanges.

Advantages of Listing on the BSX

2.70 The key advantages of the BSX are:

- efficient, time sensitive admission process;
- reasonable fee structure;
- listed Bermuda companies enjoy free transferability of their securities;
- responsive and approachable;
- international standards of issuer regulations;
- premier location;
- high regulatory and operational standards;
- Launch and List facility agreed between the BMA and the BSX enables formation and listing approvals of investment funds to run concurrently;
- dematerialising securities through the Bermuda Securities Depository (BSD) removes the need for physical delivery and settlement;
- use of the NASDAQ OMX X-stream trading platform (as used in over 50 countries);
- securities listed on the BSX are free from stamp duty on transfer in Bermuda;

- flexibility – for example, the BSX is popular with hedge funds because there are no minimum capital requirements or investment restrictions (with the exception of disallowing a fund to take control of its underlying investments).

Securities Listed on the BSX

2.71 Many different instruments can be listed on the BSX, including interests in investment funds. Securities that have a primary listing on a recognised exchange may also obtain a secondary listing on the BSX.

CONFIDENTIALITY LAWS

2.72 Where a company is a mutual fund company, the register is not publicly available for inspection. A register of directors and officers is however so available.

2.73 A limited partnership and LLC's register of limited partners/members is prima facie available for inspection by all members/limited partners, however, this can be trumped by provisions of the partnership or operating agreement (as the case may be). There is no ability to withhold the identities of the general partner(s) or manager(s) of a limited partnership or LLC.

2.74 Absent a right in the trust deed, there is no right to receive a register of unitholders of a unit trust.

2.75 Vehicles in Bermuda are not required to maintain a register of charges, although such registers are maintained by the ROC and Registry General and are publicly available for inspection.

ANTI-MONEY LAUNDERING LAWS

2.76 The Proceeds of Crime Act 1997 (POCA), the Anti-Terrorism (Financial and Other Measures) Act 2004 (Anti-Terrorism Act), the Proceeds of Crime (Anti-Money Laundering and Anti-Terrorist Financing) Regulations 2008 (AML/ATF Regulations), the Proceeds of Crime (Anti-Money Laundering and Anti-Terrorist Financing Supervision and Enforcement) Act 2008 (Supervision and Enforcement Act) and the Financial Intelligence Agency Act 2007 make up the key elements of Bermuda's anti-money laundering (AML) and anti-terrorist financing (ATF) legislation.

2.77 Bermuda has worked hard to enhance its AML and ATF legal framework so as to ensure that it complies with the 2012 revised recommendations and corresponding 2013 methodology of the Financial Action Task Force (FATF) and other international AML standards.

2.78 Of most relevance in the context of a fund is the requirement that, if any person resident in Bermuda knows or suspects or has reasonable grounds for knowing or suspecting that another person is engaged in criminal conduct or is involved with terrorism or terrorist property and the information for that knowledge or suspicion came to their attention in the course of business, such as administering the fund, the person is required to report such knowledge or suspicion to (i) the Financial Intelligence Agency (FIA) (pursuant to POCA if the disclosure relates to criminal conduct or money laundering), or (ii) a police officer of the rank of constable or higher pursuant to the Anti-Terrorism Act if the disclosure relates to involvement with terrorism or terrorist financing and property. These reports are called Suspicious Activity Reports and should be filed electronically via the FIA's online reporting system, goAML. Any such report is not treated as a breach of confidence or of any restriction upon the disclosure of information imposed by any enactment or otherwise and the fund's offering documents will often highlight that an investor shall have no claim whatsoever against a fund's investment manager, administrator or the fund itself in respect of any such required disclosure.

2.79 In order to comply with Bermuda's legislation and related regulations, a fund that is authorised under the IFA, is a Class A or Class B exempt fund or specifically excluded under section 6 of the IFA (or more specifically, its operator), is required to adopt and maintain AML policies and procedures. To assist regulated institutions with AML/ATF compliance, the BMA has published an updated set of guidance notes in September 2016 that can be relied upon to instate appropriate policies and procedures.

2.80 Whilst a fund may, and commonly does, delegate the maintenance of its AML/ATF procedures (including the acquisition of due diligence information) to its administrator, the fund retains ultimate responsibility for ensuring that AML procedures and laws are being adhered to. In order for such delegation to be permissible, the administrator must be located in a jurisdiction which has at least equivalent AML regulations as those found in Bermuda or require the administrator to adopt Bermuda-compliant policies and procedures under a service level agreement whilst being periodically monitored for adherence to Bermuda requirements via testing of the administrator's AML/ATF controls, systems and procedures. However, it is the responsibility of the fund to ensure equivalence given that the BMA has not issued a list of which jurisdictions meet that standard.

2.81 Prior to the launch of a Class A or Class B exempt fund or a fund that is specifically excluded under section 6 of the IFA, where not already so registered or otherwise licensed, the operator must register as a non-licensed person with the BMA. In order to so register, the BMA must be satisfied with respect to its AML policies and procedures (or those upon which it is relying eg the administrator). As part of an application to be an authorised fund, there is a requirement to describe the fund's AML and ATF policies and procedures to ensure compliance with the AML/ATF Regulations.

2.82 In all cases, the fund must be in a position to monitor the business relationship with its subscribers. This includes screening all subscribers against international sanctions lists. In order for a fund to follow such procedures, subscribers will likely be required to provide evidence to verify their source of funds, identity, residential address, date and place of birth and nationality of any individual. If the subscriber is a legal entity or arrangement such as a group of directors, trustees, or beneficial owners, the fund will need to identify not only the legal structure of that entity or arrangement but also the individuals who comprise that entity or relationship, specifically understand the control or ownership structure, identify beneficial owners and verify directors and other persons exercising control over the management of the entity or arrangement. It is relatively standard to note in a fund's offering memorandum the right to gather such information and set out what may happen in the event of delay or failure on the part of the subscriber to provide the same.

CONCLUDING REMARKS: WHAT ARE THE JURISDICTION'S UNIQUE SELLING POINTS?

2.83 Bermuda is a jurisdiction, uniquely located between the UK and US, therefore able to provide advice in a time zone convenient to both. That advice is provided in respect of a flexible and well-developed set of laws and regulations drafted with the needs of industry at heart including a statutorily clear ability to launch a fund on a same day basis. The BSX is one of the most appealing offshore securities exchanges for the listing of equities, investment fund structures, fixed income structures, and hedge fund structures. With its premier reputation in the insurance sector, Bermuda also offers unparalleled access to the insurance-linked securities markets. As the race to the top in terms of regulatory compliance continues, Bermuda is well placed to service its existing client base and attract new business.

CHAPTER 3

THE BRITISH VIRGIN ISLANDS

GENERAL DESCRIPTION OF THE JURISDICTION

3.01 The British Virgin Islands (**BVI**) are a group of islands in the Caribbean located about 65 miles east of Puerto Rico, north of the Leeward Islands and adjacent to the US Virgin Islands. The largest and most populated island is Tortola, the capital of which is Road Town, the financial centre of the BVI.

3.02 The BVI is a British Overseas Territory and an internally self-governing dependence, with a ministerial system of government adopted in 1967. The UK remains responsible for the BVI's foreign policy, defence and internal security. The official and spoken language is English. The local currency is the US dollar and there are no exchange controls, nor is there any stock exchange in the BVI. The BVI is in time zone GMT minus four hours or five hours, depending on the time of the year.

3.03 The substantive law of the BVI is based on English common law, complemented by local statutes, and its legal system is based on that of England and Wales, with an ultimate appeal to the English Privy Council. English common law is persuasive, but not binding, in the BVI Courts.

3.04 As a British Overseas Territory, the BVI participates in most international organisations through the UK. However, it is also a member of a number of international organisations in its own right, including being an associate member of both CARICOM and the OECS.

KEY MANDATORY REQUIREMENTS

3.05

- All mutual funds (as defined in the BVI Securities and Investment Business Act 2010 (**SIBA**) and set out in detail below) must be registered or recognised with the BVI Financial Services Commission (the **FSC**). The definition of mutual fund under SIBA includes most open-ended BVI hedge funds (ie funds in which investors do have the right to redeem their fund interests on demand in accordance with the fund documents).
- Closed-ended funds (ie funds in which investors do not have the right to redeem their fund interests on demand) are generally not regulated in the BVI. However, BVI managers of closed-ended funds are regulated under SIBA.

- Any person or entity undertaking 'investment business' in or from within the BVI must be regulated to do so, unless a relevant exemption applies. 'Investment business' under SIBA includes activities such as investment management and fund administration.
- The BVI has strict anti-money laundering laws and the acceptance of subscription monies into a fund is subject to anti-money laundering regulations.

RECENT DEVELOPMENTS

3.06 The BVI recently introduced two new types of open-ended funds in the BVI, being the 'incubator fund' and the 'approved fund'. These funds are specifically aimed at start-up managers and/or smaller, private offerings. Incubator and approved funds are discussed in further detail below.

THE REGULATION OF INVESTMENT BUSINESS

Regulator

3.07 The FSC is the local financial services regulator in the BVI. The functions of the FSC are numerous, but its primary function is to supervise and regulate entities that are authorised, licensed, registered or recognised under BVI financial services legislation. The FSC also oversees the recognition or registration of open-ended funds, fund managers and those marketing investment funds in the BVI that fall within the scope of SIBA or the Mutual Funds Regulations 2010 (as amended) (the **Regulations**).

3.08 The FSC's Licensing and Supervisory Committee is responsible for assessing all applications for licences and certificates to operate in and from within the BVI. The committee also maintains ongoing supervisions of authorised entities (including BVI mutual funds, managers and administrators) to ensure continuous compliance with relevant laws and regulations.

3.09 There is no central bank or other relevant regulator for private funds in the BVI.

SIBA contain restrictions on (i) carrying on 'investment business' in or from within the BVI; and (ii) acting as a mutual fund in or from within the BVI.

Regulation overview

3.10 Investment business – SIBA provides that any person carrying on 'investment business' (which includes acting as the manager of a mutual fund and managing investments belonging to another person involving the exercise of discretion (other than as a manager of a mutual fund)) in or from within the BVI must be licensed or approved to do so by the FSC. Subject to limited exceptions, this means that any BVI entity acting as the manager of a fund (whether open-ended or closed-ended) must be licensed or approved to do so by the FSC. Generally, a non-BVI company does not need to be authorised by the FSC to act as the manager of a BVI fund, unless it has a physical presence in the BVI or solicits a person in the BVI to provide the fund management services. BVI investment managers may either be licensed by the FSC under SIBA or approved by the FSC pursuant to the Approved Manager Regulations 2012 (as amended) (an **Approved Manager**). Please see below for further details.

3.11 Funds – SIBA prohibits from carrying on business as a mutual fund (defined below) in or from within the BVI, unless the fund is registered or recognised with the FSC under SIBA or the Securities and Investment Business (Incubator and Approved Funds) Regulations 2015 (the **AF Regulations**) (as relevant).

INVESTORS

3.12 The statutory and regulatory framework in the BVI has typically attracted funds that seek investment from high net worth individuals and other sophisticated and institutional investors rather than funds aiming to raise money through retail channels, though there are regulatory categories that would facilitate the registration with the FSC of funds wishing to raise money in this way.

SETTING UP A FUND

Types of fund

3.13 There are five categories of open-ended 'mutual' funds in the BVI, being private funds, professional funds, public funds, incubator funds and approved funds. Closed-ended funds fall outside of the scope of BVI funds law and are therefore not generally regulated in the BVI.

Definition of a 'mutual' fund under SIBA

3.14 A mutual fund (**mutual fund**) is defined under SIBA as a company or any other body, a partnership or a unit trust incorporated, formed or organised, whether under the laws of the BVI or the laws of any other country which:

(a) *collects and pools investor funds for the purpose of collective investment, and*

(b) *issues fund interests that entitle the holder to receive on demand or within a specified period after demand an amount computed by reference to the value of a proportionate interest in the whole or in a part of the net assets of the company, the partnership, the unit trust or other similar body, as the case may be.*

3.15 This includes an umbrella fund whose shares are split into a number of different class funds or sub-funds, and a fund that has a single investor that is a fund not registered or recognised under SIBA. The definition of fund interest under SIBA excludes debt and, therefore, funds issuing debt rather than equity interests will generally fall outside of the scope of SIBA.

Professional funds

3.16 Professional funds are the most popular BVI investment funds product and are aimed at high net worth, professional investors.

3.17 The key features of a professional fund are:

- investors must be professional investors or exempted investors (see 'eligible investors' below for definitions);
- minimum investment is US$100,000 or its currency equivalent (unless the investor is an exempted investor (being the manager, administrator, promoter or underwriter or an employee of such));
- can launch for up to 21 days prior to obtaining FSC recognitions, so long as the application is lodged with the FSC within 14 days of launch;
- must have a manager, administrator, auditor and custodian or obtain exemption(s) from such requirement. The functionaries do not need to be BVI based but must be from a recognised jurisdiction (see below for table of recognised jurisdictions); and
- must file annual audited accounts with the FSC or obtain an exemption from such requirement.

Private funds

3.18 Private funds are also very popular with investors. They are aimed at offerings made on a private basis only.

3.19 The key features of a private fund are:

- maximum of 50 investors or invitations to subscribe for, or purchase, interests in the fund are made on a private basis only. A 'private basis' is defined under SIBA as including an invitation that is made: (i) to a specified person (however described) and is not calculated to result in fund interests becoming available to other persons or to a large number of persons; or (ii) by reason of a private or business connection between the person making the invitation and the investor;
- no minimum investments;

- no investor eligibility requirements;
- requires FSC prior consent to launch;
- must have a manager, administrator, auditor and custodian or obtain exemption(s) from such requirement. The functionaries do not need to be BVI based but must be from a recognised jurisdiction (see below for table of recognised jurisdictions); and
- must file annual audited accounts with the FSC or obtain an exemption from such requirement.

Public funds

3.20 A public fund is a mutual fund which is not a professional fund or a private fund. The product is generally utilised by managers looking to make retail offerings and is therefore subject to more stringent regulation and scrutiny. Public funds fall outside of the subject of this chapter so are not covered in further detail.

Incubator funds

3.21 An incubator fund is an open-ended fund that is designed for start-up managers who are looking to come to market quickly and cost efficiently to create an initial track record over a set period of time.

3.22 The key features of an incubator fund are:

- it can have a maximum of 20 investors, who must be 'sophisticated private investors' (see below for definition);
- the minimum investment for each investor is US$20,000; and
- the net assets must not exceed US$20,000,000 or its equivalent in any other currency.

3.23 An incubator fund is authorised to initially operate for a period of two years, which may be extended to three years on application to the FSC. At the end of the initial two-year period, or if the incubator fund has more than the authorised number of investors or net assets for an incubator fund, it must either convert to an approved fund, professional fund or private fund or liquidate.

Approved Fund

3.24 An approved fund is an open-ended fund that is designed for small, private funds or friends and family funds. Unlike the incubator fund, there are no eligibility requirements, no minimum level of investment is required and there is no limit to the time that it may exist as an approved fund (so long as it does not breach any of the relevant limits as described below).

3.25 The key features of an approved fund are:

- it can have a maximum of 20 investors; and
- the net assets must not exceed US$100,000,000 or its equivalent in any other currency.

Recognised foreign fund

3.26 An overseas fund that is not a BVI fund and wants to promote itself in or from within the BVI, or solicit an individual within the BVI to subscribe for or purchase any of its fund interests, must apply to the FSC for, and be granted, recognition as a recognised foreign fund before undertaking such regulated activity. Once recognition is granted, the recognised foreign fund may then only undertake such regulated activities in accordance with the provisions of SIBA. A non-BVI fund is not deemed to be soliciting individuals within the BVI if the subscription or purchase of fund interests is made as a result of an approach made by the individual to the non-BVI fund without any solicitation being made by or on behalf of the non-BVI fund.

STRUCTURE

3.27 A private or professional fund can be established as a BVI business company, a limited partnership or a unit trust. An incubator or approved fund can be established as a BVI business company or a limited partnership. BVI business companies and limited partnerships are most commonly used as the vehicle for a BVI closed-ended fund.

3.28 Companies are by far the most common vehicle used for open-ended funds in the BVI. A BVI business company is subject to the BVI Business Companies Act 2004 which is widely regarded as one of the most modern and progressive company law regimes in the world.

3.29 Every BVI business company is required to have a BVI registered agent and registered office and a company is incorporated by its proposed BVI registered agent filing memorandum and articles of association, signed by the BVI registered agent as incorporator, with the BVI Registrar of Corporate Affairs together with a 'consent to act' as registered agent and paying the annual government fee (detailed below). Subject to the receipt by the BVI-registered agent of all necessary client take-on information, the incorporation of a BVI company can generally be done on a same-day basis.

3.30 A BVI international limited partnership (**ILP**) is required to have a BVI-registered agent and registered office. An ILP does not have a separate legal personality and is formed by at least one general partner and one limited partner signing articles for the ILP and giving them to the proposed BVI-registered agent. The registered agent must then sign a memorandum for the

ILP and file it with the FSC and pay the registration fee (detailed below). An ILP is formed pursuant to the BVI Partnership Act 1996 (as amended). ILPs are more commonly used for closed-ended funds and private equity funds than open-ended funds.

3.31 Unit trusts are not commonly used for the establishment of closed-ended or open-ended funds in the BVI. A unit trust is formed though a declaration of trust by the trustee alone or by a trust deed executed by both the trustee and the investment manager.

SEGREGATED PORTFOLIO COMPANIES

3.32 A segregated portfolio company (**SPC**) is a single legal entity within which may be established various segregated portfolios. The assets and liabilities of each segregated portfolio are legally separate from those of other segregated portfolios. An SPC is formed in a similar manner to a business company except that only private, professional or public funds (or certain insurance companies) may be incorporated as SPCs and the prior written consent of the FSC is required to incorporate an SPC.

ELIGIBLE INVESTORS

Professional funds

3.33 SIBA provides that the fund interests in a professional fund shall only be issued to professional investors or exempted investors. A professional investor is defined under SIBA as a person:

- whose ordinary business involves, whether for that person's own account or the account of others, the acquisition or disposal of property of the same kind as the property, or a substantial part of the property, of the fund; or
- who has signed a declaration that he or she, whether individually or jointly with his or her spouse, has net worth in excess of US$1 million (or its currency equivalent) and that he or she consents to being treated as a professional investor.

3.34 An exempted investor (**Exempted Investor**) is the investment manager, administrator, promotor or underwriter of a fund, and employee of the investment manager or promoter, or such other person as the FSC may specify from time to time.

Private funds

3.35 There are no eligibility requirements for approved funds.

Incubator funds

3.36 An investor in an incubator fund must be a 'sophisticated private investor' which is defined under the AF Regulations as being 'a person who has been invited to invest in an incubator fund and the amount of his or her initial investment is not less than US$20,000'.

Approved Fund

3.37 There are no eligibility requirements for approved funds.

AUTHORISATION PROCEDURE

3.38 The authorisation process for recognition or registration of a BVI fund depends on the type of fund. Details for each category are set out below.

Private and professional funds

3.39 An application for recognition of a private and professional fund shall be sent to the FSC in the approved form and shall specify:

- the address of the fund's place of business in the BVI;
- the name and address of each of the fund's directors;
- the name and address of the fund's authorised representative;
- if the fund is a unit trust, the name and address of the trustee;
- the address of any place of business that the fund may have outside the BVI;
- the name and address of the fund's auditor;
- the name and address of each of the fund's functionaries;
- whether the fund has issued, or intends to issue, an offering document;
- in the case of a foreign fund, written details of the nature and scope of the fund's business; and
- such other information as may be required by the approved form.

3.40 The application must be accompanied by:

- a copy of the fund's constitutional documents;
- a copy of the fund's certificate of incorporation, formation or registration or equivalent document;
- details in relation to exemption applications (if any);
- a copy of the offering document (if relevant); and

- if the fund is not issuing an offering document, an explanation as to why and how relevant information will be provided to investors.

3.41 A professional fund may carry on business for up to 21 days before obtaining FSC recognition, so long as the application for recognition is lodged with the FSC within 14 days of launch. This means it is possible for professional funds to come to market very quickly in the BVI. Unlike a professional fund, a private fund must obtain its FSC recognition before launch. However, in our experience, this is usually a fairly quick process that takes a couple of weeks.

Incubator and approved funds

3.42 An application for approval of an incubator fund or approved fund shall be sent to the FSC in the approved form and shall include the following information:

- details of the applicant and the intended date to commence business;
- the name and address of each of the fund's directors and a CV for each director;
- the name and address of the fund's authorised representative;
- proof of classification; and
- details of the fund's administrator (for an approved fund only).

3.43 The application must be accompanied by:

- the constitutional documents specifying whether the applicant intends to be an incubator fund or approved fund;
- a written description of the investment strategy of the proposed incubator fund or approved fund;
- a written warning which the incubator fund or approved fund will issue to investors or potential investors as provided in the AF Regulations; and
- such other information as may be required in the prescribed form.

3.44 Incubator and approved funds can commence business within two (2) days from the date the FSC receives a complete application in accordance with the AF Regulations.

SUPERVISION

3.45 BVI funds have a number of statutory requirements and continuing obligations. It is not possible to list all such continuing obligations in this chapter but they include the below in relation to ongoing filings and record keeping:

Filings

3.46 A private or professional fund is required to make various filings with the FSC including but not limited to filing:

- changes to its place of business;
- amendments to its offering or constitutional documents;
- a notification of the appointment of a new functionary; and
- a notification of the change of directors.

Record-keeping

3.47 A private or professional fund is required to maintain records that are sufficient:

- to show and explain its transactions;
- to enable its financial position to be determined with reasonable accuracy, at any time;
- to enable it to prepare such financial statements and make such returns as it is required to make under BVI law; and
- if applicable, to enable its financial statements to be audited.

3.48 Such records must be retained for a period of at least five years after completion of the relevant transaction.

Incubator and approved funds

3.49 Incubator and approved funds must be approved by the FSC and pay an annual approval fee (detailed below). Incubator and approved funds have limited ongoing obligations, which include the requirement to have at least two directors (one of whom must be an individual) and an authorised representative, and notifying the FSC within 14 days of key changes to the funds in accordance with the AF Regulations.

INVESTMENT RESTRICTIONS

3.50 No investment restrictions are imposed on the investment powers of BVI funds, making each category suitable for use as hedge and other alternative investment funds.

FEES

Application fees

3.51 Private or professional fund: US$700.

3.52 Incubator or approved fund: US$1,000.

Annual FSC fees

3.53 Private or professional fund: US$1,000.

3.54 Incubator or approved fund: US$1,000.

Annual registry fees

3.55 For a company:

3.56 US$1100 if the fund is authorised to issue in excess of 50,000 shares.

3.57 US$350 if the fund is authorised to issue up to a maximum of 50,000 shares.

3.58 For a limited partnership: US$500.

ACCOUNTS/AUDIT REQUIREMENTS

3.59 A BVI private or professional fund is required to have an auditor and file audited financial statements on an annual basis within six months of the end of the fund's financial year, or have obtained an exemption from the requirement to do so. It is also required to file a 'mutual funds annual return' with the FSC on an annual basis.

3.60 Incubator and approved funds are required to make semi-annual returns to the FSC regarding the fund's assets and the number of investors and file annual financial statements to the FSC. There is no requirement for the financial statements of an incubator or approved fund to be audited.

SETTING UP A LOCAL MANAGEMENT COMPANY/INVESTMENT MANAGER

3.61 Fund management is a regulated activity under BVI law pursuant to SIBA. SIBA provides that any person carrying on 'investment business' (which includes acting as the manager of a mutual fund and managing investments belonging to another person involving the exercise of discretion (other than as manager of a mutual fund)) in or from within the BVI must be licensed or approved to do so by the FSC.

3.62 Subject to limited exceptions, this means that any BVI entity acting as the manager of a fund (whether open-ended or closed-ended) must be licensed or approved to do so by the FSC. Generally, a non-BVI company does not need to be authorised by the FSC to act as the manager of a BVI fund, unless it has a physical presence in the BVI or solicits a person in the BVI to provide the fund management services.

3.63 BVI investment managers may either be licensed by the FSC under SIBA or approved by the FSC pursuant to the Approved Manager Regulations 2012 (as amended) (an approved manager). The approved manager product is by far the most popular option, and given there are very few new applications for SIBA licensed investment managers following the introduction of the popular approved manager regime in 2012, this chapter focuses on the approved manager regime.

3.64 A BVI investment manager is not required to have any physical presence in the BVI, other than a BVI registered office, registered agent and authorised representative. It must, at all times, have at least two individual directors but there is no requirement for the directors to be BVI resident.

Approved managers

3.65 The BVI approved manager product is an attractive 'regulatory light' option for qualifying investment managers and advisors. The application process for approval is generally quick and straightforward making it an appealing and popular option for both start-up and existing qualifying investment managers and advisors.

3.66 BVI business companies and ILPs who wish to undertake Approved Business (as defined below) are eligible to apply to the FSC for approval to act as an Approved Manager.

3.67 An Approved Manager may act as investment manager or investment advisor to either:

- private or professional funds and their qualifying feeder funds and affiliates with less than US$400 million assets under management;
- closed-ended funds from either the BVI or a 'recognised jurisdiction' (please see below for details of recognised jurisdictions), which have the characteristics of a private or professional fund, and their qualifying feeder funds and affiliates with less than US$1 billion of assets under management; or
- open-ended funds incorporated, formed or organised in a 'recognised jurisdiction' (please see below for details of recognised jurisdictions), which have equivalent characteristics to a private or professional fund with less than US$400 million assets under management.

3.68 An applicant who wishes to apply to the FSC for approval to act as an Approved Manager (the **Applicant**) must lodge a completed application form and supporting documents with the FSC at least seven days prior to the date it intends to commence Approved Business, unless the FSC accepts a shorter period in writing. The Applicant is then permitted to commence Approved Business for a period of up to 30 days which can be extended for an additional 30-day period either on application to the FSC or at the FSC's own volition. In the event the FSC does not grant approval during this time, the Applicant must cease carrying on Approved Business at the end of the initial or extended period as the case may be.

3.69 The application form must be accompanied by the following supporting documents and application fee (currently US$1,000):

- a copy of the Applicant's constitutional documents;
- the details of each director or general partner and senior officer of the Applicant;
- the details of each person who owns or holds an interest in the Applicant;
- a written declaration by the Applicant that each director, general partner, senior officer and each person who holds at least a 10% interest in the Applicant (as applicable) is 'fit and proper' in accordance with the Regulatory Code 2009;
- the number and details of each fund the Applicant intends to act for upon commencement of Approved Business (including the name, address and place of incorporation or registration of each fund);
- the date on which the Applicant intends to commence Approved Business;
- a copy of the investment advisory or investment management agreement between the Applicant and each fund;
- a written confirmation as to which individual(s) will be carrying out the day-to-day investment business functions of the Applicant;
- a written confirmation as to whether or not the Applicant has delegated or intends to delegate any of its Approved Business functions. If so, the application must outline the functions that have been delegated or that the Applicant intends to delegate and provide a copy of the agreement relating to the delegation;
- a written confirmation from the Applicant's legal practitioner that the legal practitioner has agreed to act for the Applicant; and
- a written declaration by the Applicant's authorised representative or legal practitioner that the application for approval as an investment manager is complete and meets the application requirements of the Approved Manager Regulations.

3.70 A successful applicant will be issued with a Certificate of Approval to act as an Approved Manager and registered in the register of approved investment managers by the FSC. It will then be obliged to pay the annual license fee (currently US$1,500) at the time of approval and then, going forward, on an annual basis.

Renewal of Approved Manager status and annual fees

3.71 Approved Manager status may be renewed annually, subject to (a) payment of the annual license fee (currently US$1,500), and (b) submission of an annual return in the approved form, each by 31 January in each calendar year.

3.72 The annual return is required to:

- state that the Approved Manager is not in breach of the requirements of the Approved Manager Regulations;
- confirm that each director, general partner, senior officer and shareholder holding a 'significant interest' in the Approved Manager is 'fit and proper' in accordance with the Regulatory Code, 2009; and
- provide, as at 31 December of the previous year, details of (a) each Fund for which it provides services; (b) the assets under management of each Fund; (c) the number of investors in each Fund; and (d) any significant complaints received by the Approved Manager.

3.73 Where the FSC is required or considers it necessary to comply with any reporting obligation, it may require an Approved Manager to provide the FSC with such further information as the FSC may consider fit.

Restrictions on an Approved Manager

3.74 An Approved Manager is subject to various restrictions, particularly in relation to the business it undertakes and its assets under management. An Approved Manager may only undertake Approved Business. In the event an Approved Manager manages both open-ended and closed-ended funds, the Approved Manager's aggregated assets under management for open-ended and closed-ended funds shall be segregated and treated separately for the purpose of calculating the statutory limitations on its assets under management. If an Approved Manager ceases to qualify as such under the Approved Manager Regulations, it shall not take on any new business and immediately notify the FSC that it is no longer qualified to act as an Approved Manager. It then has a period of three months within which to cease carrying on Approved Business. In addition, where an Approved Manager has assets under management in excess of the permitted statutory limitations, it must notify the FSC within seven days of exceeding such amount. It shall then cease to qualify as an Approved Manager, unless within three months of the date it ceased to qualify as an Approved Manager:

- it no longer exceeds the statutory limitations;
- it submits an application to obtain a full license as an investment manager under SIBA; or
- the FSC provides written approval that it may continue to act as an Approved Manager.

Ongoing obligations of an Approved Manager

3.75 Change in information – An Approved Manager must notify the FSC within 14 days of the change of any information submitted with the original application form, providing details of the change and a written declaration as to whether or not the change complies with the requirements of the Approved Manager Regulations. An Approved Manager must also notify the FSC of any matter which has or is likely to have a 'material impact' or a 'significant regulatory impact' on the Approved Manager or the Approved Manager's conduct of Approved Business.

3.76 Authorised Representative and number of directors – An Approved Manager is at all times required to have a BVI authorised representative and, if it is a corporate entity, at least two directors (at least one of whom must be an individual). In the case of an Approved Manager constituted as a limited partnership, the partnership must, at all times, have at least one general partner.

3.77 Financial statements – An Approved Manager is required to prepare unaudited financial statements which comply with prescribed accounting standards and give a fair and true view of the matters to which they relate. Such financial statements must be signed by a director (or general partner, in the case of a partnership) and must be accompanied by a director's certificate and a report on the affairs of the Approved Manager made in respect of the relevant financial year. The financial statements and supporting documents must be submitted to the FSC within six months of the end of the financial year to which they relate. In limited circumstances, it is possible to apply for and gain an exemption from the requirement to submit financial statements.

OTHER KEY SERVICE PROVIDERS

3.78 The BVI hosts a highly skilled workforce of lawyers, accountants, corporate administrators and insolvency experts. Most of the major offshore law and accountancy firms have offices in the BVI. However, other than the requirement to have a BVI registered office/agent and authorised representative, there is generally no requirement for a BVI fund to have any other BVI based functionaries. The requirements are as outlined below:

3.79 A private or professional fund is required to have:

- at least two directors (at least one of whom must be an individual);
- a BVI registered office, registered agent and authorised representative;
- a manager, custodian and auditor (unless an exemption is obtained); and
- an administrator.

3.80 An incubator or approved funds is required to have:

- at least two directors (at least one of whom must be an individual); and
- a BVI registered office, registered agent and authorised representative.

3.81 An incubator fund is not required to have a manager, administrator, custodian or auditor. An approved fund must have a third-party administrator but it is not required to have a manager, custodian or auditor.

3.82 Where required, the fund manager, administrator, custodian and auditor do not need to be BVI based, but must be from a 'recognised jurisdiction'. The current list of recognised jurisdictions is:

Argentina	Cayman Islands	Germany	Italy	New Zealand	Sweden
Australia	Chile	Gibraltar	Japan	Norway	Switzerland
Bahamas	China	Greece	Jersey	Panama	UK
Bermuda	Curacao	Guernsey	Luxembourg	Portugal	USA
Belgium	Denmark	Hong Kong	Malta	Singapore	
Brazil	Finland	Ireland	Mexico	Spain	
Canada	France	Isle of Man	Netherlands	South Africa	

3.83 Under SIBA, a custodian is defined as a person to whom the fund property is entrusted for safekeeping. The custodian must be functionally independent from the fund manager and fund administrator or, where the custodian is the same person as the fund manager or fund administrator be a company having systems and controls that ensure that the persons fulfilling the custodian function are functionally independent from the persons fulfilling the fund management or fund administrator functions.

TAX REGIME

3.84 Funds are not subject to any income or capital gains taxes in the BVI and no capital or stamp duties are levied in the BVI on the issue, transfer or redemption of fund interests (assuming that the fund does not own an interest in land in the BVI). Shareholders who are not tax resident in the BVI will not be subject to any income or capital gains taxes in the BVI, with respect to the fund interests owned by them and dividends received on such fund interests, nor will they be subject to any estate or inheritance taxes in the BVI.

CONFIDENTIALITY LAWS

3.85 There is very little information publicly available on a BVI company or ILP. There is no requirement to publicly file copies of statutory registers (such as the company's register of members or register of directors) and this information will only be provided to third parties with the fund's consent. However, the BVI has signed up to a number of tax information exchange agreements and was an early subscriber to the Common Reporting Standards and FATCA, and therefore information is available to governments and other bodies in accordance with those rules.

3.86 There is no statutory confidentiality law in the BVI. However, whilst it is not binding, English and other common law is persuasive in a BVI Fund and the BVI may owe a common law duty of confidentiality to a person on whom it holds confidential information. A duty of confidentiality may also be owed by a BVI fund to a person on whom it holds or manages confidential information under a contractual relationship or by operation of law.

ANTI-MONEY LAUNDERING LAWS

3.87 The BVI has some of the strictest and most stringent anti-money laundering laws (AML) in the world. Under BVI law, any person carrying on 'relevant business' (which includes the business of a mutual fund or providing services as a manager or administrator of a mutual fund in the BVI, is subject to a number of obligations under BVI AML laws. These obligations include, but are not limited to, conducting client due diligence (**CDD**) checks prior to entering into a client relationship, identifying and verifying clients and obtaining relevant CDD documents, appointing a Money Laundering Reporting Officer (MLRO), record keeping requirements and employee training.

3.88 However, it is recognised under BVI AML law that the process for the subscription and redemption of fund interests may be delegated to a non-BVI third party administrator. In these circumstances, BVI law provides that the fund will be accepted to be compliant with the relevant AML requirements if the following two conditions are met: firstly, the fund administrator or fund manager performs requisite CDD requirements; and secondly, that the fund administrator or fund manager, as applicable, complies with the anti-money laundering and terrorist financing obligations of a jurisdiction that is recognised under BVI AML laws and such recognised jurisdiction is treated as having anti-money laundering/combating the financing of terrorism AML/CFT measures equivalent to those established under BVI AML laws.

CONCLUDING REMARKS: WHAT ARE THE JURISDICTION'S UNIQUE SELLING POINTS?

3.89 The BVI is one of the most popular offshore jurisdictions for investment funds.

3.90 It is internationally recognised as a well-regulated jurisdiction with a robust legal system that actively engages and cooperates with foreign governments and supranational bodies to ensure that its regulations meet international standards.

3.91 Due to the BVI's modern and progressive company law regime, BVI business companies are the most commonly used offshore vehicles in the world and are very familiar to international investors.

3.92 The BVI hosts a highly skilled workforce of lawyers, accountants, corporate administrators and insolvency experts.

3.93 Compared with other jurisdictions, the BVI is extremely cost effective for incorporating, launching and maintaining investment funds. For this reason, the BVI appeals to both large, existing fund managers and smaller start up managers.

3.94 An investment fund incorporated in the BVI is not subject to any income, withholding or capital gains taxes in the BVI.

3.95 There are no requirements for directors, officers, managers, administrators or custodians to be based in the BVI. There are also no restrictions in the BVI on commercial matters, such as investment objectives, trading strategies, or leverage, trading or diversification limits.

CHAPTER 4

THE CAYMAN ISLANDS

GENERAL DESCRIPTION OF THE JURISDICTION

4.01 The Cayman Islands are situated in the western Caribbean, 480 miles south of Miami and 180 miles northwest of Jamaica. The Islands are five hours behind Greenwich Mean Time, in the Eastern Standard Time zone. The Islands benefit from state-of-the-art telecommunications facilities and direct flights are available from a number of major international centres, including London and New York.

4.02 The Cayman Islands are a British Overseas Territory and have a history of stable government. The British government retains responsibility for internal security, defence and external affairs for the Islands, which otherwise are self-governing. Prudent economic policies and a strong financial services sector have resulted in the Islands enjoying an Aa3 sovereign risk rating, from Moody's, with an attendant 'stable' outlook. Residents of the Islands enjoy a high standard of living.

4.03 Cayman Islands law derives from English common law, supplemented by local legislation. The courts system is well developed and experienced. Major civil cases are heard in the Grand Court with appeals to the Cayman Islands Court of Appeal and ultimately to the Privy Council in London. It is common practice for leading advocates from the UK to appear before the Cayman Islands courts on major litigation matters.

4.04 There are no exchange control restrictions or regulations in the Cayman Islands. Funds can be freely transferred in and out of the Islands in unlimited amounts, subject to checks as to source of funds required by an anti-money laundering regime which conforms to international standards. The Cayman Islands dollar is tied to the US dollar and the latter is freely accepted and used within the local economy.

4.05 The Cayman Islands is one of the world's leading offshore jurisdictions for the establishment of investment funds. As at December 2016, there were over 10,500 funds (predominantly hedge funds) registered with the Cayman Islands Monetary Authority (**CIMA**) under the Mutual Funds Law (the **Mutual Funds Law**). There are also significant numbers of private equity and other closed-ended alternative investment funds registered in the Cayman Islands but which are not required to register with CIMA and so verifiable numbers are not available.

KEY MANDATORY REQUIREMENTS

4.06 The Cayman Islands' regulatory regime is focussed on investment business – whether the activities of an investment manager/advisor or those of a collective investment scheme – and seeks to focus on sophisticated activities involving sophisticated high net-worth or institutional investors. Accordingly, the regime is streamlined and focused, and easily navigated.

4.07 Key themes and mandatory requirements are:

- The Mutual Funds Law regulates the activities of open-ended funds (see further below), which are registerable with CIMA in one of three regulatory brackets, or which otherwise may avoid regulation entirely; closed-ended funds may, but they are not required to, register with CIMA as mutual funds.
- Funds registered with CIMA as mutual funds (ie any such fund in one of the three brackets noted) must appoint a CIMA-approved auditor to sign-off the annual financial statements of the mutual fund, within six months of each financial year end.
- The processing of investor subscriptions and redemptions, including related cash handling and payment processing, must comply with Cayman Islands laws and regulations as to anti-money laundering and the prevention of terrorist financing; in practice mutual funds are administered by a third party administration services provider which will act as registrar and transfer agent and will either comply with the Cayman Islands legal and regulatory framework or that of its location of establishment (if such framework is subject to oversight by an overseas regulatory authority which is on CIMA's approved list).
- CIMA's Statement of Guidance on matters of governance should be adhered to by all mutual funds; the Statement of Guidance does not prescribe a one size fits all framework for good governance of mutual funds but rather it seeks to establish a baseline, which mutual funds often will exceed in practice. As a general statement, directors of mutual funds – whether based in the Cayman Islands or overseas – are required to register with CIMA before they may be appointed as a director of a mutual fund.

RECENT DEVELOPMENTS

4.08 Following the implementation by the European Union of the Alternative Investment Fund Managers Directive (**AIFMD**) in July 2013, the Mutual Funds Law and other related legislation has been updated to accommodate the requirements of the AIFMD, both in terms of alternative investment funds and alternative investment fund managers, to ensure that Cayman Islands domiciled and regulated funds and managers are not impeded from accessing European Economic Area markets.

4.09 The Organisation for Economic Co-Operation and Development (the **OECD**) has been actively engaged in working towards exchange of information on a global scale and has published a global Common Reporting Standard for multinational exchange of information pursuant to which many governments, including the Cayman Islands, have now signed multilateral agreements. A common implementing timetable saw the first exchanges of information in 2017, with further countries committed to implementing the new global standard by 2018.

4.10 The Cayman Islands introduced new legislation in 2017 to enable the establishment of a limited liability company (**LLC**) akin to a Delaware LLC, though with themes and flexibility which are associated with, and familiar to, users of the Cayman Islands. In practice, the LLC has become popular initially with private equity managers for structuring co-investment and carried interest vehicles, and as holding companies for investment management groups.

THE REGULATION OF INVESTMENT BUSINESS

Regulator

4.11 CIMA is the regulatory body responsible for supervision of financial services in the Cayman Islands, and is also the enforcement agency for breaches of the financial laws and regulations of the Cayman Islands. CIMA's remit is to ensure the protection of investors and its approach to regulation, consistent with other International Organization of Securities Commissions (**IOSCO**) member regulators, is informed by this commitment to protecting investors.

4.12 The mission of CIMA is to regulate and supervise the financial services industry in order to maintain a first-class financial system within the Cayman Islands, and its interface with the international financial system. Impliedly, therefore, CIMA has regard to international standards and the need for operational freedom by financial services providers and for the maintenance of a dynamic and competitive industry.

4.13 Since mid-2009, CIMA has been a full member of IOSCO, the principal global standard setting body for the regulation of securities markets which seeks to promote cooperation and information exchange, standard setting and surveillance, and mutual assistance. The Cayman Islands is also a member of the OECD Global Forum on Transparency and Exchange of Information for Tax Purposes, as well as being a member of the Caribbean Financial Action Task Force.

Regulation of investment funds

4.14 The Mutual Funds Law is the principal legislation relevant to the regulation of investment funds in the Cayman Islands. Investment managers established and/or based in the Cayman Islands will also need to comply with the Securities Investment Business Law (the **SIB Law**), and all investment funds and service providers must also comply with relevant anti-money laundering legislation and regulations as well as those aimed at the prevention of terrorist financing.

Definition of 'mutual funds'

4.15 The Mutual Funds Law refers to open-ended investment funds (and therefore principally hedge funds) as 'mutual funds' and as such defines a 'mutual fund' as a company, unit trust or partnership incorporated or otherwise carrying on business in the Cayman Islands that issues equity interests for the purpose of pooling investor funds, with the aim of spreading investment risk and enabling investors to receive profits or gains from investments. The scope of regulation extends to Cayman Islands incorporated or established master funds which have one or more CIMA regulated feeder funds and hold investments and conduct trading activities. The remainder of this guide will refer to open-ended investment funds as 'mutual funds'.

Scope of the Mutual Funds Law

4.16 The following exclusions or exemptions from the Mutual Funds Law apply:

(i) investment funds with only one investor fall outside the definition of a 'mutual fund', as there is no pooling of investor funds.

(ii) closed-ended investment funds or private equity vehicles which do not allow investors to require the redemption or repurchase of their interests in those funds, also fall outside the definition of 'mutual fund'.

(iii) investment funds with 15 investors or fewer, the majority in number of which have the power (together) to appoint or remove the operators of the investment fund (ie the directors, the general partner or the trustee, as the case may be), are exempt from the licensing and registration provisions of the Mutual Funds Law. This exemption does not apply to CIMA regulated master funds.

Categories of regulation

4.17 Three categories of mutual funds are required by the terms of the Mutual Funds Law to subject themselves to regulation by CIMA. Such mutual funds are referred to in this guide as:

(a) Licensed mutual funds – This is the least common type of regulated mutual fund, as it involves an approval process such that the mutual fund itself is licensed (as opposed to being able to rely on the license of the administrator in the case of type (b) administered mutual funds or being exempt from obtaining the license in the case of type (c) registered mutual funds). In granting a licence, CIMA will consider whether:

(i) each promoter is of sound reputation;

(ii) the administration of the mutual fund will be undertaken by persons who have sufficient expertise and who are fit and proper to be directors, managers or officers (as the case may be); and

(iii) the business of the fund and the offer of equity interests will be carried out in a proper manner.

(b) Administered mutual funds – Instead of applying for its own licence, a mutual fund may seek to rely on the existing licence of a licensed mutual fund administrator based in the Cayman Islands. This type of mutual fund is favoured by investment managers who wish to have a minimum initial subscription per investor that is lower than US$100,000, but who prefer not to go through the approval process outlined above. An administered mutual fund is the only type of regulated mutual fund which must appoint a mutual fund administrator based in the Cayman Islands; licensed mutual funds and registered mutual funds may appoint an administrator in any jurisdiction. For an administered mutual fund, the selected administrator undertakes the responsibility of being satisfied of the same matters that CIMA considers for a licensed fund (outlined above), and provides the principal office of the mutual fund at that administrator's office in the Cayman Islands. A licensed administrator must report to CIMA if it has reason to believe that a fund for which it provides the principal office is acting in breach of the Mutual Funds Law or may be insolvent or is otherwise acting in a manner prejudicial to its creditors or investors.

(c) Registered mutual funds – This is the most common type of investment fund registered with CIMA. Registered mutual funds are exempt from the requirement to be licensed or administered on the basis that either (i) each investor must subscribe for equity interests in an amount not less than US$100,000 or (ii) the equity interests of the fund are listed on a stock exchange recognised by CIMA.

(d) EU connected funds – Additionally, for the purpose of Cayman Islands funds qualifying for AIFMD passports, CIMA is working with the Ministry of Financial Services to create an 'opt-in' regime for a new category of mutual fund which wishes to market in the EU or EEA. Legislation has been published for these purposes but it is not yet in force.

Requirements under the Mutual Funds Law

4.18 All mutual funds other than master funds must have a current offering document, which must describe the equity interests of the mutual fund in all material respects and must contain all material information to enable a prospective investor to make an informed decision as to whether or not to subscribe for these equity interests.

4.19 All regulated mutual funds (unless it is a master fund which has no offering document) are required to file their offering document with CIMA, together with the prescribed particulars. Master funds which have no offering document must submit prescribed particulars to CIMA. The 'prescribed particulars' include details of material service providers (including directors, investment manager, auditors, lawyers and brokers) and the liquidity terms of the equity interests being offered.

4.20 All regulated mutual funds must, so long as there is a continuing offering, update their offering documents (or in the case of a master fund, the prescribed particulars) within 21 days of any material change, and must re-file the updated offering document and/or the prescribed particulars with CIMA within such 21-day period.

4.21 All regulated mutual funds must have their accounts audited annually, and such audited financial statements must be filed with CIMA in electronic format within six months of the year end of the relevant mutual fund, together with an annual return form including prescribed details, signed by a director. Such audited financial statements must be signed-off by an approved Cayman Islands-based auditor. In practice, this causes little difficulty because all of the main accounting firms have offices in Cayman. The bulk of the preparatory work will invariably be done by the audit firm in the place in which the fund's records are physically located (usually the office of the manager or administrator) and then the Cayman audit firm will sign-off on the audited financial statements.

4.22 CIMA has released a Statement of Guidance which establishes key principles of good governance which must be observed by each Cayman Islands regulated mutual fund. Such principles require, inter alia, the board of directors or other governing body to properly oversee the activities of the fund's service-providers, suitably identify, disclose and manage all conflicts of interest and meet at least twice a year or otherwise more frequently as determined by the size, nature and complexity of the fund.

INVESTORS

4.23 There are no restrictions on the number of investors that may be admitted to a Cayman investment fund, whether a mutual fund subject to regulation by CIMA or a fund which falls outside of the scope of the Mutual Funds Law. However, as noted above the mutual funds regime seeks to attract sophisticated high net worth or institutional investors and so a minimum initial investment amount may apply (as noted above for a registered mutual fund) thereby establishing a financial hurdle to access.

SETTING UP A FUND

Companies

4.24 Companies are the most common vehicle for open-ended mutual funds. The majority of Cayman Islands companies issue shares of a stated par value (although no par value shares are permitted). Dividends or other distributions are payable to investors from amounts standing to the credit of a company's share premium account, subject to the company being solvent, even if no profits are available. Shares in a Cayman Islands company may also be redeemed or repurchased out of capital, again subject to solvency considerations.

Unit trusts

4.25 Cayman Islands trust law is based on English common law and therefore interpreted according to English case law, as modified by any Cayman case law. Under a unit trust arrangement, investors (or unit holders) contribute funds to a trustee which holds those funds on trust for the unit holders, and each unit holder is directly entitled to share pro-rata in the trust's assets.

Limited partnerships

4.26 Limited partnerships are the most common vehicle for closed-ended funds or private equity funds. They are also sometimes used in master-feeder structures. Cayman limited partnerships are governed by a combination of equitable and common law rules (based on English common law) and also statutory provisions, pursuant to the Exempted Limited Partnership Law.

SUPERVISION

Companies

4.27 The management of a private company is delegated by the shareholders to the directors pursuant to the company's articles of association. There are no statutory restrictions on the minimum or maximum number of directors of a Cayman Islands company, although for registered mutual funds, CIMA has a policy of preferring at least two individual directors. Decisions of directors are taken by a simple majority at board meetings or unanimously by written resolution. The manner of appointment of directors and the number of directors is regulated by the company's articles of association. There are no statutory qualifications for directors, and directors need not be residents of the Cayman Islands. However, directors of companies acting as funds or carrying out securities investment business are required to be registered with or licensed by CIMA. Every company must keep at its registered office a register containing the names and addresses of its directors and officers, send a copy to the Registrar of Companies and notify the Registrar of Companies within 60 days if any change takes place in the directors and officers.

Limited partnerships

4.28 The general partner (the **GP**) is the operative legal entity responsible for managing the business of the exempted limited partnership (**ELP**) and is ultimately liable for all debts and obligations of the ELP to the extent that the ELP has insufficient assets. The GP will sign all contracts on behalf of and in the name of the ELP. The GP must be a Cayman resident individual, a Cayman registered company, a foreign company or foreign partnership registered in Cayman or another ELP. No additional licences or approvals will be required for the GP, and the GP may have any number of directors who will not be required to be resident in Cayman or to meet in Cayman.

Unit trusts

4.29 The trustee (the **Trustee**) is the legal entity tasked with the proper management and administration of the trust property, and therefore its business. Practically speaking, trustees of unit trusts will contract on behalf of the trust on a limited recourse basis to shield itself from liability to make whole any losses in the trust portfolio. As with GPs of limited partnerships, the Trustee of a unit trust will enter into all contracts on behalf of and in the name of the trust. The trustee need not be a Cayman entity.

INVESTMENT RESTRICTIONS

4.30 There are no investment restrictions imposed upon mutual funds by law or regulation in the Cayman Islands, and these are a question for the commercial bargain between investor and fund and often the subject of negotiation and side letter terms.

FEES

4.31 All regulated mutual funds must pay an application fee and an annual fee each year in January (currently approximately US$4,270 for funds other than registered master funds, for which the fee is approximately US$3,050).

SETTING UP A LOCAL MANAGEMENT COMPANY/INVESTMENT MANAGER

4.32 An investment fund in the Cayman Islands is not required to have an investment manager based in the Cayman Islands. If, however, an entity wishes to establish itself as an investment manager in the Cayman Islands, it will need to comply with the provisions of the SIB Law. Broadly, the SIB Law provides that the investment manager will need to be licensed by CIMA unless it is managing the assets of only certain categories of high net worth or sophisticated investors, in which case it will be able to take advantage of an annual exemption filing instead. An exemption form must be filed with CIMA in January each year and the annual exemption filing fee is approximately US$6,100. The definition of 'sophisticated investors' includes mutual funds regulated by CIMA, so that the majority of investment managers are in practice able to take advantage of the exemption filing.

FUND ADMINISTRATORS

4.33 A fund administrator must obtain a mutual fund administrator's licence to carry on business in the Cayman Islands in relation to mutual funds. Excluded from the definition of mutual fund administration are, inter alia, the activities of the general partner of a partnership and the provision of a registered office at which statutory and legal records are kept or company secretarial work is undertaken.

4.34 An applicant must satisfy CIMA that it:

(1) has available sufficient expertise to administer regulated investment funds;

(2) is of sound reputation; and

(3) will administer regulated funds in a proper manner.

4.35 A mutual fund administrator must maintain a net worth of at least US$490,000 and have a principal office in the Cayman Islands with two individuals or a body corporate resident or incorporated in the Islands as its agent.

4.36 A licensed mutual fund administrator may act for an unlimited number of funds.

4.37 A mutual fund administrator may apply to administer a limited number of related mutual funds (currently a maximum of ten). A restricted licensee need only have a registered office in the Islands and there is no minimum net worth requirement.

TAX REGIME

4.38 The Cayman Islands has no direct taxation of any kind. There are no income, corporation, capital gains, withholding taxes or death duties. Under the terms of relevant legislation, it is possible for all types of fund vehicles – the company, the unit trust and the limited partnership – to apply to the government of the Cayman Islands for a written undertaking that they will not be subject to various descriptions of direct taxation, for a minimum period, which in the case of a company is currently twenty years and, in the case of a unit trust and limited partnership, fifty years.

LOCAL STOCK EXCHANGE

4.39 The Cayman Islands Stock Exchange (**CSX**) was established in 1997 to provide a highly competitive listing facility for Cayman's specialist products, mutual funds and debt securities. Since then the CSX has expanded its facilities for listing of derivative warrants, depositary receipts and Eurobonds. The CSX currently has approximately 1,000 listings with a market capitalisation over US$150 billion.

ANTI-MONEY LAUNDERING LAWS

4.40 The Cayman Islands has long committed to implementing best international practice and is fully compliant with the requirements of the OECD and the Financial Action Task Force.

4.41 Three pieces of primary legislation, the Proceeds of Crime Law (the **PCL**), the Money Laundering Regulations (the **Regulations**) and, more recently, the Anti-Corruption Law (the **ACL**) provide the platform for anti-money laundering protection in the Cayman Islands. This legislation is supported by the Guidance Notes which are issued and updated by CIMA.

The PCL

4.42 The first version of the PCL was known as the Proceeds of Criminal Conduct Law (the **PCCL**) and was introduced in September 1996. This introduced all-crimes legislation and complemented the Misuse of Drugs Law which had been in place since 1989 and which had focused on the movement of funds generated by the drug trade. The PCCL was drafted to achieve three objectives. First, to allow local restraint and confiscation orders. This ensures that assets can be frozen pending an investigation and confiscated on conviction. Second, the introduction of offences designed to actively discourage any local assistance that may be provided by third parties. No longer is liability limited to the persons who commit the predicate crime. The third area addressed by the PCCL relates to the enforcement of foreign orders.

4.43 The PCCL was the first all-crimes money laundering legislation in the region and enacted in substance the 'suspicious transaction' reporting obligations and onward disclosure practice of the UK Criminal Justice Act. The 'all-crimes' description is tempered by the requirement of dual criminality. In other words, if the predicate offence occurred in a foreign jurisdiction, the offence must be one that would similarly be an offence in the Cayman Islands. Criminal conduct is defined in the PCL as 'conduct which constitutes an offence to which this Law applies or would constitute such an offence if it had occurred in the Islands'. The PCL's aim was to improve effectiveness and bring the legislative framework in line with changing needs and with international standards. The PCL consolidated the law relating to the confiscation of proceeds of crime and in relation to mutual legal assistance in criminal matters. The PCL also sought to widen confiscation orders and extend the powers of enforcement of orders in other jurisdictions outside the Cayman Islands.

The ACL

4.44 The ACL was originally enacted in January 2010 and it complements the PCL and the Regulations. It was drafted to repeal offences created under the Penal Code relating to corrupt practices and to meet OECD obligations relating to combating bribery of foreign public officials in international business transactions. It extends powers in respect of disclosure of information and provides for the protection of informers. The ACL established a commission known as the Anti-Corruption Commission (the **Commission**). The Commission's primary function is to receive, investigate and consider any report of a corruption offence and any suspected conspiracy to commit an offence under this law.

The Regulations

4.45 The Regulations have been introduced to ensure conformity with worldwide 'know your client' and general compliance standards. The Regulations have introduced offences to which financial services providers may be subject even if they do not have any clients that are dealing with the proceeds of criminal conduct. These offences will apply simply because the procedures as set out in the Regulations have not been followed. The Regulations supplement the offences that have been created under the PCL. They specifically cover the areas of client identification, record keeping, internal reporting and training and awareness.

Guidance Notes

4.46 CIMA has issued Guidance Notes on the Prevention and Detection of Money Laundering and Terrorist Financing in the Cayman Islands (the **Guidance Notes**). The Guidance Notes provide specific information on the operational practices CIMA considers are required to comply with national and international expectations. CIMA states in the introduction to the Guidance Notes that they go beyond the requirements of the money laundering Regulations. Whilst the financial service provider may not be liable for prosecution for a breach of the Guidance Notes, CIMA has indicated that it expects all institutions conducting relevant financial business to pay due regard to them. Further, the Guidance Notes, whilst not having statutory force, may be taken into account by the courts in determining whether a party has complied with the Regulations. The Guidance Notes are reviewed and updated from time to time by CIMA, in consultation with the private sector, to address current issues and developments both locally and internationally.

CONCLUDING REMARKS: WHAT ARE THE JURISDICTION'S UNIQUE SELLING POINTS?

4.47 The Cayman Islands offers a regulatory framework of flexibility, both for investment managers/advisors as well as for investment funds. The regulatory philosophy of CIMA is unobtrusive, and provided it is satisfied that investor interests are being accommodated and protected, it tends to be non-interventionist.

4.48 The quality and experience of the legal, administrative and accounting service providers within the Islands supports the investment funds industry both within the Cayman Islands as well as through a network of international offices in Europe and Asia, ensuring that users of the Cayman Islands funds industry are supported round the clock, throughout the year.

4.49 The establishment and registration of a mutual fund in the Cayman Islands is able to be done in quick order, and certainly within the timeframe within which all compliance and counterparty arrangements can be satisfied and put in place.

4.50 There are no requirements for mutual funds to have Cayman-based directors or officers, managers, administrators or custodians; accordingly, funds and their sponsors have tremendous flexibility to implement the structures which they and their investors require to best satisfy their investment and distribution goals, unimpeded by bureaucracy and red tape.

4.51 Correspondingly, there are no restrictions on commercial matters such as a fund's investment objectives, trading strategies or leverage, trading or diversification limits. Such commercial matters are for the fund's sponsor to determine provided that full disclosure of such matters (and all associated risk factors) is made in the offering document.

CHAPTER 5

FRANCE

GENERAL DESCRIPTION OF THE JURISDICTION

5.01 France has a population of approximately 66 million and is one of the world's leading economies. It is bordered on the west by the Atlantic Ocean, on the south by Italy, the Mediterranean Sea, Spain and the principalities of Monaco and Andorra, on the north by the English Channel, Belgium and Luxembourg, and on the east by Germany and Switzerland. High-speed train connections between Paris and London and Paris and Luxembourg have facilitated contacts between these leading financial centres.

5.02 The French Republic is a parliamentary democracy. The official language is French, although several other languages are spoken in border regions. In the financial sector, English is widely used as the working language. Metropolitan France is in the same time zone as its Continental European neighbours (Greenwich Mean Time plus 1 hour). France adopted the euro on 1 January 2002. Exchange controls and foreign investment restrictions have been largely abolished in France, although some vestiges remain.

5.03 France is one of the founding member states of the EU and is also a member of the Organisation for Economic Cooperation and Development, the seat of which is located in Paris.

5.04 Asset management in France represents, at the end of 2016, almost EUR3,800 billion under management, with EUR1,800 billion in French funds and approximately EUR2,000 billion in foreign funds or mandates. France is the leader in continental Europe and ranked among the top worldwide countries in terms of asset management.

5.05 The French market is very active and grows rapidly (up to 4.7% of assets under management in one year). There are currently 630 management companies and circa 11,000 investment funds in France. More than 50% of the portfolio management companies market their investment funds abroad and more than EUR500 billion are managed for clients who are based abroad.[1]

1 Rapport d'Activité 2016, Association Française de la Gestion Financière (the French Professional Association of Asset Managers).

KEY MANDATORY REQUIREMENTS

Key issues which might discourage a promoter or require advance planning

5.06 Non-French European management companies authorised under the Undertakings for Collective Investment in Transferable Securities (**UCITS**) and/or the Alternative Investment Fund Managers (**AIFM**) Directive can benefit from a European 'marketing passport' for the European funds they manage which allows for the marketing of those funds in France (which in the case of alternative investment funds (**AIFs**), only applies to marketing to professional investors).

5.07 Restrictions on marketing exist where the management company is not licensed in an EU country, or, for AIFs, where marketing without a passport or marketing to retail investors is envisaged. For these situations, the marketing of funds in France is subject to the prior authorisation of the French regulator, the *Autorité des Marchés Financiers* (**AMF**). As a consequence, it is generally considered that there is no private placement regime in France.

5.08 In order to relax the constraining marketing rules operating in France, a pre-marketing regime was introduced by the AMF in July 2016. Pursuant to this pre-marketing regime, management companies (or third parties acting on their behalf) contemplating offering a new fund in France, may measure interest in the fund by pre-marketing to a maximum of 50 prospective investors provided that such investors are (i) professional investors or (ii) non-professional investors whose initial subscription is at least EUR100,000. The pre-marketing regime enables the management company to provide potential investors with draft by-laws, private placement memoranda, term sheets or fact sheets regarding the relevant fund.

5.09 The provision of fund administration in France is by French banks and their subsidiaries which typically provide management companies with various services including custody services, legal and accounting services, reporting, valuation and net asset value calculation services, centralisation of orders.

5.10 French managers must pay an annual fee to the AMF for the French funds they manage. Foreign UCITS and AIFs authorised for marketing in France must also (for each sub-fund if applicable) pay a fee to the AMF for each fund (or sub-fund). This fee is due on the day on which the application for authorisation is made in the first year, and on 30 April in subsequent years.

5.11 Foreign UCITS authorised for marketing in France must appoint a centralising correspondent established in France under the conditions set out by the AMF. This centralising correspondent must provide the following financial services: (i) processing subscription and redemption requests for French investors (ii) paying coupons and dividends, (iii) making information documents available to investors, and (iv) providing specific information to investors in the cases stipulated by the AMF.

RECENT DEVELOPMENTS

ELTIF

5.12 Pursuant to the entry into force of the European Long-Term Investment Funds Regulation (EU) 2015/760 (**ELTIF Regulation**), French legislation was amended to allow French funds to adopt the ELTIF regime. Since 2016, French investment funds, including, specialised professional funds (*FPS*), professional private equity funds (*FPCI*) and securitisation vehicles (*organismes de titrisation*) are authorised to request the ELTIF label with the prior approval of the AMF. As a consequence, these French ELTIF funds are now entitled to grant loans to eligible companies. French law has also been modified in order to allow certain French funds to grant loans to non-financial companies under certain conditions, even if such funds are not authorised under the ELTIF label. As a result, French investment funds authorised to grant loans are exempted from the French banking monopoly rules that only permits duly licenced credit institutions or financial companies to grant loans directly to borrowers.

The Société de Libre Partenariat (SLP): a new French alternative fund

5.13 The SLP is a new French legal form of investment fund, created with the aim of making the French asset management industry more attractive, both to French and international institutional investors. The SLP is a new category of FPS under the legal form of a *société en commandite simple*.

5.14 The main goal of the creation of the SLP was to establish a new category of fund similar to the English limited partnership or to the Luxembourg *société en commandite simple/spéciale* (the '**SCS**'/'**SCSp**')

5.15 The SLP addresses key demands of foreign investors, among others by allowing operating rules similar to those applied abroad (ie the distinction between a general partner and limited partners), having a legal personality, and benefiting from a tax treatment that is more likely to be understood by investors' own tax authorities. Overall, the SLP is a flexible vehicle, and benefits from the following:

(i) as for all FPS, the SLP does not need prior approval by the AMF, as it is only declared to the AMF after the fund's creation;

(ii) latitude as to the content of the SLP's by-laws, which can be drafted in English and remain confidential;

(iii) the ability to invest in all asset classes;

(iv) great flexibility as to the SLP's investment rules (eg, diversification, leverage etc) and fund terms (eg liquidity terms, governance rules etc);

(v) the ability to issue different types of shares (including carried interest shares), with various voting and financial rights; and

(vi) the ability to establish an umbrella fund with segregated sub-funds.

THE REGULATION OF INVESTMENT BUSINESS

The local financial regulator

5.16 The financial regulator in France is the AMF, an independent public body, which ensures the protection of savings, investors' information and the proper functioning of financial markets. In particular, the AMF regulates, authorises and monitors participants (credit institutions authorised to provide investment services, investment firms, French management companies, French branches of foreign management companies, financial investment advisors, direct marketers) and products in France's financial markets (French investment funds and foreign investment funds passported or authorised for marketing purposes in France).

5.17 The AMF has the power to conduct inspections and enquiries and, when practices are found to contravene its general regulations or professional obligations, its disciplinary commission may impose disciplinary sanctions and fines against management companies, their managers and employees.

5.18 The AMF coordinates its activities with other French regulators, especially in the banking and insurance sectors. In particular, the AMF and the *Autorité de Contrôle Prudentiel et de Régulation* (**ACPR**) have set up a Joint Unit to enhance oversight of financial product marketing in France with the aim of improving investor protection.

5.19 The AMF plays an important role in international bodies including the International Organization of Securities Commissions (**IOSCO**) and the Financial Stability Board (**FSB**). The AMF also cooperates closely with foreign authorities conducting investigations and inspections.

5.20 The AMF contributes actively to ESMA's preparatory work on European Union rules to (i) ensure effective and harmonised implementation of European Union rules, (ii) favour cross-cutting, consistent and stable European Union rules and (iii) promote the European Union's place in a multipolar world.

5.21 The AMF consults regularly with professionals, investors and academics in an effort to take financial regulation forward. In particular, the AMF Board has set up consultative commissions which comprise around 20 experts devoted to a specific area, for example the protection of retail investors and the regulation of asset management and institutional investors.

The central bank

5.22 Since 1 January 1999, the European Central Bank (**ECB**) has been responsible for conducting monetary policy for the euro area.

Other relevant regulators

5.23 The French *Autorité de contrôle prudentiel et de résolution* (**ACPR**) is responsible for supervising the banking and insurance sectors in France. The ACPR is an independent public body, and is in charge of preserving the stability of the financial system and protecting customers, insurance policyholders, members and beneficiaries of the persons that it supervises (such as investment services providers).

INVESTORS

5.24 The French market is characterised by an important entrepreneurial landscape, among the largest in Europe, in terms of the number of management companies and in terms of diversity of services required. It also has a significant number of large management companies (37 management companies manage more than EUR15 billion, 13 of which manage more than EUR50 billion), and four French groups which rank among the largest asset management groups in the world.

5.25 France offers a wide variety of institutional investors, such as insurers, public institutions, social welfare groups, pension funds, mutual insurance companies, etc. The retail market is also very active with banks, insurers and independent financial advisors offering distribution networks.

SETTING UP A FUND

Types of French fund

5.26 French regulation includes two main categories of regulated investment funds:

(i) UCITS in the form of either (a) an unincorporated contractual fund (*Fonds Commun de Placement*, FCP), or (b) an investment company with variable capital (*Société d'Investissement à Capital Variable*, SICAV).

(ii) AIFs in the form of either (a) a FCP, or (b) a SICAV, or (c) a **SLP**.

Form of French funds

SICAV

5.27 SICAVs are investment companies, having legal personality, whose purpose is the management of a portfolio of financial instruments and deposits. The registered office must be in France. They are organised as stock corporations including public limited companies (*sociétés anonymes*) or simplified joint-stock companies (*sociétés par actions simplifiées*) allowing investors to benefit from shareholder's rights.

5.28 Specific regulations relating to SICAVs give investors in SICAVs enhanced rights, in particular relating to disclosure.

5.29 SICAVs are managed by a board of directors and a *directeur géneral* (managing director) (*société anonyme*) or by a president (*société par actions simplifies*). SICAVs can be structured as self-managed funds, subject to the licensing of the manager by the AMF. They may also opt to not be self-managed and to delegate management of their assets to a duly authorised management company, which is the prevailing market practice.

5.30 SICAVs have a variable capital, with simplified corporate rules. They must have an initial share capital of at least €300,000. SICAVs can have several categories of shares with various different rights and can be structured as umbrella funds with two or more segregated sub-funds.

5.31 The SICAV is treated as a tax-exempt entity for French tax purposes.

FCP

5.32 In contrast to SICAVs, FCPs require the co-ownership of financial instruments and deposits by investors. An FCP is a contractual fund with no legal personality. An FCP is necessarily managed and represented by a duly authorised management company to act as manager of the fund. The management company represents the FCP with respect to third parties and may act in legal proceedings to defend the rights of the unitholders. The nature of the relationship between the unitholders and the FCP is contractual.

5.33 FCPs also have a variable capital. They can have several categories of units with different rights and can be structured as umbrella funds with two or more segregated sub-funds. At the time of its creation, the initial capital of an FCP must be at least EUR300,000.

5.34 The FCP is treated as a tax transparent vehicle for French tax purposes.

SLP

5.35 The SLP is organised as a *société en commandite simple*, a commercial company vehicle in the form of limited partnership, but with a simplified regime. The SLP benefits from a separate legal personality and has a governance structure mainly based on:

- two different categories of partners: *associés commanditaires* (limited partners) whose liability is limited to the amount of their capital contributions to the fund and *associé commandité* (general partner) whose liability is unlimited;

- a manager; and
- a management company.

5.36 As an AIF with legal personality, the SLP may either:

(i) be self-managed, in which case, the SLP must satisfy the requirements applicable to any other management company; or

(ii) delegate its portfolio management to a management company, which is the prevailing market practice.

The SLP is also treated as a tax transparent vehicle for French tax purpose.

Categories of French investment funds

UCITS funds

5.37 UCITS, either in the form of SICAVS or FCPs are governed by the UCITS IV and V Directives, transposed into the French Monetary Financial Code (MFC) and the General Regulation of the AMF (RGAMF).

5.38 French UCITS are authorised and monitored by the AMF which reviews the funds primary regulatory documents: the key investor information document ('KIID') and prospectus, to which must be attached the rules (for an FCP) or the articles of association (for a SICAV); and the fund's advertising materials. The authorisation procedure for the creation of a UCITS takes approximately one month.

AIFs

5.39 The management of AIFs is governed by the AIFM Directive, transposed in 2013 into the French regulations. As set out in the AIFM Directive, AIFs are collective investment undertakings that raise capital from a number of investors with a view to investing it in accordance with a defined investment policy for the benefit of those investors; and that are not UCITS. Article L.214–24 of the French MFC lists the following categories of French AIFs:

(i) AIFs open to non-professional investors;

(ii) AIFs restricted to professional investors;

(iii) Employee investment undertakings;

(iv) securitisation vehicles; and

(v) 'Other AIFs', any entity not regulated by the AMF which qualify as an AIF, eg, third country AIFs.

5.40 The French regulations further characterises funds open to non-professional investors and to professional investors, as follows:

(A) French AIFs open to retail investors are:

(i) retail investment funds (*'fonds d'investissement à vocation générale'*, FIVG);

(ii) private equity funds (*'fonds de capital investissement'*), including retail private equity investment funds (*'fonds de capital risque'*, FCPR), retail venture capital funds (*'fonds communs de placement dans l'innovation'*, FCPI), and retail local investment funds, (*'fonds d'investissement de proximité'*, FIP);

(iii) real estate collective investment undertakings (*'organismes de placement collectif immobilier'*, OPCI) and real estate investment funds (*'sociétés civiles de placement immobilier'*, SCPI);

(iv) funds of alternative funds (*'fonds de fonds alternatifs'*);

(v) employee investment undertakings including employee investment funds (*'fonds communs de placement d'entreprise'*, FCPE) and corporate savings plans (*'sociétés d'investissement à capital variable d'actionnariat salarié'*, SICAVAS); and

(vi) closed-end investment funds (*'sociétés d'investissement à capital fixe'*, SICAF).

(B) French AIFs restricted to professional investors are:

(i) professional investment funds (*'fonds professionnels à vocation générale'*, FPVG);

(ii) professional real estate collective investment undertakings (*'organismes professionnels de placement collectif immobilier'*, OPPCI);

(iii) professional specialised investment funds (*'fonds professionnels spécialisés*, FPS') including the SLP;

(iv) professional private equity funds (*'fonds professionnels de capital investissement'*, FPCI);

(v) securitisation vehicle.

5.41 Subscriptions to such professional funds are restricted to eligible/ professional investors who qualify as:

(i) professional clients or treated as professional clients within the meaning of the Directive 2004/39/EC of 21 April 2004 on Markets in Financial Instruments and national regulations;

(ii) investors for which the subscription or acquisition of units is performed in their name and on their behalf by an investment services provider acting as part of an asset management investment service.

5.42 Eligibility requirements affect French investors and investors located in other EU member states. For investors located outside of the EU, French professional funds are restricted to investors who can be qualified as professional investors under the legislation of the State where they are located.

5.43 Subscriptions to FPCI and FPS (including the SLP) are also open to specific French investors who are able to meet the following conditions:

(i) investors whose initial subscription is equal to €100,000 or more;

(ii) investors, natural persons and legal entities, whose initial subscription is equal to €30,000 or more and who meet one of three specific criteria[2];

(iii) executives, employees or legal person investors acting on behalf of the management company of the fund or the management company itself.

5.44 These funds could also be open to retail investors, under some conditions, if they have obtained the ELTIF label.

5.45 Other AIFs – According to the MFC, 'other AIFs' are AIFs that are not expressly mentioned in Article L. 214–24 II of the MFC. This category of investment funds groups together French entities that meet the definition of an AIF under the AIFM Directive and which were not regulated before the implementation of the AIFM Directive.

5.46 There are two situations in which an entity that qualifies as an 'other AIF' must be managed by a portfolio management company and must appoint a depositary for the custody of their assets:

(i) Where the total asset value exceeds the AIFM Directive thresholds (ie, 500 million euros in assets and 100 million euros in case of leverage); or

(ii) Where the total asset value is below the abovementioned thresholds, and if at least one of the unitholders or shareholders of such 'other AIF' does not meet the definition of a professional investor.

5.47 If the above mentioned conditions are not met, the 'other AIF' will not be required to be managed by a regulated management company.

5.48 Pursuant to instruction no. 2014-02, the AMF specifies:

2 Such an investor shall: (a) provide technical or financial assistance to unlisted companies falling within the scope of the fund in view of their creation or development, or (b) provide assistance to the investment fund management company in identifying potential investors or contribute to the objectives pursued by the company with regard to research, selection, monitoring or disposal of investments, or (c) have acquired knowledge about private equity by being a direct equity investor in unlisted companies or by subscribing to a retail private equity investment fund that is not advertised or promoted, a professional specialised fund, a professional private equity investment fund or an unlisted venture capital firm.

- the minimum information that shall be disclosed to investors prior to subscription of shares or units of 'other AIFs';
- the content of the annual report of other AIFs.

AUTHORISATION PROCEDURE

5.49 French investment funds (UCITS and AIFs) require AMF prior authorisation before being launched and marketed. Certain major modifications of such funds are also subject to AMF prior approval.

5.50 Certain funds aimed at professional investors (such as the FPS (including SLP)), and the FPCI are not subject to AMF prior approval before being launched and marketed. These two categories of funds are only subject to a process of notification to the AMF. Modifications made during the life of the fund are not subject to AMF approval but must be notified to the AMF.

SUPERVISION

5.51 French regulated funds mentioned above are subject to the supervision of the AMF. This includes the funds authorisation procedure, reporting to the AMF (including net asset value and annual management reports) and inspection by the AMF of the asset management companies.

APPOINTMENT OF A CUSTODIAN

5.52 French investment funds must appoint a single authorised custodian, who can only be selected from the following organisations: (i) the *Banque de France*, (ii) the *Caisse des Dépôts et Consignations*, (iii) credit institutions having a registered head office in France or established in a Member State of the European Union or of the European Economic Area acting through its branches established in France, and (v) investment firms, under certain conditions, having their registered head office in France.

5.53 Certain 'Other AIFs' which are below the AIFM Directive thresholds and which are only subscribed by professional investors (within the meaning of MiFID) are not under an obligation to appoint a custodian.

INVESTMENT RESTRICTIONS

5.54 French investment funds, depending on the nature of their assets, and depending on whether they are open to retail investors or restricted to professional investors, may have to comply with investment ratios and investment restrictions as set out under the provisions of the MFC.

5.55 Such rules apply to regulated funds such as UCITS and certain AIFs which are similar to UCITS such as FIVG (dedicated to retail investors) or FPVG (dedicated to professional investors, with a lighter regime than FIVG). These rules also apply to private equity or real estate funds available to retail investors.

5.56 FPCI funds are subject to very light regulation and must comply with simple and unburdensome ratio constraints.

5.57 FPS (including the SLP) are considered to be very attractive by asset managers as they do not have to comply with any restrictions or investment ratios and can invest in a wide variety of assets. This flexibility allows FPS to offer a wide range of investment strategies. FPS offer:

(a) full freedom to determine their eligible assets (eg, financial instruments, real estate, commodities, tangible assets, debt);

(b) full freedom to determine their investment strategy (eg, investment rules, diversification of assets, permitted levels of leverage, investment style etc); and

(c) full freedom to determine their terms (eg, subscription terms, redemption and sales conditions etc).

FEES

5.58 Investors may be required to pay entry and exit fees (as determined freely by the manager), management fees and transactions costs. Information relating to cost and associated charges must be provided to the investors.

ACCOUNTS/AUDIT REQUIREMENTS

5.59 French regulated investment funds must prepare annual account and financial statements. The manager has discretion to decide the dates of the fund's fiscal year. The annual financial statements of French regulated investment funds must be certified by a statutory auditor.

5.60 An annual report shall be made available to investors each year and shall be notified to the AMF.

SETTING UP A LOCAL MANAGEMENT COMPANY/INVESTMENT MANAGER

Incorporation

5.61 A French management company may be incorporated in any form but is generally set up in the form of a French commercial company ie a public company (*société anonyme*), a simplified stock company (*société par actions simplifiées*) or a stock limited partnership (*société en commandite par actions*). The most common form is the simplified stock company.

5.62 For simplified stock companies, requirements for incorporation are very limited. The company must establish its by-laws in compliance with French corporate law. There may be one or several shareholders. The minimum capital requirement is one euro (even if the AMF regulations require a higher minimum capital). The company must have its place of business located in France. The company shall be managed and represented by a chairman. One or several directors must also be appointed by the chairman or by the shareholders. The company must have a statutory auditor appointed by its shareholders for a term of six years.

5.63 French companies must be registered with the local commercial court before they can begin their activities. The timing for this registration is around 3–4 days and it costs less than EUR500.

Authorisation/licensing

5.64 UCITS and AIFs in France (excluding 'Other AIFs' with assets below the AIFM Directive thresholds with only professional investors), must be managed by a licensed management company, duly authorised to manage UCITS or AIFs.

5.65 Pursuant to French law, portfolio management companies are investment firms whose primary function is to provide portfolio management services for third parties, which include management of one or several UCITS or AIFs. The portfolio management company's activity is based on an authorisation granted by the AMF. Such authorisation may include access to a European passport in order to provide portfolio management services on a cross-border basis. Indeed, French portfolio management companies have full freedom of establishment and freedom to provide services across the European Union.

5.66 In order to set-up a portfolio management company, an application must be submitted to the AMF. This must include a description of the programme of operation (*programme d'activité*) of the company, which will describe its activities, the services it intends to provide, its potential clients and its structure for distributing instruments, and the main organisational rules governing the company. Among the various specific requirements, portfolio management companies must use adequate and appropriate human and technical resources that are necessary for the proper management of its activities and to satisfy the most efficient protection of client's interests. The application submitted by the company when applying for licensing with the AMF must specify the following elements: (i) the type of investment strategies implemented by the portfolio manager, (ii) the description of procedure for the projected allocation of orders (decision-making methodology, order routing, flow of information, etc) and (iii) the counterparty selection policy.

5.67 The management company shall also adhere to and be a member of a French professional association (such as the *Association Française de la Gestion Financière* (AFG), or the *Association Française des Investisseurs pour la Croissance* (AFIC)).

5.68 As required by EU regulations, the minimum capital requirement of French portfolio management companies is the greater of (i) EUR125,000 plus 0.02% of the assets under the management of the company over EUR250 million and (ii) a quarter of fixed overheads in the previous year. The minimum capital must be fully paid in cash as from the licensing of the management company. It must have the appropriate and sufficient financial means to conduct its activities.

5.69 Portfolio management companies shall disclose to the AMF the identities of their direct or indirect shareholders and the amounts of their holdings. The AMF assesses the quality of the company's shareholders, having regard to the need for sound and prudent management and the proper performance of its own supervisory responsibilities.

5.70 Portfolio management companies must be effectively managed by responsible managers ('*dirigeants responsables*') with at least one full-time manager. By way of exemption, a portfolio management company may be effectively managed by a single person when managing no more than EUR20 million.

5.71 Responsible managers must demonstrate to the AMF that they possess the necessary good repute and suitable experience for their role, for the purpose of guaranteeing sound and prudent management.

5.72 The portfolio management company must employ at least three individuals working full time within the company, and at least two of these individuals must be portfolio managers working full time within the company. The AMF assesses the experience of the portfolio managers, which must be in line with the investment strategies to be implemented by the company.

5.73 The portfolio management company must ensure that the portfolio managers have the appropriate level of qualification and skills as well as a sufficient level of knowledge. In that respect, portfolio managers are required to pass a professional expertise test. Only responsible managers can hold the position of portfolio manager.

5.74 A compliance officer must be appointed. Depending on the size of the portfolio management company and the amount of assets under management, one of the responsible managers may be appointed as the compliance officer. Such function may be outsourced to an external provider acting under the responsibility and control of the responsible managers. Compliance officers are required to hold a professional licence.

5.75 Depending on the type of investment strategy that is implemented by the portfolio managers, portfolio management companies may be required to appoint analysts (for credit derivatives, alternative multi management), legal counsel (for credit derivatives) and/or a risk control officer (for alternative strategies).

5.76 The application file for licensing must contain a detailed description of the material resources of the company. The AMF monitors companies' systems to ensure that they are efficient and reliable, in particular with regard to the security of transactions.

5.77 The AMF authorises and monitors portfolio management companies during the course of their lifetimes. Portfolio management companies are required to inform the AMF over the entire course of their existence of any changes/modifications made to their initial authorisation file. These modifications are subject either to prior authorisation after examination by the AMF or to notification of the modification to the AMF, depending on the facts and circumstances.

ACCOUNTS/AUDIT REQUIREMENTS

5.78 The management company shall, each fiscal year, draw up annual financial statements and file these with the local commercial court, once they have been approved by the shareholders of the company. The annual financial statement of the portfolio management company must be certified by a statutory auditor and must be provided to the AMF.

SUPERVISION

5.79 A French management company is subject to the supervision and the control of the AMF.

5.80 Each year, the French management company shall provide the AMF with various types of information, including its annual financial statement, the calculation of the amount of its regulatory capital, an annual report on its management of conflict of interests, and information related to the investment funds managed and the amount of assets under management.

5.81 The AMF is authorised to conduct investigations and audits on the management company. It can investigate all aspects of the business of the company in order to verify whether the company complies with the applicable regulations. After such investigation, the AMF can initiate procedures against the management company in order to obtain regularisation of any compliance issues, or, if there is a significant breach, impose penalties against the management company and/or its directors or employees.

FEES

5.82 Each fiscal year, French management companies must pay annual fees to the AMF calculated on the basis of their total assets under management.

OTHER KEY SERVICE PROVIDERS

5.83 A management company which manages French investment funds must appoint a custodian for each fund it manages. In France, there are several large French and foreign banks which offer custodial services (see below).

5.84 The same bank providing custodian services will generally also offer fund administration services, including accounting and preparation of annual financial statements, calculation of net asset value, administration of the register of shareholders (including the management of subscription, redemption, transfers of shares, etc), administrative work related to shareholders (communication to investors of net asset value of shares, providing tax information or tax documentation, etc) and regulatory reporting.

5.85 A large part of these services are not regulated and could be provided by service providers which are not banks, and for some services, by service providers which are not located in France.

5.86 There is no obligation for the management company or the funds it manages to use an external accountant, even if the annual financial statements of the management company and of the funds are required to be reviewed and certified by a statutory auditor. In practice, most French management companies work with external accountants.

5.87 There are many service providers acting in France as consultants who specialise in compliance and regulatory work. Excluding the biggest management companies, small and medium French management companies usually outsource some of the work related to compliance and internal controls to such services providers.

5.88 Companies with activities outside France may be domiciled in France but management companies must always be operational in France with sufficient human and material resources located in France in order to conduct their activities and to obtain their licence from the AMF.

5.89 The French regulations authorise schemes pursuant to which a management company can manage a fund but is permitted to outsource to an external financial advisor, French or foreign, a large part of the work related to sourcing, studying and analysing portfolio investments. Some French management companies offer this type of service which can be useful for financial advisors who are not in a position to set up a fully compliant management company themselves.

5.90 According to EU regulations, French management companies must appoint a custodian for each fund they manage. The custodian is in charge of safekeeping the funds' assets and ensuring that the management company's decisions comply with the fund's documentation, the regulation applicable to the fund and the management company, that the fund is conducted in the best interests of the investors.

5.91 French management companies must comply with EU regulations with regards to their relationships with prime brokers, which may be located in France or outside of France. They are required to apply principles of best selection and best execution, supervision and control, and manage any conflict of interests with such services providers.

TAX REGIME

Registration taxes

5.92 The subscription, redemption or sale of French investment funds is generally exempt from all registration taxes.

Value-added tax (VAT)

5.93 In France, the management of French AIFs is generally exempt from VAT.

5.94 Related advisory investment services should also be VAT exempt (ECJ case C-275/11, GfBk and Official Administrative Answer, *Rép Min Cayeux*).

French income tax regime applicable to foreign investors into French funds

5.95 French funds are generally 'transparent' for income tax purposes. In other words, French funds are not themselves subject to any taxation and the French tax authorities 'look through' the funds for the purpose of determining the type of income received by the investor when the fund makes a distribution.

Capital Gains Tax

5.96 Foreign investors are generally not subject to capital gains tax in France: either (i) on the sale or redemption of their fund shares, or (ii) on the distribution of capital gains realised on the sale of shares of French portfolio companies, provided however that the investor does not own, directly or indirectly, more than 25% of the rights to the profits in the underlying portfolio company sold.

5.97 Nevertheless, foreign investors domiciled, established or incorporated in a jurisdiction included in the list of non-cooperative States or territories (the '**NCST**') are subject to a 75% tax in France on capital gains derived from the sale of shares of a French company, irrespective of their level of ownership in that company.

5.98 If the fund realises a capital gain on the sale of a foreign (ie, non-French) company, the country in which that company is resident may impose a tax, by withholding or otherwise, on the gain realised.

Ordinary Income

5.99 Foreign investors will be taxed upon receipt of the income received from the fund according to the nature and the source of the income received (*look through approach*), namely:

- French source income can be subject to French withholding tax. Dividends 'redistributed' by the fund to a foreign investor are generally subject to withholding tax at the rate of 30%; whereas French source interest is generally not subject to withholding tax in France (75% withholding applicable in the case of payment into a NCST).
- Foreign source income (ie, income from sources outside of France) is not subject to any income tax or withholding tax in France when it is 'redistributed' by the fund to a foreign investor.

Double tax treaties

5.100 France is a member of OECD and has signed double tax treaties with a large number of states and territories in order to avoid double taxation for investors, French or foreign.

5.101 However, French funds are generally not regarded as 'tax resident' in France for the application of double tax treaty provisions.

BEPS

5.102 France is a member of the OECD and the G20. France applies regulations related to Base Erosion and Profit Shifting (BEPS) as recommended by these international organisations.

5.103 France has implemented into French tax law several regulations related to BEPS.

5.104 France has signed a multilateral agreement, which includes exchanges of tax information with other states' signatories.

LOCAL STOCK EXCHANGE

5.105 Euronext Paris, formerly known as the '*Bourse de Paris*', is the Paris Stock Exchange. The CAC 40 Index which includes 40 equities selected among the top 100 by market capitalisation and the most active listed equities, is the main benchmark for Euronext Paris. Euronext Paris offers a wide range of equities, futures, options, and interest rate products, and has a new, in-house clearing arrangement underway.

CONFIDENTIALITY LAWS

Banking and professional secrecy

5.106 France's confidentiality and banking secrecy laws are governed by the MFC and the Criminal Code. A bank or financial institution may disclose a customer's confidentiality information only where it is required to do so by law. Confidential information may be disclosed to the Banque de France, the tax and customs authorities, the ACPR, the AMF, any parliamentary investigation commission, and to a judge in criminal or insolvency proceedings. Money laundering regulations may also permit a disclosure of confidentiality information in certain situations (obligation of reporting of any suspicious or unusual transactions, see below). Employees from investment and banking services providers are required to report to the ACPR and AMF any failings of their obligations.

The Register of beneficial owners

5.107 Pursuant to the fourth anti-money laundering (AML) Directive and the Sapin Law II on Transparency, Anti-Corruption and Economic Modernisation enacted on 9 December 2016, France implemented provisions related to the keeping of beneficial ownership registers. French corporates and other legal entities are required to disclose to the trade and company registry updated adequate, accurate and current information on identity of beneficial owners. The information on beneficial ownership is accessible to competent authorities and TRACFIN (see below), entities subject to the anti-money laundering and counter financing of terrorism (AML/CFT) obligations, and any person or organisation that can demonstrate a legitimate interest.

The Public Register of Trusts

5.108 Pursuant to the fourth AML Directive, under French Law, trustees are required to obtain, hold and provide beneficial ownership information to the French Ministry of Economy and Finance, when the settlor or beneficiary of the relevant trust has its tax domicile in France. The information on trust beneficiaries is accessible in all cases to competent authorities (including Tax and Customs, the AMF, the ACPR), a judicial authority, and TRACFIN or entities subject to the AML/CFT obligations.

ANTI-MONEY LAUNDERING LAWS

5.109 The EU AML Directives have been implemented in France into the MFC. The Fourth AML Directive has been transposed into French law. Management companies having activities in France are subject to the AML French regulation and the supervision of the AMF.

5.110 The Treasury Department supervises AMF activities through the French Financial Intelligence Unit, TRACFIN (*Traitement du Renseignement et Action Contre les Circuits Financiers Clandestins*). It serves as a national centre for the receipt and analysis of suspicious transaction reports issued by professionals listed under Article L.561-2 of the MFC and other information relevant to money laundering, associated predicate offences and financing of terrorism, and for the dissemination of the results of that analysis. TRACFIN also publishes Annual Activity and Analysis Reports providing an overview of the participation of professionals subject to the AML/CFT framework and the trends and risks of money laundering and financing terrorism.

5.111 The main obligations of portfolio management companies under the AML regulation consist of:

(i) Know-Your-Customer requirements;

(ii) implementation and performance of ongoing supervision;

(iii) reporting of suspicious or unusual transactions.

CONCLUDING REMARKS: WHAT ARE THE JURISDICTION'S UNIQUE SELLING POINTS?

5.112 France offers various advantages to help set up portfolio management activities:

- a large community of asset managers and professional service providers dedicated to financial service activities, including a number of global participants;

- a large pool of potential investors, ranging from retail investors to large institutional clients;
- active and comprehensive regulators and lawmakers, especially in the context of implementation of EU regulations and international standards into French regulation, with a well-balanced objective to provide strong protection and a safe environment to investors and to allow entrepreneurs to be innovative, competitive and to grow their businesses.

CHAPTER 6

GERMANY

GENERAL DESCRIPTION OF THE JURISDICTION

6.01 The Federal Republic of Germany is Europe's most populous nation. Since reunification in 1990, it has expended a large amount of money and effort into becoming the fourth-largest economy in the world and the largest economy in Europe. In January 1999, it became one of the first countries to swap its own domestic currency for the European common currency — the euro.

6.02 This central European country has Berlin as its capital and is divided into 16 states. The financial centre is widely considered to be Frankfurt, which is home to the European Central Bank and the country's most famous stock exchange, although many other exchanges also operate within the country — for example, the Bavarian stock exchange in Munich.

6.03 The economy has steadily recovered from the 2008 global crisis and, thanks to past reforms, the labour market has proved strong. Germany has high material living standards, low income inequality and scores well in most dimensions of well-being.

KEY MANDATORY REQUIREMENTS

6.04

- Private funds which according to German understanding would be alternative investment funds, can generally be established through the typical vehicles available for German investment funds: i) a Sondervermögen ('investment fund') or a Spezial-Sondervermögen ('special fund') operated by a Kapitalverwaltungsgesellschaft ('capital management company' or **KVG**), that manages the portfolio of the fund either itself or by a separate regulated entity to act as portfolio manager, or ii) an investment stock company with variable capital or fixed capital or in the form of a limited partnership (**InvKG**).
- Fund managers must generally be licensed although a light regime (registration) is available for sub-threshold AIFMs.
- Fund rules must be in the German language.
- Sufficient substance must be available in Germany for the purposes of being granted a licence to manage funds.
- A depositary must be appointed for each private fund.

RECENT DEVELOPMENTS

6.05 In 2016, Germany introduced a framework for direct lending funds by enacting the UCITS V Implementation Act. The changes implemented by this act also allow certain non-German (particularly EU) funds to enter the German direct lending market. The revised regulatory framework triggered substantial interest in the debt fund industry, particularly in relation to foreign funds engaging in lending activities with German borrowers. Furthermore, institutional investors continue to show growing interest in this asset class and seem receptive to investing in attractive debt fund strategies.

THE REGULATION OF INVESTMENT BUSINESS

6.06 The country operates on a system of civil law. Germany has a large and diverse asset management sector to which it applies a well-developed and comprehensive regulatory framework.

6.07 On 22 July 2013, the Investment Act 2003 as amended in 2007 was replaced and repealed, when the Kapitalanlagegesetzbuch (**KAGB**) entered into force, implementing Directive 2011/61/EU (Alternative Investment Fund Managers Directive or **AIFMD**) in Germany.

6.08 With the KAGB, the supervision of German investment funds and their management companies as well as the marketing of funds, has been put on a completely new basis. The new Investment Code applies to managers of open-ended funds as well as managers of closed-ended funds. It distinguishes between fund types defined as either Undertakings for Collective Investment in Transferable Securities (**UCITS**) or as Alternative Investment Funds (**AIF**). German private funds therefore qualify as AIFs.

6.09 The German Federal Financial Services Supervisory Authority *(Bundesanstalt für Finanzdienstleistungsaufsicht* or **BaFin**) is the main regulatory authority for the regulation of funds and their managers. BaFin is seen as a well-respected and authoritative body which maintains close contact to the asset management industry and supervises it in a firm but fair manner.

INVESTORS

6.10 A variety of investor groups invest in German (private) funds that are dedicated to institutional investors only. The most important of these investor groups are insurance companies, followed by pension schemes, credit institutions and other types of companies, which include industrial foundations as well as employer and business associations.

6.11 The fund sector is one of the most important managers of pension capital in Germany. Life assurance companies and pension funds have committed more than 33% of their total capital to investment funds. For occupational pension schemes, the figure is around 38%. Funded retirement provisions are inconceivable without investment funds. They are at the very core of the German pension system.[1]

SETTING UP A FUND

6.12 As described above, all German investments fall into one of two categories: UCITS funds or AIFs. Therefore a private fund would be considered to be an AIF. A further key distinction in Germany between open ended and closed-ended funds. Open-ended funds can be UCITS or AIFs, while all closed-ended funds are AIFs.

6.13 Investment funds in Germany are generally considered in the context of an investment triangle, comprising investors, the fund and the depositary.

6.14 Private funds may be launched through the following vehicles:

- *Sondervermögen*;
- *Spezial-Sondervermögen*;
- Investment stock corporations with fixed or variable capital;
- Limited investment partnership (*Investmentkommanditgesellschaft* or InvKG).

Sondervermögen

6.15 These are pools of assets which are established by KVGs. They have no legal identity of their own and their assets are held separately from those of the KVG. *Sondervermögen* can be likened to a fonds commun de placement in France, Luxembourg or Belgium.

6.16 The legal basis for these asset pools is a contract between the KVG and the investors in which the fund rules, including the basis on which the KVG holds and invests the assets, are laid down. Sample fund rules have been prepared by the German Association of Investment and Asset Management and have been approved by BaFin.

Spezial-Sondervermögen

6.17 Private funds can be established as Spezial-Sondervermögen (special funds). According to the KAGB, these are funds whose units are only held by professional and semi-professional investors. There is no maximum for the

1 Source: German Investment Fund Association.

number of investors, although funds must have no more than 100 investors in order to qualify as a special fund for investment tax purposes. As institutional funds, special funds are subject to less burdensome regulatory requirements than ordinary investment funds. Although the contractual rules and conditions must be filed with BaFin, its approval is not required.

Investment stock corporation

6.18 Open-ended funds can also be established as an investment stock corporation with variable capital (*Investmentaktiengesellschaft mit veränderlichem Kapital*). This legal form can be likened to Luxembourg's investment company with variable capital (société d' investissement à capital variable) or SICAV. The investment stock corporation with fixed capital (*Investmentaktiengesellschaft mit fixem Kapital)* can be used for closed-ended funds.

Limited investment partnership (Investmentkommanditgesellschaft or 'InvKG')

6.19 The InvKG, can be structured either as open-ended or closed-ended investment funds. An InvKG is a separate legal entity and therefore is treated as an incorporated undertaking in legal terms. Therefore, the partnership itself holds its assets and can assume its own liabilities.

ELIGIBLE INVESTORS

6.20 The KAGB distinguishes three types of investor categories: the professional, the semi-professional and the retail investor.

6.21 With regard to the definition of a professional investor, the KAGB refers to the definition of professional clients in Annex II of Directive 2004/39/EC on markets in financial instruments.

6.22 A semi-professional investor within the meaning of the KAGB is any investor:

- who commits to investing a minimum of €200,000;
- who states in writing in a separate document from the contract to be concluded for the commitment to invest, that he is aware of the risks associated with the envisaged commitment or investment;
- whose expertise, experience and knowledge was assessed by the fund management company or the distribution company appointed by it, and such assessment is not based on the assumption that the investor possesses the market knowledge and experience of those investors mentioned in Annex II, Section I of Directive 2004/39/EC;

- regarding whom the fund management company or the distribution company appointed by it, in light of the nature of the intended commitment or investment is sufficiently convinced that he is capable of making his own investment decisions and understanding the risks involved and that such a commitment is appropriate for the respective investor; and
- to whom the fund management company or the distribution company appointed by it, confirms in writing that it has made the assessment mentioned above and the prerequisites regarding the investor's capabilities in relation to the intended commitment are fulfilled; or
- certain institutions under public law.

6.23 Furthermore, directors and employees of the management company who invest in a fund managed by the management company or a member of the management board or board of directors of an externally managed investment company who invest in the externally managed investment company are semi-professional investors within the meaning of the KAGB, as well as any investor who commits to investing a minimum of €10 million in an investment fund.

6.24 The category of retail investors comprises all investors that do not qualify as professional or semi-professional investors.

AUTHORISATION PROCEDURE

6.25 BaFin approval is required for the fund rules of retail funds (UCITS and retail AIFs). The approval must be granted within a period of four weeks after submission of the application, provided the fund rules meet the statutory requirements.

6.26 In the case of special funds, no approval is required, a notification is sufficient. This reflects the more sophisticated nature of the investors in such funds.

6.27 There are two types of special fund: (i) general special funds, which have no limits on their eligible assets; and (ii) special funds with fixed investment conditions, which have a more limited range of eligible assets.

INVESTMENT RESTRICTIONS

6.28 The KAGB contains provisions on different sets of eligible assets and investment limits depending on the type of the fund. Generally, the investments of special funds are less restricted than those of retail funds.

Hedge Funds

Funds of hedge funds

6.29 A fund of hedge funds may generally acquire units in both domestic regulated single hedge funds and foreign investment funds with comparable investment policies. In addition to the principle of risk diversification, further precautionary rules apply; for instance, no more than 20% of a fund of hedge funds may be invested in a single fund. German funds of hedge funds cannot make use of short selling or leveraging techniques, but are permitted to use currency futures contracts

Single hedge funds

6.30 Single hedge funds may only be offered as special funds, ie they may only be marketed to professional and semi-professional investors. Single hedge funds must observe the principle of risk diversification and keep within the scope of the fund's investment policies but are not otherwise subject to any limitations on the assets they invest in. The contractual terms and conditions of the fund must, in addition, include at least one of the following: i) an increase in the investment level of the fund financed through generally unlimited borrowings, or ii) the use of derivatives (leverage) and the sale of assets which, at the time of the sale, do not belong to the fund (short sales).

Private Equity Funds

Closed-ended Investment Funds

6.31 Investment in private equity is an investment in illiquid assets. Private equity funds typically provide their investors either no redemption right or only a very limited redemption right. In the context of the KAGB private equity funds should normally be regarded as closed-ended. Closed-ended investment funds may only be set up as investment stock corporations with fixed capital or as closed-ended InvKGs. The fund can be internally or externally managed in which case an AIFM must be appointed. Typically, a German private equity fund would be set up as a closed-end special fund in the form of an InvKG established as a GmbH & Co InvKG. This structure is comparable to a closed-end LLP structure.

Closed-ended Real Asset Funds

6.32 Closed-ended funds, prior to the introduction of AIFMD were unregulated in terms of their investment policy and management, but have since been assigned in their entirety to the regulated segment under the KAGB.

6.33 Both closed-ended mutual funds and closed-ended special funds must invest their funds primarily in assets that are not financial instruments within the meaning of the KAGB. This requirement is meant to differentiate (liquid) open-ended and (illiquid) closed-end funds. With regard to closed-ended mutual funds, it is supplemented by a restricted list of eligible assets for reasons of investor protection. While stronger product-based constraints are intended for mutual funds, they only apply to special funds on a limited basis.

6.34 Alongside real estate, ships and aircraft, closed-ended funds may acquire plants for the generation of electricity from renewable energies, holdings in public private partnership project companies as well as holdings in special purpose companies, which hold the aforementioned assets. In addition, they may acquire shares and stock in other (regulated) closed-ended funds. Direct investments in (other) holdings (inter alia, private equity holdings) are not permitted.

6.35 As mentioned above investments of a closed-ended special fund are widely unrestricted. Such funds may invest in any asset of which the market value can be assessed.

ACCOUNTS/AUDIT REQUIREMENTS

6.36 The accounting standards for contractual type investment funds, are set out in the KAGB and are further specified in the German Law on Investment Fund Accounting (**KARBV**).

6.37 The provisions of the German Commercial Code (**HGB**) generally apply with regard to the annual financial statement of an investment limited partnership or an investment stock corporation. These provisions are supplemented or modified by specific accounting requirements under the KAGB and KARBV.

SETTING UP A LOCAL MANAGEMENT COMPANY/INVESTMENT MANAGER

6.38 Fund managers in Germany are established as KVGs. KVGs are undertakings whose business is the management of funds. They supply services or ancillary services to funds and require a licence from BaFin to operate under the German Investment Code.

6.39 ***Legal form***: They can be formed as stock corporations (**AG**), limited liability companies (**KVGs**) or limited partnerships with a limited liability company as general partner (**GmbH & Co KG**).

6.40 ***Minimum share capital***: The minimum initial capital for a KVG is €125,000 for an external KVG and €300,000 for an internal KVG, although this increases as funds under management increase.

6.41 ***Management***: KVGs in the form of an AG and a GmbH require both a management board and a supervisory board (normally a supervisory board is not required for a GmbH under ordinary corporate law). If the KVG is established as a GmbH & Co. KG, an advisory board is required. The management board is responsible for the day-to-day running of the company and must have at least two members with adequate experience of investment management business. The supervisory board must have at least three members appointed by the shareholders to oversee the actions of the management board, who must also be suitably qualified and of sufficient standing. Furthermore, one member of the supervisory board must be independent of the shareholders, their affiliated companies their business partners.

6.42 The duty of both boards is to the investors. A KVG must act only in the interest of the investors and must, at all times, ensure that it has the appropriate knowledge and skills to do so. This requirement can be met by employing competent staff or delegating to third parties if necessary.

6.43 An application for a KVG licence must be submitted by the KVG's management. The application must be made in writing, although no special form is prescribed.

6.44 Applicants are recommended to liaise with BaFin prior to making a licence application. For this purpose, it is helpful for the shareholder of the entity, together with the designated managing director, to meet with BaFin. The meeting would generally be arranged by the KVG's advisors who would also accompany the applicant. The KVG must have its registered seat in Germany. The application must include the applicant's name, address and legal structure, the names of at least two managing directors and the anticipated date of commencement of business.

The following must also be included in the application:

- suitable proof that the KVG has the required capital to commence business operations;
- fit and proper information on the managing directors;
- information on the professional qualifications of the managing directors;
- Information on the identities of the shareholders above a qualifying participation in the AIFM, information to assess their reliability and the extent of their participation;
- information on persons with whom the KVG has close links and the amounts of their holdings in the KVG;
- a viable business plan;
- information on the KVG's remuneration policies and practices;
- information on arrangements made for the delegation or sub-delegation to third parties;
- information on the investment strategies;
- the fund rules and the memorandum and articles of association for every fund the KVG intends to manage;
- information on the depositary for each fund the KVG intends to manage; and
- prospectuses for each fund the KVG intends to manage.

6.45 The reporting obligations set out in the KAGB include both reports on the level of the KVG itself and on the level of the individual investment fund. A German KVG is obliged to inform BaFin on an ongoing basis of the main instruments in which it is trading, including the fund's investment strategies and geographical and sectoral investment focus, the markets of which it is a member or where it actively trades and the diversification of the fund's portfolio, including its principal exposures and most important concentrations.

6.46 Additionally, a KVG is obliged to provide BaFin with the following information: i) the percentage of the fund's assets which are hard to value due to their illiquid nature; ii) any new arrangements for managing the liquidity of the fund; iii) risk management systems employed by the fund and the current risk profile of the fund; iv) information on the main categories of assets in which the fund invested and the results of periodic stress tests under normal and; v) exceptional circumstances.

Timescales

6.47 An applicant will be informed, within three months of the submission of a complete application, whether or not authorisation has been granted. This period of time can be extended by another three months if BaFin deems it necessary due to particular circumstances of the individual case. The KVG may commence business as soon as authorisation has been granted. Reasons must be given where authorisation is refused by BaFin.

FEES

6.48 The licence application for a KVG that will manage private funds is subject to a fee of €10,000–€40,000.

SUB-THRESHOLD KVGS

6.49 A tailored approach is taken to registered management companies, which are those falling below the relevant threshold of the AIFMD and/or the KAGB. Where the registered KVG manages only special AIFs, the management company is subject only to registration and reporting requirements. Where the registered KVG also manages retail AIFs, it is subject to a broader set of rules covering, inter alia, conduct and organisational requirements, and depositary obligations.

OTHER KEY SERVICE PROVIDERS

6.50 A depositary must be appointed for every private fund. The depositaries bear primary responsibility for the safekeeping of a fund's investment, in particular, financial instruments that can be entered into an account for financial instruments on the depositaries' books and all financial instruments that can be physically transferred to the depositary. For all other non-depositable assets, the obligation to verify the legal ownership relationship applies in place of the deposit requirement.

6.51 Another primary duty of the depositary is to provide proper monitoring of the fund's cash flows.

6.52 In addition to this, depositaries must also perform certain oversight and approval duties with regard to certain transactions for a fund.

6.53 A depositary for a German private fund can be either a credit institution or a financial services institution which holds a license for limited custody business. For financial services institutions acting as depositary, the initial capital has to be at least €730,000. A derogation is provided for certain types of closed-ended AIF such that a trustee can be engaged as depositary if the trustee meets certain personal and professional requirements (eg, having sufficient financial guarantees in the form of capital and liability). BaFin has issued a circular in which the obligations on trustees are detailed further.

GERMAN MASTER-KVG-STRUCTURE

General concept

6.54 German institutional investors (banks, family offices, insurance companies and pension funds) prefer not to invest into retail funds but into tailor made dedicated funds. Moreover, they like to use structures which gives them a maximum degree of transparency, and the flexibility to change the managers of 'their' funds if they are dissatisfied with their performance. Such funds, generally set up as special funds, under German law are funds that can be held exclusively by professional or semi-professional clients. Over the last decade, a business model called Master-KVG-model has been developed which gives the German institutional investors a simple, standardised structure, which offers maximum flexibility as regards manager selection.

German fund structure – Investment triangle

6.55 As discussed above, German funds are established on the basis of an investment management agreement between the KVG, the depositary (**Depotbank**) and the investor. The KVG is responsible from a regulatory perspective for the administration and the asset management of the fund. The depositary acts independently of the KVG and solely in the interests of the investors. It keeps in custody and supervises the fund's assets on blocked accounts which enables the depositary to review and supervise transactions for the account of the respective fund.

6.56 Furthermore, the depositary issues and redeems the fund units and is in the case of a distributing fund also responsible for distributions by the fund to the investors. The calculation of the issuance and redemption price of the fund units is carried out in cooperation with the KVG. The investor invests his money on the basis of the general and special fund terms (*Allgemeine und Besondere Anlagebedingungen*). In the case of a special fund the investor, the KVG and the depositary agree that the investor subscribes the fund units. The fund itself as a pool of assets managed by the KVG has no legal personality of its own. The predominant number of German funds are established under the contractual model based on the contractual relationship between the investor and the KVG according to the fund rules. The relationship between the investor, the KVG and the custodian is called the investment triangle.

Appointment of an asset manager in a Master-KVG structure

6.57 In a typical situation, the institutional investors instruct a Master-KVG to set up a fund administered by the KVG and to delegate the management of the assets of the fund to a third party asset manager. The KVG would still administer the fund. The KVG would therefore enter into an investment agreement with the asset manager which, from a regulatory perspective, is an outsourcing agreement since the management of the assets of the fund is a task which is material to the performance of the business operations of a KVG.

NEW GERMAN TAX REGIME

6.58 With effect from January 2018, a totally revised German investment tax law (**New GITA**) has entered into force. It is equally applicable to domestic and foreign funds and in addition to which (among other provisions):

- The former highly punitive lump-sum taxation for German investors in non-tax transparent funds has been abolished for most funds (with the exception of certain so-called "special funds" with a restricted catalogue of eligible assets and which are set up exclusively for not more than 100 institutional investors).
- There generally will no longer be a requirement that investment funds subject to the New GITA file an annual German tax return.
- Significant specific partial tax exemptions will be afforded to German taxable investors in investment funds that qualify as so-called *Aktienfonds* (equity funds); *Mischfonds* (mixed funds) and *Immobilienfonds* (real estate funds). These types of funds are described in more detail below.

Categories of Covered Investment Funds

6.59 The New GITA applies to ***all*** *Investmentfonds* (investment funds) regardless of their origin. In general, these funds may be organised in either corporate form (*eg*, German AG, Irish PLC or ICAV, Luxembourg S.A.) or contractual form (*eg*, German Sondervermögen, Luxembourg FCP, Irish unit trust). However, partnership structures cannot qualify as *Investmentfonds* and will continue to fall under the ordinary income taxation rules.

There are different subcategories of privileged *Investmentfonds*: an *Aktienfonds* is an investment fund that, according either to its predefined contractual terms (*Anlagebedingungen*) or upon factual proof after each business year end, on an ongoing basis invests at least 51% of its value in *Kapitalbeteiligungen* (generally, equity participations in corporations that are either listed or subject to certain minimum taxation of earnings in the country where domiciled). A *Mischfonds* is an investment fund that, according to its contractual terms or upon factual proof, on an ongoing basis invests at least 25% of its value in *Kapitalbeteiligungen*. An *Immobilienfonds* is an investment fund that, according to its contractual terms or upon factual proof, invests at least 51% of its value in real estate and qualifying real estate companies (*Immobiliengesellschaften*).

Tax Treatment of ordinary (opaque) investment funds

Fund-Level

6.60 Investment funds are generally treated as opaque, non-transparent, corporations, which are subject to a reduced flat rate tax on specific German-sourced income (primarily German dividends and certain German real estate related income). A precondition for an upfront reduction of the withholding tax is the application for a so-called 'fund status certificate' which is issued by the relevant tax authorities and has to be presented to the individual dividend paying agent(s) of the fund. The presentation of such a fund tax certificate in advance (which is valid for 3 years) may avoid the necessity of conducting expensive withholding tax reclaim procedures.

Investor-Level

6.61 For German taxable investors, distributions received from the fund, as well as gains resulting from the redemption/disposal of fund units, are subject to tax. The former punitive taxation for income received from non-transparent funds is abolished.

With respect to accumulated income, a certain minimum amount (so-called *Vorabpauschale*), calculated according to a specific formula is, on an annual basis, subject to tax at the investor level. However, this minimum tax applies only if a fund`s distributions in the relevant year are lower than the amount of the *Vorabpauschale* calculated.

A key benefit for German taxable investors is that the New GITA will introduce significant additional reductions of the investor`s tax base in *Aktienfonds,*

Mischfonds and *Immobilienfonds*, depending on the fund category and type of investor. There are basically two options for a fund in order to prove compliance with the relevant limits for classification as such funds. Either the fund manager may bind himself ex ante through fixed obligations in the statutes to keep the necessary thresholds or he has to make sure to have monitored the relevant investments throughout the year on the basis of regular holding lists in order to be able to confirm it ex-post at business year end towards the German investor directly or via data providers like Bloomberg/WM Data etc.

Tax Treatment of (transparent) so-called "special funds" for institutional investors

6.62 In order to secure specific, applicable, tax exemptions, some institutional investors (especially corporate tax payers) might opt to follow the tax regime of a so-called 'special fund'. Special funds must not have more than 100 investors altogether and are not allowed for investment by private persons. Additionally they have a limited catalogue of eligible (long-only) investments and may hardly be used for alternative investment strategies. Special funds are regarded as tax transparent under the New GITA and continue to be required to file annual German tax returns (similar to the former regime which existed until the end of 2017).

LOCAL STOCK EXCHANGE

6.63 A decentralised exchange landscape developed in Germany, with regional centres that reflect the federal state system. Regional exchanges operate in Berlin, Düsseldorf, Frankfurt, Hamburg, Hanover, Munich and Stuttgart.

6.64 The best known German stock exchange is the Frankfurter Wertpapierbörse (**FWB**), the Frankfurt Stock Exchange. The FWB is one of the world's largest trading centres for securities. With a share in turnover of more than 85%, it is the largest of Germany's seven stock exchanges. The FWB is operated by Deutsche Börse AG.

CONFIDENTIALITY LAWS

6.65 Confidentiality in Germany is governed by the highly-developed and sophisticated Data Protection Act 2003 (as amended on 28 April 2017). New data protection legislation is in the final stages of being finalised in Germany and is set to expand on the EU's new General Data Protection Regulation (**GDPR**).

ANTI-MONEY LAUNDERING

6.66 German anti-money laundering regulation derives, for the most part, from two pieces of legislation. On 26 June 2017, an act implementing the Fourth EU Anti-Money Laundering Directive, for the execution of the EU Funds Transfer Regulation and for the reorganisation of the central department for financial investigations became effective. The act reforms and restates the former version of the German Anti-Money Laundering Act (**GwG**).

6.67 Section 261 of the Criminal Code sets out the offence of money laundering.

6.68 Germany is also a member of the Financial Action Task Force on money laundering and as such, has signed up to their recommendations.

CONCLUDING REMARKS: WHAT ARE THE JURISDICTION'S UNIQUE SELLING POINTS?

6.69 Germany is the strongest economy in Europe and one of the largest worldwide. Few countries are as tightly connected into the world economy as Germany is. The fund sector is one of the most important managers of pension and other institutional capital in Germany. During the first six months of the year 2017, the German fund industry recorded net inflows of €79.1 billion, making this the second highest result for new business in any single half year since 2015.[2] A well-developed infrastructure, efficient capital markets, and a high level of legal security contribute to putting Germany in a leading position in international location comparisons.

2 Source: German Investment Fund Association.

CHAPTER 7

GUERNSEY

GENERAL DESCRIPTION OF THE JURISDICTION

7.01 The Bailiwick of Guernsey comprises the inhabited islands of Guernsey, Alderney, Sark, Herm, Jethou and Brecqhou (referred to herein together as Guernsey or the Bailiwick). The islands are situated in the Bay of St. Malo, with their closest point being eight miles from the Cherbourg peninsula, and they are in the same time zone as the UK. The island of Guernsey is approximately 24.3 sq. miles and has a resident population of around 63,000. The capital of Guernsey is St. Peter Port. The official language is English, and the official currency is the pound sterling.

7.02 The islands are self-governing possessions of the Crown and allegiance is given to Queen Elizabeth II. As such, the Bailiwick of Guernsey is part of the British Isles, but independent of the UK. The island of Guernsey has its own government, known as the States of Deliberation (the States) which legislates at insular and local level on all matters, including the raising and expenditure of taxes. The UK Government in Westminster may legislate, with consultation, on behalf of the islands on matters relating to defence, foreign policy and broadcasting.

7.03 The States comprises the Bailiff (*ex officio* president) HM Attorney-General, HM Solicitor General and 40 peoples' deputies, including two representatives of Alderney. The States is also the executive body in the island and following a fundamental reform of the machinery of government in Guernsey, approved by the States in 2003, the States now has 10 departments responsible for, among other things, health, home affairs, education, the environment and social services. Each department is headed by a minister, and each minister has a seat on the Policy Council which is chaired by the Chief Minister who is elected by the States. The Policy Council has ultimate responsibility for the policy of the States and will oversee the interaction between the various departments.

7.04 Guernsey is neither a member, nor an associate member, of the European Union. The Bailiwick's relationship with the EU is governed by Protocol 3 on the Channel Islands and the Isle of Man to the Treaty of Accession of 1972. The effect of this protocol is that the Bailiwick falls within the common customs area and the common external tariff, but is not required to comply with EU Directives and is free to maintain an independent fiscal policy.

KEY MANDATORY REQUIREMENTS

7.05

- No fund can be established in Guernsey without the prior consent of, or registration with, the Guernsey Financial Services Commission.
- A promoter who is new to Guernsey must be able to show a demonstrable track record in the promotion and management of funds.
- No Guernsey body may provide services to a fund, whether established in Guernsey or elsewhere, without a licence.
- Licensees are subject to certain conduct of business rules and minimum capitalisation requirements.
- No person from outside Guernsey may provide investment services from within Guernsey without a licence.
- All open-ended funds must appoint a designated administrator, designated trustee or custodian each licensed and resident in Guernsey (but subject to certain concessions in respect of private investment funds (**PIF**s) and hedge funds as set out below).
- All PIFs, whether open-ended or closed-ended, must appoint a manager licensed and resident in Guernsey, in addition to its designated administrator.
- The acceptance of subscription monies from prospective investors is subject to international standard 'customer due diligence' regulations.

RECENT DEVELOPMENTS

7.06 Guernsey launched a new fund product in 2016, the Private Investment Fund (as more particularly described below).

The Regulation of Investment Business

7.07 Investment business in Guernsey is overseen by the Guernsey Financial Services Commission (the **Commission**). The Commission was established by the States of Guernsey by statute as a body corporate in 1988 with the task of taking such steps as it considered necessary for the development and effective supervision of finance business in the Bailiwick of Guernsey and, as well as regulating investment business, it is also responsible for the supervision of banks, insurance companies and fiduciaries.

INVESTORS

7.08 Guernsey is a leading funds domicile with over 50 years' experience as an international finance centre. At the end of September 2017, the overall value of institutional and retail funds under management and administration in Guernsey stood at £269 billion. From an investor prospective Guernsey has an excellent reputation as an attractive funds jurisdiction, due to its fiscal neutrality and robust yet flexible regulatory framework with a strong focus on corporate governance and high quality of service providers.

SETTING UP A FUND

7.09 For the purposes of Guernsey law, a fund is a collective investment scheme, and a collective investment scheme is defined as i) any arrangement relating to property of any description (including money) the purpose or effect of which is to enable investors to participate in, or receive profits or income arising from, the acquisition, holding, management or disposal of the property, or sums paid out of such profits or income; and ii) in which the investors do not have a day-to-day control over the management of the property to which the arrangement relates (whether or not they have any right to be consulted or give directions); and under which: i) the contributions of the investors and the profits or income out of which payments are to be made to them are pooled; or ii) the property in question is managed as a whole by, or on behalf of, the person responsible for its management. Funds may be open-ended or closed-ended, and may be set up under the provisions of the Protection of Investors (Bailiwick of Guernsey) Law 1987 (as amended) (**the POI Law**) as either authorised schemes, registered schemes, or as PIFs (as described below).

7.10 The Commission's application fees for open and closed-ended funds are currently £3,435 and annual fees of £3,435 also apply.

Authorised open-ended schemes

7.11 There are three classes of authorised open-ended funds: Class A, Class B and Class Q. Class A Schemes are those which comply with a detailed rule book which enables them to be recognised under Section 270 of the UK Financial Services and Markets Act 2000, so that they can be promoted to the public in the UK in the same way as if they were UK-authorised unit trusts.

7.12 Class B Schemes are usually, but not necessarily, those which are marketed on a restricted basis to institutional or professional investors. The rules governing Class B Schemes lay down requirements as to the information which must be contained in the principal documents and the Scheme Particulars, but do not impose specific restrictions on investment and borrowing powers and are generally designed to be flexible, while at the same time reflecting best practice. The overriding requirement is that the assets of a Class B Scheme must be invested with the aim of spreading risk, so the manager must adopt and adhere to an investment objective and investment and borrowing restrictions designed to achieve this.

7.13 Class Q Schemes may only be marketed to qualified professional investors and are subject to a relatively short set of rules, which do not lay down any requirements as to what must be included in a Scheme's principal documents and which prescribe much simpler requirements than the Class B Scheme Rules as to the information which must be made available in information particulars to prospective investors. As with Class B Schemes, the property of a Class Q Scheme must be invested to provide a spread of risk and in accordance with the limits or restrictions disclosed in the information particulars.

7.14 For the purposes of the Class Q Rules, a qualifying professional investor is:

- a government, local authority or public authority in the Bailiwick of Guernsey or elsewhere;
- a trustee of a trust which, at the time of investment, has net assets in excess of £2 million (or currency equivalent);
- a body corporate or limited partnership, if it, or any holding company or subsidiary of it, has, at the time of investment, net assets in excess of £2 million (or currency equivalent); or
- an individual who has, together with any spouse, at the time of investment, a minimum net worth (which excludes that individual's main residence and household goods) of £500,000 (or currency equivalent).

Authorised closed-ended schemes

7.15 As a result of amendments to the POI Law which were brought into force in 2008, closed-ended funds, which previously had not been within the scope of the POI Law, became subject to regulation under the Authorised Closed-Ended Investment Schemes Rules 2008 made by the Commission pursuant to powers conferred on the Commission by the POI Law. These Rules which, broadly speaking, have put on a statutory footing the policy which the Commission previously applied to closed-ended funds, set out requirements on:

- administration;
- custody;
- conflicts of interest;
- contents of information particulars;
- accounting and audit requirements; and
- notifications.

7.16 A closed-ended fund is not required (as open-ended schemes are, subject to any applicable concessions) to appoint a custodian to hold the fund's assets, but the Commission does need to be advised of, and be satisfied with, the proposed arrangements for the safe custody of the fund's assets.

Registered collective investment schemes

7.17 The Commission introduced the concept of registered closed-ended funds in 2008. Registered funds are not reviewed or approved in any way by the Commission, but simply registered subject to the condition that the prospectus, other offering or explanatory memorandum contains a statement to the effect that the fund has been dealt with in accordance with the registered fund rules (as described below) and that, accordingly, no documents have been reviewed by the Commission. The Commission instead relies on certain warranties given by the proposed designated administrator to the fund. Following amendments made to the POI Law, the registered fund route can now extend to open-ended funds. Notwithstanding that registered funds are not regulated by the Commission, they are nevertheless subject to the Registered Collective Investment Schemes Rules 2015 and the Prospectus Rules 2008. The former contain regulations on administration, custody, conflicts of interest, accounting and audit requirements and notifications, and the latter contain regulations on the information to be contained in prospectuses and other offering or explanatory memoranda to be issued by, inter alia, registered funds.

7.18 The registered fund route offers a fast track registration process (typically three working days) lfor the launch of a fund where authorisation is not deemed to be a material consideration for potential investors. However, it is not a way around the Commission's overriding policy on acceptable promoters which is more fully described under 'Authorisation Procedure', below. This applies with the same force as it applies to authorised funds, but the responsibility for judging the acceptability of the promoter lies with the proposed designated administrator of the fund rather than with the Commission.

Private Investment Funds

7.19 The Commission launched its private investment fund (**PIF**) regime in November 2016 to further increase the diversity of fund products available in Guernsey and to continue to facilitate and incubate market access by new managers and promoters. The PIF regime is intended to offer managers and promoters a more cost effective and less burdensome regulatory product in Guernsey whilst at the same time ensuring that investor protection is sufficiently maintained, with a strong focus on corporate governance, including, inter alia, managing conflicts of interest.

Key features of a PIF:

7.20

- Each PIF must be registered under the POI Law with the Commission and is subject to the Private Investment Fund Rules 2016 which contain regulations on, inter alia, management, administration, custody, conflicts of interest and notifications;

- The fund can be open or closed-ended and take a variety of legal forms (as described under 'Structure', below);
- There is a choice as to whether an offer document is used by the fund;
- The fund can admit up to a maximum of 50 investors; however, there is no limit on the number of investors to which the fund can be marketed;
- A Guernsey licensed manager must be appointed to manage the fund together with a Guernsey licensed designated administrator;
- There is no requirement to appoint a custodian to the fund; however, if the fund is open-ended a designated custodian must be named under the POI Law – in practice this can be the designated administrator but it does not have to be a Guernsey licensed and resident body;
- The Commission offer a fast track application process of 24 hours;
- A PIF is not subject to additional restrictions on investment or borrowing (although it may elect to include restrictions in its constitutional or offering document (if any)).

Hedge funds

7.21 In terms of Guernsey products, hedge funds can be either open or closed-ended (although the majority tend to be open-ended schemes). The Commission operates a flexible approach in the case of funds targeted at institutional and/or expert investors, for example, a reputable prime broker can be appointed as the designated custodian or trustee and the Commission will not require the prime broker to take on formal duties of oversight over the fund manager.

STRUCTURE

7.22 Funds are typically structured as either unit trusts, companies or limited partnerships. The principal features of these are as follows:

Unit trusts

7.23 A unit trust is not a separate legal entity but is constituted by an agreement in writing, commonly known as a 'trust instrument', between a manager and a trustee. This trust concept has been recognised in Guernsey for over 100 years and trusts generally are now governed by the provisions of the Trusts (Guernsey) Law 2007, as amended.

7.24 The assets of a unit trust are held by its trustee and are managed by the manager, who may appoint one or more investment managers/advisers to assist it. Contracts in relation to the management and administration of the trust fund will be entered into by the manager, whereas the trustee will enter into contracts in relation to the assets themselves, such as bank deposits, borrowings and security agreements.

Companies

7.25 Companies are incorporated under the provisions of the Companies (Guernsey) Law 2008 (as amended) (**the Companies Law**). The liability of shareholders in Guernsey companies may be limited by shares or by guarantee or by a combination of shares and guarantee, or it may be unlimited. The form usually chosen for investment funds is a company limited by shares. Fund companies, which are established as open-ended so that investors have the right to realise their investment in the company, will normally issue redeemable shares to facilitate this. Under the Companies Law, companies are not required to have an authorised share capital and may choose to have the power to issue an unlimited number of shares (subject in some circumstances to having authority from its shareholders to do so) with either a par value or no par value.

7.26 In addition to the traditional type of limited liability company, the Companies Law also permits the incorporation of protected cell companies which are particularly well suited for use as umbrella funds and incorporated cell companies. The umbrella structure, under which a company segregates its assets into separate class funds, each with its own investment activity, has been a familiar feature in the offshore fund world for many years. While this has worked well in practice, there is no distinction between class funds in law and, notwithstanding the separation of assets between class funds, the potential exists for the assets of profitable class funds to be taken to cover losses in an insolvent class fund.

7.27 The Companies Law provides that the assets of a protected cell company shall be either cellular assets or non-cellular assets. It is the duty of the directors of the company to keep cellular assets separate and separately identifiable from non-cellular assets, and to keep cellular assets attributable to each cell separate and separately identifiable from cellular assets attributable to other cells. This statutory ring-fencing of assets and liabilities also means that it is possible to pay dividends out of profitable cells even if other cells are unprofitable. Incorporated cell companies are similar to protected cell companies, but go a stage further in that each cell is a separate company in its own right with its own constitution and capital structure.

7.28 All companies formed under Guernsey law have a separate legal personality and are capable of suing and being sued in their own name. Management and control is vested in a board of directors although, particularly in the case of open-ended companies, it is often the case that an investment management will be delegated to a management company.

Limited partnerships

7.29 Limited partnerships, which are now the favoured vehicles for closed-ended private equity funds, are established under the provisions of the Limited Partnerships (Guernsey) Law 1995 (as amended). A limited partnership can only be created by a written partnership agreement and cannot come into existence until it has been registered in the register of limited partnerships maintained by the Registrar of Companies at the Guernsey Registry. An unusual feature of Guernsey's partnership law is that the general partner may make an election at the time of registration as to whether or not the partnership is to have a separate legal personality.

7.30 A limited partnership consists of one or more general partners who are admitted to the partnership as general partners in accordance with the partnership agreement and who are jointly and severally liable for all debts of the partnership without limitation; and one or more limited partners who are admitted to the partnership as limited partners in accordance with the partnership agreement, who upon entering the partnership contribute, or agree to contribute, to the capital thereof a specified sum and are not liable for any debts of the partnership beyond the amounts contributed or agreed to be contributed. Among the features which make the Guernsey limited partnership attractive to fund promoters are the following:

- there is no limit on the number of limited partners who may be members of a limited partnership;
- a person may be both a general partner and a limited partner, and a body corporate or a partnership may be a general partner or a limited partner;
- the general partner is not required to be resident in Guernsey;
- although the partnership is registered in a public register which is open to inspection, the names of the limited partners do not appear on it; and
- a limited partnership can distribute both capital and profits without formality, provided that the partnership is solvent before and after the distribution.

AUTHORISATION PROCEDURE

7.31 Prior to the introduction of registered schemes and PIFs, there was only one, three-stage, way to obtain approval for a fund, whether open or closed-ended. This process is still the only means of getting certain funds authorised but now, as already noted above, registered schemes and PIFs are dealt with under a streamlined process. In addition, a fast-track process is available for the authorisation of funds which are to be promoted exclusively to certain categories of professional investors.

7.32 Following the traditional authorisation route, the first stage is an application for approval in principle, which involves the completion and submission of a form GFA. The form sets out, among other things, details of the nature and purpose of the scheme, the names and addresses of the proposed manager and trustee/custodian and the fees to be borne by the scheme. If the promoter is new to the island, there is an Introductory Checklist which must also be submitted. The new promoter will first have to satisfy the Commission as to its acceptability, before the Commission will go on to consider whether it is prepared, in principle, to approve the proposed fund. The forms can be downloaded from the Commission's website, www.gfsc.gg.

7.33 The Commission's policy in relation to new promoters is one of selectivity. This means that only promoters of the first rank are encouraged. Normally, a demonstrable track record in the promotion and management of investment funds is required and the authorisation of intended promoters by regulatory authorities in other jurisdictions is not, in itself, generally sufficient. The Commission's due diligence process will usually involve scrutiny of the most recent report and accounts of the applicant or, if the applicant is newly established, the personal background and investment experience of the individuals behind the applicant. The Commission will also make enquiries with any relevant regulators in the applicant's home jurisdiction; this can sometimes delay the approval process, as some regulators can be slow to respond.

7.34 Assuming the promoter is acceptable to the Commission and outline approval for the proposed fund is given, an application for interim consent must be made. This must be accompanied by a copy of the proposed prospectus or explanatory memorandum in as near to final form as possible. When all the documents are in final form and any queries raised by the Commission have been dealt with to the Commission's satisfaction, the application for final consent is made by letter. This must be accompanied by copies of all the material documents certified to be true copies of the originals and a printed copy of the prospectus or explanatory memorandum.

7.35 An open- or closed-ended fund which is only to be offered to 'qualified investors' (which broadly means professional investors, experienced investors and knowledgeable employees) is eligible to be approved by the Commission as a 'Qualifying Investor Fund'. Somewhat confusingly, the conditions to be satisfied to be classed as a qualified investor are not quite the same as the conditions to be satisfied by an investor in a Class Q Scheme, so it does not necessarily follow that a Class Q Scheme will always be eligible to be approved under the Qualifying Investor Fund regime. Under this regime, the Commission's policy of selectivity still applies, but the responsibility for undertaking the necessary assessment is assumed by the prospective Guernsey administrator. Once the administrator has satisfied itself that the promoter meets the acceptability criteria, all that is necessary when the fund is ready to launch is for the administrator to submit an application for approval of the fund as a Qualifying Investor Fund, accompanied by certified copies of the material documents in final form together with a cheque for the application fee. The Commission has indicated that it will use best endeavours to issue the necessary consent within three working days. In respect of collective investment schemes, the Commission may only grant final authorisation if it is satisfied that the scheme will meet the specific requirements of Schedule 3 to the POI Law, and these are:

- the scheme must comply with all rules made under the POI Law applicable to the class of authorised or registered collective investment scheme which it is declared to be;
- the name of the scheme must not be undesirable or misleading;
- the purposes of the scheme must be reasonably capable of being successfully carried into effect;
- the scheme which is promoted or otherwise described as an open-ended investment scheme must entitle investors either:
  - to have their units redeemed or repurchased at a price related to the net value of the property to which the units relate; or
  - to sell their units on a recognised investment exchange at a price not significantly different from that mentioned in the point immediately above; and
- the manager and the trustee or custodian of the assets of a scheme which is promoted or otherwise described as an open-ended investment scheme must each be a body corporate.

OTHER KEY SERVICE PROVIDERS

7.36 All collective investment schemes must have a designated administrator and all open-ended collective investment schemes must also have a designated trustee/custodian incorporated and resident in Guernsey (excluding any concessions applicable to PIF's and hedge funds). It has been the practice for a promoter to establish its own management company to act as manager (a principal manager for the purposes of the rules) and, historically, it was the Commission's policy to insist on this. Following a full-scale review of Guernsey's investment business by an independent committee set up by the Commission, this policy requirement has now been dropped. It is difficult to avoid this in practice, in any event, if the fund is to be structured as a unit trust, since a unit trust is usually constituted by a written instrument between a manager and a trustee. Invariably, where a principal manager has been appointed, it will delegate investment management back to an investment manager in the promoter's group or to a third-party investment manager, and will delegate administration to a Guernsey-based fund administrator which acts as designated administrator. In most cases, the principal manager will not have a physical presence or staff on the island.

7.37 In a Class B Scheme, the designated trustee/custodian has a dual function, i) to safeguard the assets and ii) to exercise oversight of the management and administration of the fund by the manager. In a Class Q Scheme, the role of the designated trustee/custodian is broadly limited to that of responsibility for the custody of scheme property and ensuring that any sub-custodians which it may appoint are fit and proper.

7.38 The requirement that open-ended funds must have a Guernsey resident and incorporated custodian, potentially gives rise to a problem to certain type of funds, for example a hedge fund, which intends to employ the services of a prime broker. The Commission has, in the past, dealt with this on an ad hoc basis, but is prepared to grant derogations depending on the risk profile of the fund, the intended investor base and the standing of the proposed prime broker. It is, however, an essential requirement that the prime broker can demonstrate that it will segregate the fund's assets and keep them segregated from the assets of other funds and its own funds.

7.39 The POI Law makes it a criminal offence, subject to certain exceptions, for any person to carry on, or hold himself out as carrying on, any controlled investment business in or from within the Bailiwick of Guernsey without a licence issued by the Commission. In addition, it is an offence for a Bailiwick body to carry on, or hold itself out as carrying on, any controlled investment business from in, or from within, a territory outside the Bailiwick, unless that body is licensed to carry on that business in the Bailiwick and the business would be lawfully carried on if it were carried on in the Bailiwick. Subject to limited defences, agreements entered into in contravention of the POI Law are unenforceable. An investment manager to whom a principal manager of a fund has delegated investment management responsibilities, and which is not incorporated in Guernsey, is not treated as carrying on controlled investment business in Guernsey but the principal manager itself, the custodian/trustee and the designated administrator all require a licence from the Commission to enable them to provide services to that fund.

7.40 A person is treated as carrying on a controlled investment business if he engages by way of business in any of the 'restricted activities' specified in Schedule 2 of the POI Law in connection with any 'controlled investment' identified and described in Schedule 1 of the POI Law. Category 1 of Schedule 1 identifies and describes collective investment schemes as controlled investments, and Category 2 of that Schedule identifies general derivatives and securities. Activities described in Schedule 2 for which a licence is required if carried on in connection with any controlled investment are promotion, subscription, registration, dealing, management, administration, advising and custody.

7.41 The Commission may grant or refuse an application at its discretion and, in considering whether or not to grant a licence, the Commission is required to have regard to the need to protect the public and the reputation of the Bailiwick as a financial centre. Among the matters which the Commission must take into account in reaching a decision are i) whether the applicant is a fit and proper person to carry on the business proposed, ii) the manner in which it is proposed to organise the carrying on of the business to which the application relates and iii) what, if any, economic benefit the Bailiwick is likely to derive from the conduct of the business. The Commission has the power to impose conditions on a licensee, either on the grant of a licence or at any time after its issue, and also to cancel or suspend a licence in certain specified circumstances.

7.42 The Commission's application fees for licensees are currently £2,322 with annual fees ranging from £1,661 to £2,322 depending on the type of licence held.

7.43 In terms of on-going supervision and obligations, licensees are required to comply with the Commission's prescribed rules regarding conduct of business (the Licensees (Conduct of Business) Rules 2016) and capacity adequacy (the Licensees (Capital Adequacy) Rules 2010). The former contains regulations on, inter alia, corporate governance, conflicts of interest, accounting and audit requirements, client relations including dealing with client money, complaints procedures and notifications. The latter lays down minimum financial resources requirements which vary depending on the type of business undertaken and whether or not the licensee has a physical presence on the Island. The requirements are as follows:

- The designated custodian or trustee of an open-ended collective investment scheme must have net assets of at least £4 million and minimum professional indemnity insurance (**PII**) cover of £300,000 (or three times total revenue, whichever is greater), the excess of which must not exceed 20% of the total insured.
- The designated manager of a collective investment scheme must have net assets of at least £100,000 or net assets equal to, broadly, three months' expenditure, whichever is the greater and minimum PII cover of £300,000 (or three times total revenue, whichever is greater), the excess of which must not exceed 20% of the total insured.
- Any other licensees with no physical presence or staff in the Bailiwick is required to have net assets and PII cover which, in the opinion of its directors, is sufficient to meet its commitments and to withstand the risks to which the business is subject (in practice, the Commission insist on a share capital of at least £10,000 and will only accept the contention of the directors that the company does not need PII cover in the most exceptional circumstances).
- All other licensees must have net assets of £25,000 or net assets equal to, broadly, three months' expenditure, whichever is the greater, and minimum PII cover of £250,000 (or three times total revenue, whichever is greater), the excess of which must not exceed 20% of the total insured.

7.44 In addition to the above, all licensees licensed under the POI Law are required to maintain, at all times, a liquidity requirement of £10,000 (or 10% of its annual audited expenditure, whichever is the greater).

TAX REGIME

7.45 Taxation in Guernsey is the responsibility of the States of Guernsey Income Tax Department, headed by the Director of Income Tax, and the principal legislation is contained in the Income Tax (Guernsey) Law 1975 as extensively amended since 1975. Guernsey does not currently levy any form of capital gains tax, inheritance tax or value-added tax either in respect of fund vehicles or investors in fund vehicles. The income tax position for fund vehicles is set out below:

Unit trusts

7.46 The Income Tax (Exempt Bodies) (Guernsey) Ordinance, 1989 the **Ordinance** provides that a body is exempt from income tax for any year of charge on its income (other than Guernsey-source income excluding bank deposit interest) if:

- it is a body of a description set out in Schedule 1 of the Ordinance;
- has applied for and been granted exemption; and
- meets the conditions of eligibility set out in Schedule 2 of the Ordinance.

7.47 The exemption has to be applied for annually and is subject to payment of a fee currently fixed at £1,200. Unit trusts and any companies in their beneficial ownership fall within category A of Schedule 1 and the condition of eligibility are as follows:

- there must be an agreement in place with a person resident in Guernsey for the provision of managerial and secretarial services for remuneration calculated on an arm's length basis; and
- there must be no investment in any property situated in Guernsey other than bank deposits or other exempt bodies.

Companies

7.48 A company incorporated in Guernsey is treated as resident in Guernsey in any year of charge unless it has been granted exemption under the Ordinance (as described above). Under the Ordinance, a company which derives the principal part of its capital from the issue of redeemable preference shares falls within Category B of Schedule 1 and is entitled to exemption on the same conditions as set out above for a unit trust.

7.49 If a Guernsey company has not applied for tax exempt status pursuant to the Ordinance it is subject to Guernsey income tax at the standard company rate of income tax, currently zero per cent. A Guernsey company will not pay any Guernsey income tax on its income and gains provided that no investments will be made in Guernsey property and the company will not engage in any regulated activities which fall outside the scope of the zero-rate regime.

Limited partnerships

7.50 A limited partnership, whether or not it has elected to have a separate legal personality, is transparent for the purposes of Guernsey tax. There is no requirement for the partnership to make any returns or pay any fees to the States of Guernsey Income Tax Department. It is the responsibility of each partner to determine whether he/she has any liability in Guernsey to tax. A limited partner who is resident in Guernsey for Guernsey income tax purposes is liable to income tax on his share of the profits of a limited partnership whether those profits are generated in Guernsey or elsewhere. A limited partner who is an individual not solely or principally-resident in Guernsey, or a company which is not resident in Guernsey, is not liable to tax in Guernsey on any income derived from a limited partnership's international operations (defined as business operations conducted on behalf of a limited partnership with, and investments made on behalf of, a limited partnership in, persons who are not resident in Guernsey for the purposes of the Income Tax (Guernsey) Law 1975).

Tax Transparency and Information Exchange

7.51 Guernsey is at the forefront of standards on tax transparency and information exchange.

- Guernsey has signed a Model 1 agreement with the US government in relation to the Foreign Account Tax Compliance Act (**FATCA**). A similar agreement has been signed with the UK government.
- Guernsey has also joined with 50 other jurisdictions in confirming its agreement to new global standards in automatic exchange of information, the Common Reporting Standard (**CRS**).
- To date Guernsey has signed more than 60 Tax Information Exchange Agreements (**TIEAs**).
- Guernsey has also signed tax sharing agreements, including 13 Full Double Taxation Arrangements (**DTAs**) and 12 Partial DTAs.

Base Erosion and Profit Shifting (BEPS)

7.52 In 2016 Guernsey established a BEPS working party to assess the OECD's October 2015 BEPS Action Plans, as well as scrutinise the EU Commission's 'BEPS Directive'. Discussions between the working party and local business bodies have demonstrated that Guernsey is already effectively a BEPS-compliant jurisdiction, due to Guernsey's finance sector model and regulatory framework which prevents the island being exploited significantly for BEPS and ensures equivalent outcomes to those that both the OECD and EU Commission are seeking to secure. In addition Guernsey has taken the following action:

- Guernsey has joined the BEPS Inclusive Framework;
- Guernsey signed the BEPS Multilateral Instrument on 7 June 2017 which aims to implement tax treaty-related measures to combat BEPS;
- Guernsey has signed up to the Multilateral Competent Authority Agreement (**MCCA**) to assist with the sharing of relevant information in relation to

Country by Country Reporting (**CbCR**) (Action 13), as well as broadly adopting the OECD's CbCR implementation package, to facilitate its implementation of this BEPS minimum standard; and

- Guernsey has already put in place the relevant implementing regulations for CbCR.

LOCAL STOCK EXCHANGE

7.53 The TISE (formerly the Channel Island Securities Exchange prior to a rebrand completed in March 2017) is a registered trademark of The International Stock Exchange Group Limited (**TISEG**), a Guernsey company. Its wholly owned subsidiary, also a Guernsey company, is The International Stock Exchange Authority Limited (**TISEA**) which is licensed by the Commission to operate an investment exchange under the POI Law. TISE is headquartered in Guernsey with offices also in Jersey and the Isle of Man.

7.54 The TISE provides a platform for the listing and electronic trading of a wide range of products, including trading companies, specialist debt, investment vehicles, special purpose acquisition companies and extractive industries. Provision is also made for secondary listings where a primary listing already exists on another exchange.

7.55 The TISE is an affiliate member of the International Organisation of Securities Commissions (**IOSCO**) and an affiliate member of the World Federation of Exchanges (**WFE**). The UK tax authority, Her Majesty's Revenue & Customs (**HMRC**), deems TISE to be a Recognised Stock Exchange for the purposes of investment by Self-Invested Personal Pensions (**SIPPs**) and Individual Savings Accounts (**ISAs**). HMRC's recognition also means that products listed on the TISE may be able to avail of the Quoted Eurobond Exemption (**QEE**). TISE is officially recognised by the German Federal Financial Supervisory Authority (**BaFin**) and the Australian Stock Exchange (**ASX**).

CONFIDENTIALITY LAWS

7.56 Guernsey has no banking or other secrecy laws and follows English common law with regards to the duty of confidentiality owed by a bank or other financial institution to its customers. Therefore, a bank or financial institution may breach a customer's confidentiality only where it is required to do so by law, where it is in the public interest to do so, where it is in the interests of the bank to disclose such information, or where there is express or implied consent to disclosure by the customer. There are also statutory provisions which impose an obligation to disclose what would otherwise be confidential information:

- **The Disclosure (Bailiwick of Guernsey) Law 2007, as amended and the Terrorism and Crime (Bailiwick of Guernsey) Law 2002, as amended.** The entry into the force of the Disclosure (Bailiwick of Guernsey) law 2007, as amended (the **Disclosure Law**) and the Terrorism and Crime (Bailiwick of Guernsey) Law 2002, as amended (the **Terrorism and Crime Law**) consolidated existing legislation in Guernsey concerning money laundering and financial crime reporting. Reports of suspicion of money laundering must be disclosed either under the Disclosure Law 2007 or suspicions relating to terrorism must be disclosed under the Terrorism and Crime Law. A person acting in the capacity of a financial services business or a non-financial services business will commit an offence when he fails to report that knowledge or suspicion to the Financial Intelligence Service in the form and manner prescribed under the Disclosure Law. Any disclosures made in good faith will not contravene any obligation as to confidentiality or other restriction on the disclosure of information imposed by statute, contract or otherwise.

- **The Data Protection (Bailiwick of Guernsey) Law 2001.** This law came in force on 1 August 2002 and brings Guernsey's data protection legislation into line with the European Communities (Data Protection) Regulations 2001 (which came into effect from 1 April 2001) and gives effect to certain articles of EC Directive 95/46/EC. This law, in certain circumstances, imposes obligations on the service providers to Guernsey funds in relation to the treatment of personal data accumulated by Guernsey-based administrators. An amended law is due to be in force by May 2018.

ANTI-MONEY LAUNDERING LAWS

7.57 Guernsey has been recognised by the Financial Action Task Force for its regulatory and criminal law framework following a recent review of the island's anti-money laundering procedures. The financial stability forum classify Guernsey as being in Group 1 of the offshore financial centres, due to the legal infrastructure, supervisory practises and level of co-operation with other jurisdictions.

CONCLUDING REMARKS: WHAT ARE THE JURISDICTION'S UNIQUE SELLING POINTS?

Guernsey – simple, safe and well respected

7.58 Guernsey is widely regarded as a stable, secure and trusted jurisdiction for the management and administration of a variety of fund structures, offering a robust yet practical and flexible regulatory environment with the highest quality service providers.

CHAPTER 8

HONG KONG

GENERAL DESCRIPTION OF THE JURISDICTION

8.01 The Hong Kong Special Administrative Region (**Hong Kong**) is located on the southeast coast of the People's Republic of China (**PRC**). It is part of the PRC, but under the principle of 'one country, two systems', Hong Kong's legal system is based on English common law which is different from that of the PRC.

8.02 Hong Kong is a major international financial centre, comprising an integrated network of institutions and markets which provide a wide range of products and services to local and international customers and investors. There are no exchange controls in Hong Kong. The official currency of Hong Kong is the Hong Kong dollar which, under a linked exchange rate system, has been pegged to the US dollar at a constant exchange rate since 1983.

8.03 As one of the largest asset management centres in Asia, Hong Kong continues to be a platform for international investors investing in the region. Hong Kong's combined fund management business amounted to approximately US$2,230 billion as at the end of 2015. Hong Kong is also the regional centre for portfolio management activity, including Hong Kong authorised unit trusts and mutual funds and, on a larger scale, institutional fund management. As at the end of March 2017, there were 2,203 authorised unit trusts and mutual funds in Hong Kong. As at December 2016 the net asset value of authorised unit trusts and mutual funds totalled around US$1,284 billion.

www.gov.hk/en/about/abouthk/factsheets/docs/legal_system.pdf.

www.gov.hk/en/about/abouthk/factsheets/docs/financial_services.pdf.

www.sfc.hk/web/EN/files/SOM/MarketStatistics/d02.pdf.

www.sfc.hk/web/EN/files/SOM/MarketStatistics/d03.pdf.

KEY MANDATORY REQUIREMENTS

8.04 If a private fund is managed/advised in Hong Kong:

- the promoter is advised to consider tax issues in relation to the income and profits of the fund and the management/advisory entity; and
- whether the Hong Kong management/advisory entity is required to be licensed and, if so, the type of licence that will be required.

If a private fund is marketed and distributed in Hong Kong the promoter is advised to consider:

- to whom the marketing materials and the fund will be marketed and distributed; and
- who conducts the marketing and distribution as this person must either be licensed or otherwise exempt from being required to be licensed.

RECENT DEVELOPMENTS

Open-ended fund company

8.05 To increase Hong Kong's competitiveness as a full-service international asset management centre and a preferred fund domicile, the Financial Services and Treasury Bureau of Hong Kong (**FSTB**) consulted the public on the establishment of a regulatory regime for open-ended fund companies (**OFC**) in Hong Kong to serve as an additional type of vehicle for investment funds. The Securities and Futures (Amendment) Ordinance 2016 (Amendment Ordinance) sets out the basic legal framework for the OFC regime, which was gazetted and passed in June 2016. At about the same time, the Hong Kong Securities and Futures Commission (**SFC**), Hong Kong's securities regulator, published a consultation introducing the Securities and Futures (Open-ended Fund Companies) Rules (**OFC Rules**) and Code on the Open-ended Fund Companies (**OFC Code**) detailing the legal and regulatory requirements regarding the OFC.

8.06 It is proposed that all OFCs will be required to be registered by the SFC and will be subject to the OFC Rules and OFC Code. OFCs which are intended to be offered to the retail public will also have to obtain SFC's authorisation, which includes complying with certain additional requirements as set out in the SFC Products Handbook, but private OFCs are not subject to such additional requirements and are permitted to operate flexibly to pursue investment strategies as set out in their constitutive documents and offering documents, so long as they meet the basic principles in the OFC Code.

8.07 OFCs have separate legal personality. Shareholder's liability will be limited to the amount of share capital in the OFC. They can be established as umbrella funds with separately pooled sub-funds where the assets and liabilities of each such sub-fund are segregated. OFCs must have a registered office located in Hong Kong and are governed by a board of directors who must delegate their investment management functions to an investment manager licensed by or registered with the SFC to carry on Type 9 (asset management) regulated activity. The investment manager must also comply with all applicable rules and regulations including the Securities and Futures Ordinance (**SFO**), their subsidiary legislation and the SFC's various codes and guidelines. The assets of an OFC must be entrusted to an independent custodian who satisfies the SFC's eligibility requirements.

8.08 Private OFCs will be required to predominantly invest in securities and futures (and over-the-counter derivatives when the relevant laws have been enacted) that are within the remit of Type 9 regulated activity. OFCs will be allowed a 10% de minimis limit for investing in other asset classes. As OFCs are domiciled in Hong Kong, they will be able to take advantage of its double tax treaties with other jurisdictions. Publicly offered OFCs will be exempt from profits tax on qualifying income but privately offered OFCs may be subject to profits tax in Hong Kong.

8.09 The OFC regime is expected to be implemented in 2018 after public consultations on the OFC Rules and OFC Code have concluded and upon successfully passing through the legislative process.

THE REGULATION OF INVESTMENT BUSINESS

8.10 The principal banking and financial services regulators in Hong Kong are the Hong Kong Monetary Authority (**HKMA**), the SFC, the Office of the Commissioner of Insurance (**OCI**) and the Mandatory Provident Fund Schemes Authority (**MPFA**). These entities are responsible respectively for regulation of the banking; securities and futures; insurance and retirement scheme industries.

Hong Kong Monetary Authority

8.11 The HKMA was established on 1 April 1993 by merging the Office of Exchange Fund with the Office of the Commission of Banking. The HKMA's main functions and responsibilities are governed by the Exchange Fund Ordinance and the Banking Ordinance. The HKMA reports to the Financial Secretary and is the government authority responsible for maintaining monetary policy and banking stability.

8.12 Apart from banking supervision, other functions and objectives of the HKMA include the maintenance of currency stability and the promotion of the efficiency, integrity and development of the financial system.

Securities and Futures Commission

8.13 The SFC was established in 1989 and is an independent statutory body set up to regulate the securities and futures markets. With its powers derived from the SFO and other subsidiary legislation, it maintains and promotes the fairness, efficiency, competitiveness, transparency and orderliness of the securities and futures industry, and offers protection and education to the public on financial products. Within the regulatory framework, the SFC has regulatory oversight of the Hong Kong Exchanges and Clearing Limited (**HKEx**) and its subsidiaries, namely the Stock Exchange of Hong Kong (**SEHK**), the Hong Kong Futures Exchange Limited and four recognised clearing houses.

Mandatory Provident Fund Schemes Authority

8.14 The MPFA is a statutory body set up in 1998 under the Mandatory Provident Fund Schemes Ordinance to assist Hong Kong's workforce to accumulate savings for retirement, through regulating and supervising privately managing Mandatory Provident Fund (**MPF**) schemes and overseeing the operation of occupational retirement schemes. The MPFA supervises and monitors the operation of the MPF System.

Office of the Commissioner of Insurance

8.15 Empowered by the Insurance Companies Ordinance, the OCI protects the interests of policyholders and promotes the general stability of the insurance industry. It authorises and supervises insurers and regulate insurance intermediaries through a self-regulatory system.

www.thechinfamily.hk/web/common/pdf/publication/en/IEC-quick-guide-to-hk-financial-system-and-services.pdf.

INVESTORS

8.16 Hong Kong is the world's largest offshore renminbi (**RMB**) business hub, with the world's largest offshore pool of RMB liquidity. Hong Kong plays a major role in the transformation of the RMB into an internationally accepted and widely used currency. With the development of RMB-denominated bonds, loans and equity products, Hong Kong has become the largest centre for conducting offshore RMB financing activities. Hong Kong also serves as a platform for fund management companies and financial institutions in Asia to distribute funds and other financial products to Chinese investors.

SETTING UP A FUND

Types of fund

8.17 Under existing Hong Kong laws, an open-ended investment fund is typically established in the form of a unit trust. Investment funds are rarely established under the Companies Ordinance (Cap. 622) due to restrictions prohibiting the company from varying its share capital to meet shareholder subscription and redemption requests and distributions out of profits. Closed-ended investment funds may be established in the form of limited partnerships under the Limited Partnership Ordinance (Cap. 37). In practice, these forms of Hong Kong-domiciled fund structures are rarely considered given their structural limitations and the tax advantages associated with similar offshore structures.

8.18 It is expected that Hong Kong-domiciled private funds will take the form of OFCs once the OFC regime is made available in 2018.

8.19 Investment funds which are managed in Hong Kong often take the form of offshore mutual fund companies, segregated portfolio companies (**SPC**) or limited liability partnerships for tax efficiency purposes. The key advantage in establishing a fund in a tax-neutral jurisdiction such as the Cayman Islands is that the fund's investment and trading activities, as well as any gains of the portfolio, are generally either untaxed or very lightly taxed. Standalone structures often established either in the form of Cayman Islands-exempted limited liability companies or Cayman Islands exempted limited liability partnerships with a Cayman Islands-domiciled investment manager who delegates certain powers to a Hong Kong-domiciled investment manager or advisor. The Hong Kong investment manager or advisor employs the investment team and is licensed to carry on regulated activities in Hong Kong with the SFC.

8.20 A master-feeder structure where multiple funds (established as feeder funds) invest into a single master fund vehicle is also a popular structure. Feeder funds are often established in the form of Cayman Islands or Delaware limited partnerships, LLCs, unit trusts or exempted limited liability companies. The advantage of this structure is that different feeder funds may be established to cater for different types of investors (particularly US taxable persons) and the structure provides for the flexibility to create additional feeders any time after the fund's establishment. Cayman Islands-SPCs may also be employed for umbrella structures.

AUTHORISATION PROCEDURE

8.21 Private funds, if not marketed or distributed to the Hong Kong public, are not required to be authorised. The Hong Kong public is not a reference only to the retail public or everyone in Hong Kong but can also include only a single class of persons (whether institutional, corporate or retail) in Hong Kong.

8.22 Where private funds are marketed or distributed to the Hong Kong public, they must fall within one of the relevant exemptions. The exemptions most often used are (1) if such materials concern a private fund which is or is intended to be distributed *only* to 'professional investors' (as defined below) and (2) in relation to a private fund with a corporate structure (eg a Cayman Islands exempted limited liability company, but not a unit trust or limited partnership), if the marketing materials concern a private fund which falls within any one of the exclusions set out under the definition of 'prospectus' under the Companies (Winding Up and Miscellaneous Provisions) Ordinance (**CWUMPO**) (for example, offers to 'professional investors', offers to no more than 50 persons, etc).

8.23 Under the SFO and the CWUMPO, 'professional investors' includes (1) a recognised exchange company (ie only the Hong Kong Stock Exchange at present), (2) regulated investment business professionals, (3) regulated banks, (4) regulated insurers, (5) authorised Collective Investment Schemes, (6) regulated pension schemes, (7) governments, (8) substantial trusts meeting a HK$40 million minimum asset requirement, (9) high net worth individuals or businesses meeting an HK$8 million minimum investment portfolio or a HK$40 million minimum asset requirement. For this purpose, 'regulated' or 'authorised' mean regulated or authorised by a Hong Kong or non-Hong Kong regulatory body.

Requirements on persons marketing/distributing funds

8.24 A person who markets and/or distributes funds is required to be licensed in Hong Kong if (1) the marketing and/or distribution activities are actually being carried on in Hong Kong or (2) the marketing and/or distribution activities are being carried on outside Hong Kong but such business has been actively marketed to the Hong Kong public, unless otherwise exempt.

SUPERVISION

8.25 Investment managers and advisors, fund distributors and other intermediaries carrying out regulated activities (as defined below) are all regulated by the SFC (unless the intermediary is a bank, in which case HKMA). The SFC prescribes certain standards to ensure that all licensees are fit and proper. The SFC also monitors licensees' financial soundness, compliance with relevant ordinances, codes and guidelines and handles and investigates complaints against misconduct of licensees.

8.26 The SFC sets standards for authorisation and regulation of investment products (ie investment funds authorised for retail distribution) and reviews and authorises offering documents of retail investment products that are marketed to the public.

INVESTMENT RESTRICTIONS

8.27 Whilst the SFC does not impose any strict investment or borrowing parameters on private investment funds, it is generally expected that fund managers are required to make appropriate disclosures in the fund's constitutive and offering documents. The offering document must clearly explain the types of financial instruments in which the fund will invest, the extent of diversification or concentration of investments, investment strategies, stock lending policy, the extent and basis of leverage (including the maximum level of leverage) and the related risk implications of the investment and borrowing parameters.

Fees

8.28 Given that private funds are rarely established using a Hong Kong-domiciled vehicle, fees will be those that are required for the jurisdiction in which the private fund is established or domiciled.

ACCOUNTS/AUDIT REQUIREMENTS

8.29 Given that private funds are rarely established using a Hong Kong-domiciled vehicle, accounts and audit requirements are subject to the requirements of the jurisdiction in which the private fund is constituted and/or domiciled.

SETTING UP A LOCAL MANAGEMENT COMPANY/INVESTMENT MANAGER

8.30 The SFO contains the relevant provisions relating to the licensing of securities and futures intermediaries. Schedules 1 and 5 of the SFO prescribe ten types of 'regulated activity':

- Type 1: dealing in securities;
- Type 2: dealing in futures contracts;
- Type 3: leveraged foreign exchange trading;
- Type 4: advising on securities;
- Type 5: advising on futures contracts;
- Type 6: advising on corporate finance;
- Type 7: providing automated trading services;
- Type 8: securities margin financing;
- Type 9: asset management; and
- Type 10: providing credit rating services.

8.31 In order to regulate the over-the-counter (**OTC**) market two additional types of regulated activity have been proposed by the SFC:

- Type 11: dealing in OTC derivative products or advising on OTC derivative products; and
- Type 12: providing clearing agency services for OTC derivative transactions.

8.32 Investment managers/investment advisors performing asset management or advisory activities in Hong Kong must obtain the appropriate licences from the SFC regardless of whether the fund they manage are offered to retail investors or only privately placed to professional investors. Asset management activities will need to be licensed for Type 9 (asset management) regulated activity. If the investment manager separately provides advice on securities or on futures contracts, or undertakes to deal/distribute securities, then depending on the activities it would also need to obtain (as appropriate) a Type 1 (dealing in securities), Type 2 (dealing in futures contracts), Type 4 (advising on securities) and/or Type 5 (advising on futures contracts) licence from the SFC.

8.33 To be licensed by the SFC for any regulated activity, the investment manager must satisfy that it has proper internal controls, expertise, financial resources and sound risk management systems in relation to its business and investment strategies and that it (and its senior management) is fit and proper to be licensed. The manager is also required to apply for, and obtain, a licence for at least two responsible officers (one of whom must be an executive director) for each regulated activity.

8.34 A company licensed by the SFC must also nominate a manager-in-charge (**MIC**) for each of the following eight core functions:

- overall management oversight;
- key business line;
- operational control and review;
- finance and accounting;
- risk management;
- information technology;
- compliance; and
- anti-money laundering and counter-terrorist financing.

8.35 An individual may be the MIC for more than one core function. MICs for the overall management oversight core function and key business line core function must also be responsible officers of the company whilst the MICs for the remaining six core functions need not be a responsible officer. The purpose of the MIC regime is to clearly identify individuals responsible and accountable for any regulatory breaches by the licenced company.

8.36 There are ongoing obligations which the investment manager/investment advisor must comply with upon being licenced by the SFC. The investment manager must remain fit and proper at all times, and in particular, comply with all applicable provisions of the SFO, its subsidiary legislation and codes and guidelines issued by the SFC. The investment manager is required to file its audited accounts, financial resources returns and annual returns with the SFC. The licensee must also notify the SFC of certain events and changes within a specified time limit and must obtain the SFC's prior approval before effecting certain changes, such as changing its financial year end, using a new premises for keeping of records or becoming a substantial shareholder (as defined in Schedule 1 to the SFO) of the licensed corporation.

OTHER KEY SERVICE PROVIDERS

8.37 Given that private funds are rarely established using a Hong Kong-domiciled vehicle, requirements of key service providers would depend upon the requirements of the jurisdiction of which the fund is constituted and/or domiciled.

TAX REGIME

8.38 Retail funds authorised by the SFC are exempt from profits tax. Private funds may be subject to profits tax in Hong Kong if the following three conditions are satisfied:

(i) it is carrying on a trade, profession or business in Hong Kong either on its own account or through another person acting on its behalf;

(ii) it has profits derived from such trade, profession or business; and

(iii) such profits arise in or are derived from Hong Kong.

8.39 Accordingly, non-Hong Kong sourced profits are not taxable in Hong Kong. Gains of a capital nature are also not taxable in Hong Kong.

8.40 Whether or not the fund is carrying on a business in Hong Kong is a factual determination. This determination is based on the extent to which the fund undertakes its investment activities in Hong Kong, either by itself or through another person. The extent of activities that is likely to rise to the level of 'carrying on a business in Hong Kong' is a subjective analysis.

8.41 Profits derived from the disposal of investments (except gains of a capital nature) would be regarded as having arisen in or derived from Hong Kong where the contracts of purchase and/or sale are 'effected' (ie negotiated, concluded and executed) in Hong Kong. Profits derived from the disposal of securities listed on the SEHK will be considered as having arisen in or derived from Hong Kong. Interest income arising from certain debt instruments is generally regarded as having arisen in or derived from the jurisdiction where the subscription monies were first made available to the issuers. If the subscription monies are first made available to the issuers in Hong Kong, the interest income will be considered as having arisen in or derived from Hong Kong.

8.42 There is no withholding tax imposed on dividends or interest in Hong Kong.

8.43 Under the Revenue (Profits Tax Exemption for Offshore Funds) Ordinance 2006 (**Offshore Funds Legislation**), in any tax year, a non-Hong Kong resident fund is exempt from Hong Kong profits tax on profits derived from 'specified transactions' (as defined) and 'incidental transactions' (ie transactions that are incidental to the carrying out of 'specified transactions', which must not exceed 5% of the total trading receipts from the 'specified transactions' and such incidental transactions in that tax year), that are carried out through or arranged by 'specified persons' (as defined), provided that the non-Hong Kong resident fund does not carry on any other business in Hong Kong during that tax year (**Exemption Provisions**). If, in that tax year, the non-Hong Kong resident fund carries on a business in Hong Kong other than carrying out 'specified transactions' and 'incidental transactions', the fund would not be eligible for the exemption under the taxation provisions for that tax year and accordingly, the fund will be subject to Hong Kong profits tax in respect of any profits which arose in or are derived from Hong Kong (except gains of a capital nature). At present the rate of Hong Kong profits tax is 16.5%.

8.44 Distributions by way of dividends to shareholders would generally not be subject to profits tax in Hong Kong. Any gains of a capital nature arising from the disposal or redemption of shares would also not be subject to Hong Kong profits tax, unless the shareholder in question carries on a business of acquiring and disposing of shares and financial instruments for a trading purpose (in which case, such gains would be regarded as being part of the shareholder's normal trading profits as opposed to being capital in nature, and therefore, if they arise in or are derived from Hong Kong, such gains would be subject to Hong Kong profits tax).

8.45 The 'deeming provisions' (**Deeming Provisions**) of the Offshore Funds Legislation, which aim to prevent abuse or round-tripping arrangements by Hong Kong resident investors, provide that, under certain circumstances, a Hong Kong resident investor will be deemed to have derived assessable profits in respect of his respective share of the non-Hong Kong resident fund's trading profits that are otherwise exempted under the Exemption Provisions, even where no dividends have been distributed by the non-Hong Kong resident fund. The Deeming Provisions apply if a Hong Kong resident investor, either alone or with his associates (as defined), holds a direct and/or indirect beneficial interest of 30% or more in a fund that is exempted from Hong Kong profits tax, or any percentage if the non-Hong Kong resident fund is the resident person's associate. However, the Deeming Provisions will not apply to the resident person if the Commissioner of Inland Revenue is satisfied that the beneficial interests in the non-Hong Kong resident fund are 'bona fide widely held'.

LOCAL STOCK EXCHANGE

8.46 Hong Kong's stock market was the fifth largest in the world and the third largest in Asia in terms of market capitalisation as at the end of April 2015. Hong Kong was one of the most active markets for raising initial public offering funds. In 2014, US$29.8 billion were raised. A wide variety of products are traded in the stock market, ranging from ordinary shares to options, warrants, callable bull/bear contracts, exchange traded funds, real estate investment trusts, units trusts and debt securities. As at the end of April 2015, 1,780 companies were listed on the Stock Exchange of Hong Kong, with a market capitalisation of HK$30,995.2 billion.

www.gov.hk/en/about/abouthk/factsheets/docs/financial_services.pdf.

CONFIDENTIALITY LAWS

8.47 The Personal Data (Privacy) Ordinance (**PDPO**) (Cap. 486) governs the collection and use of personal data and prevents any abuse of data that is considered as intruding on an individual's privacy. Any person or organisation collecting, holding, processing or using personal data (the **Data User**) must comply with the six data protection principles laid down in the PDPO.

8.48 The PDPO provides that personal data must be collected for a lawful purpose and Data Users must ensure that the data held is accurate and up-to-date. Unless personal data are used with the express consent of the person whom personal data is/will be collected (the **Data Subject**), the data must not be used for any purpose other than the purpose indicated at the time of collection. A Data Subject includes an individual investor or an individual working at a corporate investor or institution. Data Users must also take appropriate security measures to protect personal data from unauthorised or accidental access, processing, erasure or use by others without authority. Data Users must publicly disclose the type of personal data held by them as well as their policies on how personal data is handled. A Data Subject is entitled to request from the Data User a copy of any personal data held by the Data User and if the data contained therein is inaccurate, the Data Subject has the right to request that Data User correct the information held.

ANTI-MONEY LAUNDERING LAWS

8.49 The Anti-Money Laundering and Counter-Terrorist Financing (Financial Institutions) Ordinance (**AMLO**) (Cap. 615) is Hong Kong's main piece of legislation to combat money laundering and terrorist financing activities for financial industry. The AMLO sets out client due diligence and record keeping requirements for financial institutions. SFC licensed corporations must also comply with the SFC's Guideline on Anti-Money Laundering and Counter-Terrorist Financing (the **Guidelines**) which is intended to assist companies licensed by the SFC in designing and implementing appropriate and effective policies, procedures and controls in compliance with the AMLO and other applicable anti-money laundering and counter terrorist financing legislation.

8.50 The Guidelines require effective ongoing monitoring by financial institutions which entails reviewing customer information; monitoring customers' activities to ensure consistency with the nature of their business, risk profile and source of funds; and identifying transactions that are complex, large or unusual, or patterns of transactions that have no apparent economic or lawful purpose and that may indicate money laundering or terrorist financing. The Guidelines set out the different aspects of the business relationship that may be considered, and financial institutions are expected to adopt a risk-based approach to such monitoring, depending on the risk profile of the customer.

8.51 The Guidelines provide comprehensive guidance in relation to the identification and reporting of suspicious transactions, setting out the general principles that apply once knowledge or suspicion has been formed, as well as a non-exhaustive list of examples of various circumstances that may give rise to the suspicion of money laundering or terrorist financing.

CONCLUDING REMARKS: WHAT ARE THE JURISDICTION'S UNIQUE SELLING POINTS?

8.52 As at the end of 2016, the size of the global fund industry grew to US$69.1 trillion assets under management. Compared to North America and Europe, the Asia (ex-Japan) fund industry saw the fastest asset growth at US$6.6 trillion assets under management. As at 31 December 2016, Hong Kong's private wealth management industry's assets increased to US$666.1 billion whilst the assets managed in Hong Kong increased to US$6.823 trillion reflecting the growing capabilities and skill set of fund managers in Hong Kong. With the introduction of OFC as a new type of fund vehicle, it is likely that Hong Kong will become a popular jurisdiction for industry participants to establish new private funds given its proximity with China.

http://ignitesasia.com/c/1687263/198223?referrer_module=SearchSubFromIA&highlight=HK%20fund%20industry%20rebounds%20with%20AUM.

http://ignitesasia.com/c/1684793/197993?referrer_module=SearchSubFromIA&highlight=China%20leads%20global%20asset%20growth%20in%202016.

www.sfc.hk/web/EN/files/ER/PDF/FMAS%20Report_English_2016.pdf.

CHAPTER 9

IRELAND

GENERAL DESCRIPTION OF THE JURISDICTION

9.01 The Republic of Ireland is located in the North Atlantic to the west of the UK. It has a population of approximately 4.6 million and both English and Irish are recognised as official languages. Dublin is the capital city and main financial centre.

9.02 Ireland is a parliamentary democracy with a written constitution and publicly elected president who has predominantly ceremonial powers. The Irish government is led by a Prime Minister, known as the Taoiseach.

9.03 Ireland joined the European Single Currency on 1 January 2002, when it adopted the euro as its official currency. Ireland is a member of the European Union (**EU**) and the Organisation for Economic Co-operation and Development (**OECD**).

9.04 The key legal requirements with respect to the establishment and ongoing operation of private funds in Ireland derive from the EU Alternative Investment Funds Managers Directive (**AIFMD**). Private funds in Ireland are primarily established as qualifying investor alternative investment funds (**QIAIFs**) and are regulated by the Central Bank of Ireland (the **Central Bank**) pursuant to the Central Bank AIF Rulebook (the **AIF Rulebook**). However, they may also be established in unregulated, but AIFMD compliant, limited partnerships (**1907 LPs**) under the Limited Partnerships Act 1907.

9.05 QIAIFs and 1907 LPs may be established for the full range of private fund asset classes including hedge funds, property funds, private equity funds, venture capital funds, commodities funds, sovereign wealth funds, infrastructure funds, loan origination funds, fund of funds as well as credit and other debt funds. The 1907 LP offers investment flexibility and AIFMD compliance, without additional regulation by the Central Bank at product level. The QIAIF is regulated at product level by the Central Bank but its investment flexibility and ability to be established in corporate, contractual or partnership form are some of its key features allowing it to be a suitable investment vehicle for the broadest range of investment strategies and legal structure preferences.

KEY MANDATORY REQUIREMENTS

9.06

- An Irish fund must be authorised and regulated by the Central Bank in order to avail of Ireland's tax neutral regime whereby Irish regulated funds are exempt from Irish tax on income and gains derived from their investments and are not subject to any Irish tax on their net asset value. 1907 LPs, like other global limited partnership structures, are tax transparent.

- Each QIAIF established in Ireland is required to have an Alternative Investment Fund Manager (**AIFM**) to manage the QIAIF and have responsibility for compliance with the applicable legal requirements. Pursuant to the AIFMD, where it is proposed to delegate the discretionary investment management function, the mandate may only be given to entities that are authorised or registered for the purpose of asset management and subject to prudential supervision. For non-Irish based investment managers, the Central Bank requires there to be supervisory cooperation with the relevant supervisory authority or for the applicant entity to demonstrate the regulatory regime for asset management in the relevant jurisdiction is comparable to the Irish regime. Investment managers from numerous jurisdictions have been cleared to act for Irish regulated funds.
- 1907 LPs can be utilised for non-fund structures so are not required by law to appoint an AIFM. However, if a 1907 LP is an 'alternative investment fund' within the meaning of the AIFMD, it must comply with the requirement to have an AIFM. As the 1907 LP is not a regulated fund structure, the AIFM may appoint a delegate investment manager to manage the fund in accordance with the requirements of AIFMD without the requirement for separate approval of that investment manager by the Central Bank. However, an Irish AIFM is required to notify the Central Bank of the delegation.
- A QIAIF or AIFMD compliant 1907 LP must appoint an independent depositary to provide safekeeping of the fund's assets, oversight of the fund and monitoring of cash flows. The depositary must be approved by the Central Bank and located in Ireland. Most of the leading global depositaries have an approved entity in Ireland.
- For corporate QIAIFs and for AIFMs established in Ireland, the board of directors is required to be made up of a minimum of two Irish directors and half of the directors must be resident in the European Economic Area. Directors of corporate QIAIFs and AIFMs must be approved in advance for their position by the Central Bank. 1907 LPs must be established with an Irish domiciled general partner, but the general partner is not subject to any regulation or board composition requirements and may be changed to a non-Irish general partner after establishment.
- The substantive administration and control of the relevant fund structure must occur in Ireland.
- The acceptance of subscription monies from prospective investors is subject to EU anti-money laundering laws.

RECENT DEVELOPMENTS

9.07 Previously, QIAIFs were permitted to acquire debt securities but were prohibited from originating loans. However, QIAIFs are now permitted to originate loans subject to certain requirements. These requirements relate to matters such as the monitoring and management of credit granting, diversification of the QIAIF portfolio, stress testing and periodic reporting. These requirements are likely to be applied to all European loan origination funds in the future.

9.08 The Central Bank has also issued requirements in respect of corporate governance and delegate oversight entitled '*Fund Management Companies – Guidance*' which applies directly to Irish authorised AIFMs managing QIAIFs. Certain parts of the guidance also apply indirectly to non-Irish AIFMs managing a QIAIF. Commonly referred to as **'CP86'** (referencing the consultation paper released by the Central Bank as a pre-cursor to the official guidance), this guidance focuses on ensuring there are robust delegation and oversight structures in place for the management of QIAIFs in key areas such as investment management, risk management and distribution. It also seeks to assist the Central Bank in the ongoing supervision of funds by introducing requirements for a dedicated email address for correspondence with the Central Bank together with the obligation to maintain all key fund documentation in immediately accessible form for Central Bank inspection. CP86 is aimed at ensuring that Ireland has a robust framework for the management of QIAIFs and ensuring that there is sufficient substance within Irish AIFMs.

9.09 The Irish government has proposed draft legislation for updates to the Investment Limited Partnership structure, which is a regulated partnership structure that must be authorised as a QIAIF. The updated version of the Investment Limited Partnership will provide additional flexibility and structuring options.

THE REGULATION OF INVESTMENT BUSINESS

9.10 The Central Bank acts as the single regulatory authority for all regulated investment activity in Ireland, including investment funds, banks, insurance companies, investment firms and securities markets. It is responsible for both central banking and financial regulation in Ireland.

9.11 Within the EU, there are a number of institutions/authorities that agree regulatory policy in Europe and the Central Bank is an active member of such institutions/authorities. They include the European Banking Authority, the European Securities and Markets Authority and the International Organization of Securities Commissions (IOSCO).

9.12 The Central Bank currently publishes its supervisory requirements for QIAIFs, AIFMs and Depositaries, primarily in the form of the AIF Rulebook. As ancillary guidance, it also issues an '*AIFMD Questions and Answers*' document together with guidance notices published on its website on specific matters and periodic markets updates.

INVESTORS

9.13 Ireland has been the fund domicile of choice for nearly 900 fund managers over the past 25 years. Some of the key reasons Ireland is an attractive jurisdiction for fund managers and investors alike include:

- high regulatory standards – the Central Bank is an experienced and efficient regulator that operates within transparent timeframes;
- tax efficiency – funds and investors operate in a clear tax framework where there are no tax charges at fund level and no tax payable on distributions or redemption payments to non-Irish resident investors for regulated funds and tax transparent 1907 LPs; and
- experience – Ireland has a highly developed framework of experienced investment fund professionals ranging from administration and depositary through to professional advisory services. Irish professionals have advised across the full range of investment strategies and structures.

SETTING UP A FUND

9.14 As outlined above, private funds in Ireland are primarily established as QIAIFs, although 1907 LPs are often utilised in venture capital and private equity structures. QIAIFs are subject to very few investment restrictions in terms of asset classes and concentration limits and have no borrowing limits. However, they may only be sold to 'qualifying investors' as further explained below. As 1907 LPs are not regulated at product level, they are not subject to any restrictions with regard to investments or borrowing and need only comply with the AIFMD.

9.15 The QIAIF is a very flexible regulated investment fund and offers the following options:

- it may be structured as a standalone fund or an umbrella fund with segregated liability between its sub-funds (with the exception of the Investment Limited Partnership);
- it (or its sub-funds if structured as an umbrella) can be established as open-ended, closed-ended or open-ended with limited liquidity;
- different share classes within the QIAIF (or each sub-fund of the QIAIF) may be established based upon subscription/redemption procedures, distribution policies, fees, hedging policies and various other criteria;
- side pockets may be used for assets which become illiquid or hard to value. QIAIFs also have a range of liquidity tools available such as redemption gates;
- the QIAIF (and each sub-fund of the QIAIF) is permitted to determine whether or not it will distribute income. Where it chooses to distribute income, it is free to determine how it will do so. A QIAIF is also permitted to pay distributions out of capital, subject to appropriate disclosure;
- QIAIFs can be established on a subscription and redemption basis or alternatively on a capital commitment and draw down basis; and
- a QIAIF may establish and invest through a wholly-owned subsidiary or special purpose vehicle, subject to the Central Bank rules on such entities.

9.16 It is important to note that the term 'QIAIF' refers to the categorisation of the fund pursuant to the requirements of the Central Bank, rather than the legal structure of the fund. As noted above, the QIAIF can be formed in any of the five available corporate, contractual or partnership structures. The choice between the available structures will often depend on factors such as the targeted investor base for the fund. Certain investors may be more familiar with one structure over another or only be permitted to invest in certain structures.

QIAIF Irish Collective Asset-management Vehicle

9.17 The Irish collective asset-management vehicle (**ICAV**) is a relatively new type of corporate fund structure in Ireland which has been specifically designed for use as an investment fund. Traditionally in Ireland, the most popular fund structure was a variable capital company (**VCC**). However, the VCC is governed by general Irish company law rather than legislation that is tailored specifically to meet the needs of an investment fund. The ICAV structure has been designed to omit all of the general company law provisions which were deemed inappropriate for investment funds. It also includes some enhancements which have been specifically included to benefit investment funds.

9.18 An ICAV is a corporate entity with its own legal capacity as provided for in its instrument of incorporation. It has the capacity to enter into contracts and to sue and be sued. The management and control of the ICAV is provided by a board of directors, at least two of whom must be Irish resident (as further outlined below). An ICAV can be established as a standalone fund or as an umbrella fund with segregated liability between sub-funds and is capable of being an internally managed AIF whereby the board of directors is the AIFM, or appointing an external AIFM.

Some key distinguishing features for the ICAV include:

- amendments to the ICAV's instrument of incorporation may be implemented without the approval of shareholders, if the depositary of the ICAV is satisfied the proposed amendments will not prejudice the interests of shareholders;
- an ICAV may dispense with the requirement to hold an annual general meeting by giving shareholders at least 60 days prior written notice;
- the ICAV is structured so that it can 'check-the-box' to be treated as a partnership or disregarded entity for US federal tax purposes;
- the ICAV may prepare audited accounts on a sub-fund by sub-fund basis; and
- there is no requirement to diversify investment risk (unlike a VCC).

The ICAV has now become the corporate structure of choice and has virtually replaced the VCC for newly established funds.

QIAIF VCCs

9.19 It is still possible to establish a QIAIF as a VCC although in reality most fund managers, if seeking a corporate structure, will set up a QIAIF as an ICAV. Pursuant to the ICAV legislation it is possible to convert a VCC to an ICAV by way of continuation. However, very few VCCs have availed of this option.

9.20 A VCC is a corporate vehicle with its own legal personality and is governed in a similar manner to an ICAV. However, it is subject to Irish company law (as it applies to public limited companies generally) and does not benefit from the key features outlined above for the ICAV. Crucially it is also subject to the requirement to diversify investment risk meaning it should not be 100% invested in one single asset.

QIAIF Unit Trusts

9.21 Unit trusts may also be established in Ireland. These are contractual-type fund vehicles created by a trust deed between a manager (which can also be the AIFM) and the depositary acting as trustee. Unit trusts do not have a separate legal existence, do not have the capacity to contract, and cannot sue or be sued, but instead are legally represented by the manager and depositary.

9.22 The assets of a unit trust are held by its depositary on trust for the benefit of the unit holders and are managed by the manager. Contracts in relation to the management and administration of the unit will be entered into by the manager and, in certain cases, by the depositary as trustee.

9.23 Similar to ICAVs, a unit trust can change its constitutional document (the trust deed) without obtaining shareholder approval in circumstances where the management company and trustee certify the change does not prejudice the interests of investors. A unit trust is also not required to hold an annual investor meeting.

9.24 Unit trusts have been declining in popularity as a vehicle since the introduction of segregated liability between sub-funds for corporate structures, which had previously only been possible for umbrella unit trusts.

QIAIF Investment Limited partnerships

9.25 As discussed above, QIAIFs may also be established as an Investment Limited Partnership. An Investment Limited Partnership must have a general partner and at least one limited partner. The general partner may also be the AIFM, but this is rarely the case as the general partner has unlimited liability. As such, the general partner is generally a separate legal entity from the AIFM, and must be authorised and regulated by the Central Bank independently as an AIF Management Company (a status under Irish regulation which is not associated with the AIFMD). An Investment Limited Partnership does not have independent legal existence in the same way that an ICAV does. The Investment Limited Partnership's assets and liabilities belong to the limited partners in whatever proportion is agreed within the partnership agreement. Investment Limited Partnerships do not issue units or shares, but instead operate on the traditional partnership structure of capital accounts.

QIAIF Common Contractual Funds

9.26 The common contractual fund (**CCF**) is a contractual arrangement established under a deed, which provides that investors participate as co-owners of the assets of the fund. The ownership interests of investors are represented by 'units', which are issued and redeemed in a manner similar to a unit trust. The CCF is an unincorporated body not a separate legal entity and is transparent for Irish legal and tax purposes. As a result, investors in a CCF are considered to directly own a proportionate share of the underlying investments of the CCF, rather than shares or units in an entity which itself owns the underlying investments.

1907 LPs

9.27 1907 LPs are established under the Limited Partnerships Act 1907, which is the same legislation that establishes English and Scottish limited partnerships, albeit with fewer updates made to the legislation in Ireland since its enactment. As detailed above, 1907 LPs are capable of being fully AIFMD compliant (with the appointment of an AIFM and depositary) and, as such, are capable of availing of the marketing passport under the AIFMD. General partners of 1907 LPs are typically a newly established private limited company and are not subject to any capital requirements. 1907 LPs are not a separate legal entity and, as such, the day to day actions of the 1907 LP are carried out by the general partner on behalf of the partnership.

9.28 As 1907 LPs are not subject to the AIF Rulebook, they are capable of investing without restriction, including origination of loans. They are flexible, allowing enhanced investor negotiation (subject to the provisions of the AIFMD) and are commercially appealing with their relative ease to establish. 1907 LPs in Ireland are limited to 50 limited partners for provision of investment and loan finance and ancillary facilities structures and 20 limited partners for other purposes. 1907 LPs that are AIFMD compliant are solely available to professional clients within the meaning of the AIFMD.

ELIGIBLE INVESTORS

9.29 QIAIFs may only be sold to qualifying investors and a minimum subscription of €100,000 applies. A qualifying investor is:

(a) a professional client within the meaning of Annex II of MiFID;

(b) an investor who receives appraisal from an EU credit institution, a MiFID firm or a UCITS management company that the investor has the appropriate expertise, experience and knowledge to adequately understand the investment in the QIAIF; or

(c) an investor who certifies they are an informed investor by providing the following:

- confirmation (in writing) that the investor has such knowledge of and experience in financial and business matters as would enable the investor to properly evaluate the merits and risks of the prospective investment; or
- confirmation (in writing) that the investor's business involves, whether for its own account or the account of others, the management, acquisition or disposal of property of the same kind as the property of the QIAIF.

9.30 Within the EU, QIAIFs may only be marketed to professional investors as defined in the AIFMD unless the EU member state in question permits, under the laws of that member state, AIFs to be sold to other categories of investors as set out in (b) and (c) above.

9.31 A QIAIF is permitted to grant an exemption from the minimum €100,000 subscription requirement to the following:

(a) the management company or general partner;

(b) a company appointed to provide investment management or advisory services to the QIAIF;

(c) a director of the management company, investment company or general partner or a director of a company appointed to provide investment management or advisory services to the QIAIF; and

(d) an employee of the management company, investment company or general partner, or an employee of a company appointed to provide investment management or advisory services to the QIAIF where the employee;

- is directly involved in the investment activities of the QIAIF; or
- is a senior employee of the company and has experience in the provision of investment management services.

QIAIF AUTHORISATION PROCEDURE

9.32 One of the key benefits of the QIAIF structure is that it offers a fast-track 24-hour regulatory approval process with the Central Bank. An application for approval of a QIAIF may be filed with the Central Bank (via the Central Bank's online filing system) no later than 5pm on the business day before the proposed date of authorisation of the QIAIF. If the application is complete and the Central Bank does not raise any comments on the application, it will issue a letter of authorisation of the QIAIF by the close of business on the proposed date of authorisation. The same fast-track approval procedure applies for any new sub-funds in an umbrella QIAIF.

9.33 There are several key points to bear in mind with the fast-track QIAIF authorisation process:

- the QIAIF application for approval must reflect the agreed product parameters as outlined by the Central Bank. Any derogations from these requirements require prior discussion and approval of the Central Bank. If a proposed QIAIF has a particularly unusual feature, it is also necessary to agree this particular feature with the Central Bank prior to seeking authorisation;
- the service providers to the QIAIF (including the directors and investment manager) must already be approved or cleared to act in advance of submission of the application. Where an EU authorised AIFM is passporting services into Ireland in order to act as AIFM for the QIAIF, the relevant passporting procedures must be completed prior to submission of the QIAIF application; and
- all of the QIAIF documentation (including the prospectus, the material contracts with the QIAIF service providers, the constitutional document and the depositary agreement) must be in final, agreed form (and executed where relevant) for the purposes of submission.

QIAIF SUPERVISION

9.34 A QIAIF is subject to ongoing supervision by the Central Bank through a combination of thematic reviews and inspections in accordance with the Central Bank's 'Probability Risk and Impact System' (**PRISM**). The operation of the PRISM system provides the Central Bank with guidance on the levels of required engagement with a particular firm and a means to document their actions and judgements. Under PRISM, regulated entities receive a risk-based classification. QIAIFs are typically classified as 'low impact'.

9.35 QIAIFs are subject to ongoing reporting requirements to the Central Bank including the provision of annual audited accounts and quarterly statistical returns. Annex IV reporting pursuant to AIFMD in respect of the QIAIF may also need to be provided to the Central Bank.

QIAIF INVESTMENT RESTRICTIONS

9.36 A QIAIF is subject to very few investment restrictions but it is required to adequately disclose its investment policy within its prospectus. The investment restrictions that are applied include in summary:

(a) QIAIFs may not raise capital from the public through the issue of debt securities. However, this does not preclude the QIAIF issuing notes, on a private basis, to lending institutions to facilitate financing arrangements. Details of any such notes must be outlined in the QIAIF's prospectus;

(b) unless authorised as a loan origination QIAIF, a QIAIF is not permitted to grant loans or act as a guarantor on behalf of third parties. However, QIAIFs may acquire debt securities or securities which are not fully paid and may also enter into bridge financing arrangements where the financing extended to the QIAIF is backed by sufficiently binding commitments to discharge the financing within a time period determined by at least simultaneous triggering of obligations on shareholders to make capital contributions which they are previously contractually committed to making at the time the bridge financing is entered into;

(c) QIAIFs are not permitted to acquire shares carrying voting rights which would enable them to exercise significant influence over the management of issuing bodies, nor are they permitted to appoint an AIFM, management company or general partner who would do so. This requirement does not apply to investments in other investment funds. It is also disapplied where the QIAIF is a venture capital, development capital or private equity QIAIF, provided its prospectus indicates its intention regarding the exercise of legal and management control over underlying issuers;

(d) where a QIAIF invests in funds managed by its AIFM or its management company or by an associated or related company of either the AIFM or management company, the manager of the underlying fund must waive any sales/initial charge/redemption charge it would normally charge in respect of the investment;

(e) a QIAIF may be structured as a fund of funds and, accordingly, may invest up to 100% of net asset value (**NAV**) in other funds. Where the QIAIF proposes to invest more than 50% of NAV in one other investment fund, the underlying investment fund must either be classified as an acceptable investment fund pursuant to Central Bank criteria or the QIAIF must set a minimum subscription of €500,000 and detail in its prospectus the obligations and conditions which do not apply to the underlying unregulated fund and its manager but which do apply to the QIAIF and its AIFM. A QIAIF which invests more than 85% of NAV in a non-EU AIF may not avail of the AIFMD marketing passport.

9.37 Importantly, there are no restrictions on leverage or borrowing for a QIAIF. However, it is necessary to clearly disclose in the QIAIF's prospectus the intent to engage in obtaining leverage or borrowing and the maximum leverage levels.

FEES

9.38 The Central Bank charges an annual regulatory levy to the QIAIF. All QIAIFs are subject to a minimum levy of €1,525. QIAIFs structured as umbrella funds will also pay a contribution per sub-fund of €235 per sub-fund up to ten sub-funds and a further levy of €145 on all sub-funds above ten sub-funds, up to a maximum contribution of €5,325.

9.39 The Central Bank has announced it will introduce application fees for new QIAIF umbrellas and QIAIF sub-funds. The Central Bank intends to charge €3,000 for an umbrella UCITS application and €2,000 for each QIAIF sub-fund application capped at €23,000 for up to ten sub-funds.

9.40 1907 LPs are required to provide nominal filing fees to the Companies Registration Office for establishment and update filings for changes to the partnership.

ACCOUNTS/AUDIT REQUIREMENTS

9.41 A newly established QIAIF must submit to the Central Bank a set of accounts (whether an interim report or an annual report) within 12 months of the launch date and publish it within two months if an interim report or six months if an annual report. The first annual report must be made up to a date within 18 months of incorporation and published within six months.

9.42 On an ongoing basis, a QIAIF must publish an annual report within six months of the end of its financial year. In addition, where a QIAIF is established as a unit trust or CCF it must publish, within two months of the reporting period, a half-yearly report covering the first six months of the financial year.

9.43 1907 LPs must provide audited accounts to the Companies Registration Office in Ireland annually in accordance with the requirements of the European Communities (Accounts) Regulations, 1993.

SETTING UP A LOCAL MANAGEMENT COMPANY/INVESTMENT MANAGER

9.44 Every QIAIF or 1907 LP that is AIFMD compliant must have an AIFM. There are various entities that may be appointed as an AIFM including:

- an AIFM authorised in Ireland by the Central Bank (further details on this are outlined below);
- an AIFM authorised by the competent authority in another EU member state (which may seek to manage the fund directly via a passport or by establishing a branch in Ireland);
- for QIAIFs, establishing an internally managed QIAIF, ICAV or VCC whereby the board of directors of the ICAV or VCC is authorised by the Central Bank as the AIFM;
- 1907 LPs and QIAIFs can appoint a '*sub-threshold*' AIFM (also known as a '*registered*' AIFM) in accordance with the provisions of the AIF Rulebook.

Such entities are subject to a lighter registration and compliance regime pursuant to the AIFMD. This is on the basis such entities do not meet certain minimum thresholds outlined in the AIFMD, including, for example, they do not manage portfolios of AIFs exceeding €100million. However, in this instance, the relevant fund cannot avail of the marketing passport available under the AIFMD; or

- a non-EU investment manager may be designated as the AIFM. In this instance, the non-EU investment manager must be cleared by the Central Bank to act as discretionary investment manager for Irish funds. It is then required to comply with the provisions of the AIF Rulebook that apply in the case of a '*registered*' AIFM. However, in this instance the relevant fund cannot avail of the marketing passport available under the AIFMD.

9.45 In order to establish an Irish regulated AIFM the following matters should be considered.

9.46 *Legal Form and Substance*: An Irish AIFM needs to be a corporate entity with its registered and head office in Ireland. It will typically be established as a limited company pursuant to Irish company law. Concerns about regulatory arbitrage arising from Brexit have heightened the regulatory emphasis on form and substance.

9.47 *Directors*: The composition of the board of directors of the AIFM will, in part, be governed by the Central Bank's PRISM assessment of the AIFM. In respect of an AIFM which receives a *Medium-Low* or above impact rating from the Central Bank, the AIFM must have at least:

- three directors resident in Ireland or, at least, two directors resident in Ireland and one designated person (being a person required to carry out some of the managerial functions explained below) resident in Ireland;
- half of its directors resident in the European Economic Area (**EEA**); and
- half of its managerial functions performed by at least two designated persons resident in the EEA.

9.48 In circumstances where the AIFM has a PRISM impact rating of *Low*, the AIFM must have at least:

- two directors resident in Ireland;
- half of its directors resident in the EEA; and
- half of its managerial functions performed by at least two designated persons resident in the EEA.

9.49 Central Bank approval of all directors of the AIFM is required. In addition, there is an expectation from the Central Bank that AIFMs will adhere to a voluntary corporate governance code established by the Irish Funds association which details board composition recommendations.

9.50 An AIFM is also required to ensure that an organisational effectiveness role is performed by either an independent director or the chairperson (if independent). The purpose of the organisational effectiveness role is to ensure that there is an independent director within the AIFM who has the specific task of keeping the effectiveness of the organisational arrangements of the AIFM under ongoing review, with his or her reports being submitted to the board for discussion and decision.

9.51 *Capital:* Irish AIFMs are required to meet minimum capital requirements pursuant to the AIFMD. The minimum capital requirement for an Irish AIFM is the greater of (a) €125,000 plus 0.02% of AUM over €250 million; and (b) one quarter of fixed annual overheads. The total capital requirement for an Irish AIFM is a maximum of €10 million.

9.52 *Application Process*: A detailed application must be submitted to the Central Bank outlining background information on the proposed AIFM (ownership and management) and detailing how it will comply with the various management and organisational requirements imposed on an AIFM pursuant to the AIFMD. The AIFM will need to supply the Central Bank with a *Programme of Activity* (amongst other documents) which details how the AIFM will comply with these obligations. The Central Bank will review the complete application and issue comments. The comments must be fully addressed by the AIFM before the Central Bank authorises the entity.

9.53 *Managerial Functions*: An Irish regulated AIFM is responsible for the following ongoing oversight managerial functions:

(a) regulatory compliance;

(b) fund risk management;

(c) operational risk management;

(d) investment management;

(e) capital and financial management; and

(f) distribution.

9.54 The managerial functions are intended to be overseen and monitored on a day-to-day basis by individual Directors of the AIFM or alternatively by 'designated persons' who are appointed by the AIFM and approved to act in such role by the Central Bank. As noted above, an AIFM with a PRISM impact rating of *Low* or *Medium Low* must have half of these managerial functions performed by at least two designated persons resident in the EEA. However, an AIFM with a PRISM impact rating of *Medium Low* must also have either one designated person resident in Ireland or have a third Irish resident director.

9.55 A designated person is required to have sufficient expertise in the area they are intended to monitor. It is possible for a designated person to oversee more than one managerial function. Furthermore, the same Designated Person may carry out the managerial functions of (i) fund risk management and (ii) operational risk management. However, he or she may not perform the investment management managerial function and either the fund risk management managerial function or the operational risk management managerial function.

Continuing Obligations

9.56 An Irish regulated AIFM is subject to a range of continuing obligations such as:

- obtaining Central Bank approval for any proposed change in its direct or indirect ownership or in 'qualifying holdings' (essentially meaning 10% or more of the capital or voting rights of the AIFM);
- preparation and submission to the Central Bank of half-yearly financial and annual audited accounts. The half-yearly accounts should be submitted within two months of the half-year end and the annual audited accounts within four months of the year end. Both the half-yearly and annual audited accounts must be accompanied by a Minimum Capital Requirement Report which confirms compliance by the AIFM with the capital requirements outlined above. Annual audited accounts of the direct parents of the AIFM must also be submitted to the Central Bank; and
- notification of any change of director, name or address of the AIFM.

9.57 It is also important to note that an Irish regulated AIFM is subject to all of the standard obligations imposed on an AIFM pursuant to the AIFMD.

SUPERVISION

9.58 The Central Bank is the entity responsible for the ongoing supervision of an Irish AIFM, primarily through the ongoing oversight and PRISM procedure outlined above. The AIFM is also under an ongoing obligation to notify the Central Bank as soon as it becomes aware of:

- any breaches of applicable investment fund regulations or the requirements of the Central Bank;
- breaches of other Irish legislation which may be of prudential concern to the Central Bank or which may impact on the reputation or good standing of the AIFM;
- the commencement of any significant legal proceedings by or against the AIFM;
- any situations or events which impact, or potentially impact, on the AIFM to a significant extent;
- the imposition on the AIFM of fines by another supervisory authority; or
- a visit to the AIFM by another supervisory authority.

FEES

9.59 An Irish AIFM is subject to annual levy imposed by the Central Bank. The levy is based upon the impact category of the AIFM pursuant to the PRISM classification.

OTHER KEY SERVICE PROVIDERS

9.60 With approximately 45 authorised administration companies, 18 depositary banks and over 14,000 investment professionals employed in the investment fund industry, Ireland offers a broad choice in service provider expertise to fund promoters.

Depositary

9.61 A QIAIF or AIFMD compliant 1907 LP must appoint an independent depositary which is approved by the Central Bank and located in Ireland. A depositary must be (i) an EU credit institution, (ii) a MiFID investment firm authorised to provide custodial services and which meets certain capital requirements, or (iii) an entity subject to prudential regulation and ongoing supervision which is eligible to act as a UCITS depositary. The core responsibilities of the depositary include safekeeping of the fund's assets, oversight of the fund and monitoring cash flows. In the context of QIAIFs, the depositary is required to report to investors in the QIAIF on an annual basis as to whether the QIAIF has been operated in accordance with the prospectus and the applicable regulations. There are also strict rules imposed on a depositary on matters such as delegation and liability pursuant to the AIFMD.

Directors

9.62 The Directors of a QIAIF formed as an ICAV or VCC are subject to the same requirements as the Directors of an Irish AIFM (as outlined above).

Administrator

9.63 The AIFM may perform the fund administration and transfer agency activities itself is authorised to do so. However, the administration and transfer agency activity is frequently outsourced to an administrator. The key duties in respect of the administration function include calculation of the net asset value, maintenance of the books and records of the fund and maintenance of the investor register.

9.64 A QIAIF or 1907 LP will also typically appoint a secretary (in the context of partnerships and contractual funds this is the secretary of the management company/general partner), money laundering reporting officer and professional advisors (legal and audit). Depending on the investment strategy it would also be common to appoint a prime broker.

TAX REGIME

QIAIF Level Tax

9.65 The QIAIF is not subject to any Irish taxes on income and gains derived from investments. Where any distributions received by the QIAIF in respect of its investments have been the subject to local withholding taxes in the countries where the issuers of the investments are located, it is often possible to reduce or eliminate such withholding taxes under Ireland's network of tax treaties (outlined further below).

9.66 It is important to note that QIAIFs structured as CCFs and ILPs and 1907 LPs are, for Irish tax purposes, treated as 'tax transparent' meaning the income and gains arising for the QIAIF from its investments are treated as accruing to the investors in proportion to the value of their holding.

Investor Level Tax

9.67 Non-Irish resident investors are not subject to any Irish withholding tax in respect of a distribution of payments by the QIAIF or any redemption, cancellation or transfer of their shares.

Double Taxation Treaties

9.68 Ireland has a large network of tax treaties including over 70 countries globally. Treaty access and benefits should always be assessed on a case-by-case basis as their availability will depend on the terms of the relevant tax treaty.

Base Erosion and Profit Shifting

9.69 Within the Irish Finance Act 2015 Ireland introduced country-by-country reporting legislation following the publication of the OECD's final Base Erosion and Profit Shifting (**BEPS**) reports in October 2015. The Irish government is still actively engaging in discussions on the actions points provided for under the final BEPS report.

Irish Real Estate Funds

9.70 Ireland recently introduced a withholding tax regime in respect of certain Irish property-related distributions and redemptions made by Irish real estate funds to certain investors. Where certain thresholds are met a 20% withholding tax will be applied on distributions and redemptions made out of the profits of an Irish real estate fund.

LOCAL STOCK EXCHANGE

9.71 The Irish Stock Exchange (**ISE**) is a leading exchange for the listing of investment funds. The ISE operates a Code of Listing Requirements and Procedures which was specifically updated in line with the introduction of the AIFMD. Accordingly, the ISE will automatically accept the suitability of a QIAIF authorised by the Central Bank for the purposes of listing on the exchange. The QIAIF is technically required to publish a 'listing particulars' which must be approved in advance by the ISE. However, in most cases it is possible to use the QIAIF prospectus as the listing particulars and avoid having two separate sets of documentation.

9.72 Most QIAIF listing applications can be run concurrently with the QIAIF authorisation by the Central Bank and as such it is typically possible to have the listing complete very shortly after the authorisation of the QIAIF.

9.73 Once listed, the QIAIF is subject to continuing obligations including:

(i) the annual report and audited accounts must be sent to the ISE and shareholders within six months of the period end;

(ii) the ISE should be notified of the NAV, upon calculation;

(iii) details of controlling shareholders', directors' or investment managers' interests must be notified to the ISE; and

(iv) an annual fee is payable to the ISE.

9.74 It is also important to note that the Market Abuse Directive (**MAD**) applies to securities listed on the ISE (as an EU regulated market). MAD requires all listed entities to report interests of directors or persons closely associated with them in the listed shares and has requirements with respect to the publication of inside information.

CONFIDENTIALITY LAWS

9.75 Ireland's confidentiality and banking secrecy laws are governed by both common law and statute. The courts have held that bankers owe their customers a qualified duty of secrecy. A bank or financial institution may breach a customer's confidentiality only where it is required to do so by law, it is in the public interest to do so, it is in the interests of the bank to disclose such information, or there is express or implied consent to disclosure by the customer. The legislation governing the operation of the Central Bank also provides for a duty of confidentiality by the Central Bank to the institutions that it regulates and similar exceptions apply.

9.76 The Criminal Justice (Money Laundering and Terrorist Financing) Act 2010, as amended by Part 2 of the Criminal Justice Act 2013 (the **AML Act**) stipulates that where a 'designated person' (for example a QIAIF ICAV) under the AML Act suspects that a money laundering offence has or is being committed, the designated person must report such suspicions to the police. Where disclosures made in this regard are made in good faith, the disclosing entity will not be regarded as being in breach of its duty of confidentiality.

9.77 Ireland's Data Protection Acts 1988 and 2003 can — in certain circumstances — impose obligations on the service providers to Irish funds. These obligations mainly relate to the treatment of personal data accumulated by Irish-based administrators. New European wide general data protection regulations are due to be imposed in mid-2018.

9.78 The share register of a QIAIF is generally available for inspection by the Central Bank, the Irish Director of Corporate Enforcement and any statutory body which needs to inspect the register in order to properly exercise any of its functions. A register of beneficial ownership is also maintained as further explained below.

ANTI-MONEY LAUNDERING LAWS

9.79 The law in Ireland on anti-money laundering and the countering of the financing of terrorism (**AML'**) is governed by the AML Act. The AML Act transposes European Union Law (the Third Money Laundering Directive (2005/60/EC) and its Implementing Directive (2006/70/EC)) into Irish Law.

9.80 In addition, Ireland recently introduced the European Union (Anti-Money Laundering: Beneficial Ownership and Corporate Entities) Regulations 2016, which implemented Article 30 of the Fourth Anti-Money Laundering Directive EU 2015/849 and which took effect in Ireland on 15 November 2016. As of that date, all companies and legal entities established in Ireland are required to take all reasonable steps to gather and maintain adequate, accurate and current information of their 'beneficial owners' on an internal beneficial owner register.

9.81 The Central Bank is the competent authority in Ireland for the monitoring and supervision of financial and credit institutions' compliance with their obligations under the AML Act. The Central Bank is empowered to take measures that are reasonably necessary to ensure that credit and financial institutions comply with the provisions of the AML Act.

9.82 Since 1991 Ireland has also been a member of the Financial Action Task Force, which is an inter-governmental body established to promote measures to combat money laundering and terrorist financing.

CONCLUDING REMARKS: WHAT ARE THE JURISDICTION'S UNIQUE SELLING POINTS?

9.83 Ireland is a leading domicile for the establishment and operation of private funds. Fund promoters are attracted to Ireland due to its transparent and regulated investment environment, its efficient tax structures, the expertise of its investment professionals and service providers and the familiarity of investors with its investment vehicles.

CHAPTER 10

ITALY

GENERAL DESCRIPTION OF THE JURISDICTION

10.01 Italy is located in southern Europe and shares borders with France, Switzerland, Austria and Slovenia. There are two small independent states within Italy: the Vatican City in Rome, and the Republic of San Marino. Italy has a land area of 300,000 km^2 and a population of around 60 million. The capital is Rome and Italian is the official language.

10.02 Italy is an EU founder member and has been a member of the Eurozone since 1 January 1999, a Schengen area member since October 1997 and an OECD member since 1962.

10.03 Italy is a democratic republic, whose constitution was adopted in 1947 and entered into force in January 1948. The President of the Republic is the head of state and represents national unity.

10.04 Executive power is exercised collectively by the Council of Ministers, which is led by the Prime Minister (*Presidente del Consiglio*). The President of the Republic appoints the President of the Council of Ministers and, on his proposal, the Ministers. The Italian government is composed of a variable number of members, reflecting the parliamentary majority.

10.05 The legislative power is exercised by the Italian Parliament which is made up of 945 elected members. There are two houses, with equal rights and powers, the Chamber of Deputies (*Camera dei Deputati*) which has 630 members, and the Senate of the Republic (*Senato della Repubblica*) compromised of 315 members. The members of the Parliament are elected by all citizens and they hold office for five years.

10.06 The Italian legal system is based upon Italian civil law. The Judiciary is a branch that is autonomous and independent of all other powers and is governed by the High Council of the Judiciary (*CSM*). The court system is made up of a Constitutional Court, a court of first instance (*Tribunale*), a Court of Appeal and a Supreme Court (the *Court of Cassazione*). Challenges to acts of public bodies, including financial services regulators, can be brought before Regional Administrative Courts (*Tribunali Amministrativi Regionali*) in the first degree and on appeal before the Council of State (*Consiglio di Stato*).

KEY MANDATORY REQUIREMENTS

10.07

- The rules applicable to public offerings apply in the absence of a national private placement regime (which some member states provide) and the absence of exemptions to market units/shares of EU alternative investment funds (**EU AIFs**) to professional investors or high net worth individuals in Italy (in accordance with Article 100 of Legislative Decree no. 58 of 24 February 1998 (the Italian Consolidated Financial Law, **CFL**), the only exemption regards the application of public offering rules).
- Marketing of shares/units of EU AIFs to retail investors (other than those included among the categories of investors to which Italian Reserved AIFs can be marketed – see eligible investors below) is conditional upon the fulfilment of an authorisation procedure before Italian Authorities (in addition to the passporting procedure implementing Article 32 of the Alternative Investment Fund Managers Directive (**AIFMD**)).
- The Italian legal regime regulates exclusively the marketing of funds established in accordance with the UCITS and AIFM Directive; therefore, only funds which fall within the scope of and/or benefit from the provisions of the UCITS and AIFMD Directives may be marketed in Italy (ie passported/ authorised).

RECENT DEVELOPMENTS

10.08 With some recent legislative measures, namely, Decree Law no. 91/2014 converted into Law no. 116/2014 (*Decreto Competitività*) and lastly, Decree Law no. 18/2016, converted into Law no. 49/2016, the Italian legislator has provided, within certain limits, the possibility for Italian and EU AIFs to engage in lending activities directly to commercial borrowers (ie to subjects other than consumers).

10.09 In particular, the recent Decree Law no. 18/2016 intervened in the matter, thereby introducing under Title III, Part III of the CFL a new Chapter II-*quinquies*, entirely dedicated to Credit Funds (*FIA di credito*).

10.10 The new chapter regulates the regime applicable to Italian AIFs willing to engage in lending activities, and expressly envisages under Article 46-ter of the CFL the possibility for EU AIFs to provide lending activities to Italian commercial borrowers and/or invest in receivables in Italy, if certain conditions/ requirements are met.

10.11 In this regard it is necessary to specify that in accordance with the Italian legal regime (ie Article 4 (1) let. e) of Ministerial Decree no. 30/2015), the following activities fall within the scope of definition of 'credit funds' relevant for the provisions under Article 46-ter of the CFL:

- AIFs that directly provide loans out of the assets of the fund ('direct lending funds');
- AIFs, operating on the secondary credit market, by investing in receivables or debt certificates (*crediti e titoli di rappresentativi di crediti*), already existing and disbursed by third parties.

Conditions/requirements to be meet by the EU AIF

10.12 According to the new authorisation procedure, which implements Article 46-ter of the CFL, a non-Italian EU AIF must obtain authorisation before commencing investments in receivables or lending activities in Italy.

10.13 In this respect, the Bank of Italy may prohibit (within 60 days from the filing of the application) the EU AIF from investing in receivables and/or engaging in lending activities if the following conditions are not met:

- the EU AIF must be authorised by its competent authority to engage in credit transactions (including direct lending);
- the EU AIF must be a closed-ended AIF and the relevant rules or by-laws must be – with reference to subscription/holding of units – equivalent to those of Italian AIFs that carry out credit investment;
- the prudential provisions for risk containment and fractioning – including leverage – must be equivalent or more stringent than those applicable to Italian AIFs carrying out credit investments. The requirement of equivalence may be met also by including such rules in the by-laws or in the fund rules of the EU AIF, as long as the competent authority of the home jurisdiction ensures compliance thereof.

THE REGULATION OF INVESTMENT BUSINESS

10.14 The general rules governing the activity of asset management companies (*Società di gestione del risparmio* – **SGRs**) and funds are provided in the CFL, and in the relevant implementing regulations issued by the Bank of Italy and the *Commissione Nazionale per le Società e la Borsa* (Consob).

10.15 According to Article 6 of the CFL, the Bank of Italy and Consob act as supervisors of the SGRs/SICAVs/SICAFs (**Italian Asset Managers**) activities. In particular:

(1) the Bank of Italy supervises, inter alia:

   (a) obligations of asset managers in terms of capital adequacy, limitation of risk in its various forms and equity interests, and information to be provided to the public on the same matters and on corporate governance, administrative and accounting procedures, internal controls and remuneration and incentive plans;

(b) rules applicable to Italian undertakings for collective investments schemes (**UCIs**) regarding: (i) criteria and bans relative to the investment activity, also regarding group agreements;(ii) the prudential provisions for risk containment and fractioning, in the case of UCIs other than Italian Reserved AIFs; (iii) the layout and drafting procedures of the accounting statements which Italian Asset Managers must periodically produce; (iv) the methods for the calculation of the value of the UCI's units or shares; (v) the criteria and procedures for evaluating the assets and valuables in which the capital is invested and the frequency of said evaluation; (vi) the conditions for delegation to third parties of the evaluation of the assets in which the UCI's capital is invested and the calculation of the value of the relative units and shares;

(2) Consob supervises, inter alia:

(a) transparency, including: (i) reporting obligations; (ii) methods and criteria to be adopted in advertising and promotional communications; (iii) obligations to inform customers regarding the execution of orders, portfolio management, transactions with potential liabilities and statements of customers' financial instruments or cash equivalents held by the company; (iv) the information obligations towards investors of Italian AIFs, EU AIFs and non-EU AIFs;

(b) correctness of conduct, including: (i) obligations to obtain information from customers or potential customers for assessing the suitability or appropriateness of the transactions or services provided; (ii) measures for the best execution of client orders; (iii) obligations relating to order management; (iv) obligations to ensure that portfolio management is performed in observance with the aims of the UCI's investment policy; (v) the conditions under which incentives may be paid or received.

INVESTORS

10.16 Italy is the third economic power in the Eurozone and the eighth in the world, with a domestic market of 60 million people. Italy has a highly diversified export structure and a strong manufacturing sector with an extraordinary know-how in machine-tools and automation, fashion and design, foodstuffs and cuisine. Italy is a leading-edge research and development centre with more than 20 Italian universities ranked among the top 500 universities in the world.

10.17 Data published by the United Nations Conference on Trade and Development (UNCTAD) (World Investment Report, 2017) shows that in 2016, foreign direct investments to Italy grew to US$29 billion. Italy is definitely on the radar of foreign institutional investors, since it has earned the attention of many sovereign funds. The country remains the second most important target for sovereign wealth funds (**SWF**) in the Eurozone, whose investments in Italy amounted to US$1.9 billion in 2015 (Sovereign Wealth Fund Annual Report 2015, Sovereign Investment Lab).

10.18 As for new investment incentives to attract foreign investments, in 2017, Italy tripled the tax credit for businesses engaged in research and development. The Italian government also adopted with the 2017 Budget Law new rules (in addition to those related to the start-up visa) a 'golden visa' for foreign investors, subject to certain conditions.

SETTING UP A FUND

10.19 The domestic law is contained in the Decree of the Minister of the Economy and Finance of 5 March 2015, no. 30 (**Ministerial Decree no. 30/2015**), Regulation implementing Article 39 of the CFL on the determination of the general criteria to be met by Italian collective investment schemes, as well as in the Bank of Italy's Regulation on collective asset management of 19 January 2015, as amended by the Bank of Italy's Measure of 23 December 2016 (**Collective Asset Management Regulation**).

10.20 Italian UCIs are established as either:

(1) a contractual fund: which comprises a separate pool of assets managed by an investment manager or by an SGR and since the same is not a separate legal entity it has no registered office;

a tailor-made corporate fund vehicle: a legal separate entity that, in accordance with the Italian regulatory framework, may be established in the form of:

(a) a 'variable capital investment company' (**SICAV**): open-ended UCI constituted in the form of a joint stock company with variable capital with its registered office and general management in Italy with the exclusive purpose of the collective investment of the assets obtained by the offer of its own shares;

(b) a 'fixed capital investment company' (**SICAF**): closed-ended UCI constituted in the form of a joint stock company with fixed capital with its registered office and general management in Italy with the exclusive purpose of the collective investment of the assets obtained by the offer of its own shares and other financial instruments of equity held by the same.

10.21 In the case of multi-segment SICAVs and SICAFs, each segment represents an independent capital separate to all effects from the other segments. The assets of a single SICAV can be divided into segments composed exclusively of AIFs or UCITS.

Types of fund and investment restrictions

10.22 In accordance with Ministerial Decree no. 30/2015, the Italian regulatory framework provides for the following types of funds:

- **Italian UCITS**, which may be set up exclusively in the form of an open-ended UCI or SICAV. Italian UCITS may invest in the assets provided for under Directive 2009/65/EC, subject to the limits and criteria established by the Bank of Italy pursuant to Article 6 (1)(c) of the CFL, implementing European UCITS provisions;
- **Open-ended Italian AIFs:** open-ended AIFs (or SICAVs) which may invest their assets, subject to the prudential provisions for risk containment and fractioning by the Bank of Italy, in:
  - financial instruments traded on a regulated market;
  - unlisted financial instruments for a maximum of 20 % of their assets (units/shares of unlisted open-ended UCITS are not calculated in the 20% threshold);
  - bank deposits of money;
- **Closed-ended Italian AIFs:** closed-ended AIFs (or SICAFs) which may invest their assets (in addition to the eligible assets for open-ended Italian AIFs) in:
  - unlisted financial instruments (the 20% threshold does not apply);
  - real estate property, real estate rights, including those derived from leasing real estate contracts with translatable nature and from concessionary relationships, and shareholdings in real estate companies, units/shares of other real estate AIFs, including foreign real-estate AIFs;
  - receivables and debt securities, including engaging in direct lending activities towards commercial borrowers;
  - other goods for which there is a market, having a value which may be determined with a periodicity of at least six months;
- **Italian Reserved AIFs:** AIFs reserved to professional investors which may be set up as closed-ended or open-ended AIFs. Article 14(2) Ministerial Decree no. 30/2015 provides that Italian Reserved AIF's rules or bylaws may provide for the participation of non-professional investors (see Investors below for more details). Italian laws place no restriction on Italian Reserved AIF's investments. The only restrictions are those imposed in the fund rules or bylaws.

INVESTORS

10.23 The implementation of the AIFMD did not introduce a specific category of clients; thereby the Italian legal regulatory framework provides for the following categories of clients:

(a) Professional clients (Annex II, Part I of MiFID – Categories of client who are considered to be professionals);

(b) Opted-up professional clients (Annex II, Part II of MiFID – Clients who may be treated as professionals on request);

(c) Retail clients.

10.24 Notwithstanding the above, Ministerial Decree no. 30/2015 provides that an Italian Reserved AIF's rules or bylaws may provide for the participation of the following non-professional investors (ie retail clients):

(a) non-professional investors subscribing units/shares of the relevant AIF for a total amount of not less than €500,000 (Article 14(2) of Ministerial Decree no. 30/2015);

(b) members of the administrative body and employees of the asset manager subscribing shares/units of Italian Reserved Italian AIFs managed by them, for an amount below the €500,000 threshold (ie Article 14(4) Ministerial Decree no. 30/2015);

10.25 In addition, in accordance with Article 14(3) of Ministerial Decree no. 30/2015, Italian Reserved Real-Estate AIFs can be marketed to public entities that do not meet the requirements to be classified as public professional clients under Ministerial Decree no. 236 of 11 November 2011, where their participation is effected through the direct granting of real-estate property and rights, including concession relationships, for value enhancement of public assets pursuant to Article 33 of Decree Law no. 98 of 6 July 2011, converted into Law no. 111 of 15 July 2011.

10.26 In addition, in accordance with Article 6 of Regulation no. 345/2013 retail investors may subscribe to units/shares of the Union Venture Capital Funds Regulation (**EuVECA**) AIFs (as defined herein) upon the fulfilment of the following requirements:

- commit to investing a minimum of €100 000; and
- state in writing, in a separate document from the contract to be concluded for the commitment to invest, that they are aware of the risks associated with the envisaged commitment or investment.

AUTHORISATION PROCEDURE

10.27 The establishment of new funds and the approval of their rules/by-laws are, except for special provisions, within the competence of the administrative body of the Italian Asset Manager. Once approved, the fund rules/bylaws are transmitted to the Bank of Italy for approval. This procedure can follow two main schemes:

(1) 'in general' approval (*approvazione in via generale*): A peculiarity of the domestic market. The following fund rules/by-laws are not subject to specific approval by the Bank of Italy as they fall within the cases where approval is generally granted:

(a) UCITS and open-ended (un-reserved) AIFs rules/by-laws drawn up in accordance with the simplified regulation scheme (see Title V, Chapter I, Section II, paragraph 1 of the Collective Asset Management Regulation);

(b) fund rules/by-laws that differ from rules/by-laws of other existing funds set-up by the same asset manager only for aspects relating to subject, investment policy and expenditure regime, in the understanding that the general criteria and rules established by the Bank of Italy for such matters are observed (see Title V, Chapter I, Section II, paragraphs 3.1 and 3.3 of the Collective Asset Management Regulation);

Asset managers wishing to make use of this simplified procedure shall communicate to the Bank of Italy (in December of each year) the characteristics of the funds they intend to set-up in the following year, thereby indicating any impact on the organisational structure. The asset manager may generally approve during the year funds with characteristics other than those indicated in the annual communication. In such case, the same must inform the Bank of Italy in advance, supplementing the annual communication already sent.

(2) ordinary approval: The Bank of Italy must approve fund rules of by-laws of UCITS and AIFs other than those of Italian Reserved AIFs (as well as related amendments) where the fund rules or by-laws do not meet the requirements set out above. This approval procedure requires 60 days (30 days for Italian AIFs or UCITS established by an EU AIFM or by a company authorised pursuant to Directive 2009/65/EC in an EU state other than Italy (**EU management company**)).

10.28 As anticipated, fund rules or by-laws of Italian Reserved AIFs are not subject to the above-mentioned approval procedure; in any case, where the fund is set up as a corporate fund vehicle (ie SICAV/SICAF) the same must follow the authorisation procedure for the set-up of an Italian Asset Manager (see **10.67** and Setting up a local management company/investment manager below).

Cross border marketing

10.29 With regard to the European passport established under the UCITS and the AIFM Directives, for marketing units/shares of funds on a cross-border basis, please refer to the following passporting/authorisation procedures:

UCITS – passporting procedure

10.30 Pursuant to Article 42 of the CFL, the marketing in Italy of units and shares of an UCITS must be preceded by a communication to Consob by the authority of the UCITS home state, in accordance with the procedures set out by Regulation (EU) no. 584/2010.

10.31 Units/shares of the UCITS can be offered in Italy once the EU Management Company has received notice from the supervisory authority of home member state of origin that the letter of notice has been sent to Consob. If the offer of the UCITS is to the general public, the EU Management Company shall in any case publish the prospectus and the Key Investor Information Document (**KIID**) upon completion of the notification procedure.

10.32 For UCITS and open-ended EU AIFs, relations between investors established in Italy and the statutory and administrative headquarters of the asset manager abroad, are engaged by:

(a) a branch of the EU management company/EU AIFM established in Italy;

(b) by the asset management company, established in Italy, managing the UCITS/ open-ended EU AIF;

(c) by banks, established in Italy, qualified to act as paying agent;

(d) by intermediaries, established in Italy, in charge of the placement or marketing of units or shares of the UCITS/ open-ended EU AIF.

Non-EU AIFs

10.33 As a preliminary remark, it is worth noting that the AIFMD regime on marketing of non-EU AIFs by an EU AIFM/non-EU AIFM has not been implemented in Italy. Legislative Decree no. 44/2014 (the **Decree**), implementing the AIFMD in Italy, introduced a transitional period with respect to laws regulating the marketing of non-EU AIFs pending the entry into force of a delegated act of the European Commission referred to in Article 67(6) of the AIFMD, which will establish the passport for non-EU AIFs and non-EU AIFMs.

10.34 In this regard Article 15(1) of the aforesaid Decree states that the supervisory authorities (Bank of Italy and Consob) during the transitional period (ie until the adoption of the Delegated Act) shall retain all the powers provided by the CFL in force prior to the effective date of the Decree. It should be stressed that the regulatory framework previously in force (Article 42(5) of the former CFL, now repealed) provided for a specific authorisation procedure for foreign funds (ie EU and non-EU non-UCITS funds) which was not included in the new wording of the CFL nor in the secondary implementing legislation.

10.35 In particular, in accordance with the former secondary implementing legislation, in order to carry out the offering of shares/units of non-EU investment funds in Italy, it would have been necessary to obtain the relevant authorisation from the Bank of Italy (requirements and procedures for seeking the authorisation for offering of such funds in Italy are found in the formerly applicable Bank of Italy's Collective Asset Management Regulation of 8 May 2012 as subsequently amended).

10.36 However, considering that: (i) the updated Collective Asset Management Regulation does not provide for such authorisation procedure (ii) nor does the new

CFL provide for a rule similar to former Article 42(5), there are several uncertainties arising from the interpretation Article 15(1) of the Decree, which could substantially reduce the ability to market non-EU AIFs in Italy (notwithstanding the possibility of subscription of units/shares under a reverse solicitation scenario).

EU AIFs – passporting procedure

10.37 With regard to the cross-border marketing of EU AIFs, please note that Article 43(8) of the CFL specifies that marketing in Italy, to professional investors and to investors included among the categories of investors to which Italian Reserved AIFs can be marketed, (see Investors above), units or shares of an AIF managed by an EU AIFM authorised in an EU member state other than Italy, shall be preceded by a notification to Consob from the authority of the home member state for each EU AIF marketed.

10.38 In particular, in accordance with Article 32 AIFMD, the EU AIFM shall submit a notification (which comprises the documentation and information set out in Annex IV of the AIFMD) to the supervisory authority of its home member state of origin in respect of each AIF that it intends to market in Italy.

10.39 As for the notification letter, considering that the regulatory technical standards referred to under Article 32(8) of the AIFMD have never been published, please refer to the relevant information requested by the AIF's competent authority.

10.40 Within 20 working days after the date of receipt of the complete notification file, the home member state supervisory authority:

- shall transmit the complete notification file to Consob with a statement to the effect that the AIFM concerned is authorised to manage AIFs with a particular investment strategy; and
- notify the AIFM of the transmission.

10.41 The AIFM may start marketing from the time it receives notice of the completed transmission of the notification file to Consob.

10.42 For the sake of completeness, Consob seems to have assumed a stricter approach with respect to marketing to retail clients. In particular, as a result of the practices taken by foreign supervisory authorities (eg France does not allow marketing to retail clients of AIFs managed by Italian AIFMs) the Authority could subject marketing to retail clients to a condition of reciprocity. In addition, it is worth noting that Article 44 of the CFL (Marketing of non-reserved AIFs) states that shares/units of the AIF have to be actually sold to retail investors in the country of origin in order to be marketed to retail investors in Italy.

EU AIFs – authorisation procedure

10.43 The authorisation procedure with Consob shall be followed (in addition to the passporting procedure described under **10.37** above) when the EU AIFM intends to market its AIFs to retail investors not included among the categories of investors to which Italian Reserved AIFs can be marketed (see Investors above).

10.44 In light of the above, the following procedure shall be followed when the EU AIFM intends to market its shares to non-professional investors (ie retail investors) other than:

(a) retail investors subscribing an amount higher than the €500,000 threshold;

(b) members of the administrative body and employees of the asset manager subscribing shares or units of Italian Reserved Italian AIFs managed by them, for an amount below the €500,000 threshold (ie Article 14(4) Ministerial Decree no. 30/2015);

(c) for Italian Reserved AIFs, public entities that do not meet the requirements to be classified as public professional clients in accordance with the requirements set by (Article 14(3) of Ministerial Decree no. 30/2015).

10.45 For marketing to the categories of clients under **10.44** above, the AIFM shall follow the passporting procedure described under the section EU AIFs – passporting procedure above.

10.46 Notwithstanding the above, considering that Article 28-quarter (1) **10.47** and following, of Consob's Issuer Regulation specifies that the notification letter for the passporting procedure must contain a description of the cautionary measures taken to prevent marketing to retail investors, it is advisable to insert in the offering documentation a provision specifying that the offer in Italy is limited to MiFID professional clients and to retailers subscribing an amount over €500,000.

10.47 As for the authorisation procedure, on completion of the passporting procedure, in accordance with Article 28-novies of Consob's Issuers Regulation, the EU AIFM shall directly apply for authorisation before Consob, thereby indicating the following:

(a) the applicant's company name, registered head office and the general management;

(b) the name of the AIF or the sub-fund, the units of shares of which are to be sold in Italy;

(c) the name of the subject appointed for the payments, the subject appointed to place the units or shares in Italy and of the subject, if other than the subject appointed for the payments, who deals with the offer in Italy;

(d) the full details and legal qualification of the person who underwrites the units or shares;

(e) the list of the attached documents.

10.48 In this regard, it is worth noting that Article 44 of the CFL (Marketing of non-reserved AIFs) states that shares/units of the AIF have to be actually sold to retail investors in the country of origin in order to be marketed to retail investors in Italy.

10.49 As for the documentation requested under **10.47** (e) above, please note that the document set slight changes in relation to the nature of the relevant AIF (closed-ended AIF versus open-ended AIF) and that the relevant documentation, if drafted in a foreign language, shall be translated in Italian and shall be filed together with a certification of conformity to the original issued by the AIFM's legal representative.

10.50 Consob, in accordance with the Bank of Italy, authorises the marketing if certain conditions are met within:

- 60 days for open-ended AIFs, following the filing of the authorisation application.
- 20 days for closed-ended AIFs, following the filing of the authorisation application.

10.51 In addition to the above, we recall the consideration raised under **10.42** above on the condition of reciprocity informally requested by Consob and on the necessity that the shares/units are actually sold to retail investors in the country of origin under **10.48**.

FEES

10.52 Pursuant to Article 40 of Law 724/1999, Italian Asset Managers and EU asset managers/EU AIFMs are required to pay a supervisory fee to CONSOB. The 2017 Contribution Scheme provides for an annual supervisory contribution equal to a fixed rate of €4,000 with increases from €1,410 to €2,000 with respect to the fund/sub-funds marketed in Italy.

ACCOUNTS/AUDIT REQUIREMENTS

10.53 In accordance with Articles 2 and 3 of Ministerial Decree no. 30/2015, fund accounts are maintained by the Italian Asset Manager. For each fund managed (in addition to the ordinary accounting obligations), the Italian Asset Manager must:

(a) keep day-to-day accounts for the fund, including details of portfolio acquisitions and sales, and all issues and redemption of fund units;

(b) within four months (for UCITS)/six months (AIFs) from the end of each financial year (or in the shortest period in which proceeds are distributed), draft an investment management report, and the company's board of directors has to prepare a report on the management of the activity performed;

(c) within two months from the end of each semester, the manager has to report on the management activity carried out during the semester;

(d) periodically (in a period at least equal to the issuance of units/shares), report the NAV of each fund and its units/shares.

10.54 Additional rules are set with regards to real-estate AIFs.

10.55 Documents under **10.53** (b), (c) and (d) shall be published in the form indicated in the fund rules/bylaws and shall be provided, free of charge, to investors who ask for them. Such documents must be available to the public (publication on company's website and/or kept at the company's premises).

10.56 Auditors must certify both the Italian Asset Manager's Accounts and the reports on the fund's management activity drafted by the Board of Directors.

10.57 Italian Asset Managers are subject to the regulatory provisions regarding the statutory auditing of accounts established for 'entities subject to an interim regime' (*enti sottoposti a regime intermedio*) pursuant to Article 19-bis of Legislative Decree no. 39 of 27 January 2010. In particular, pursuant to such rules, statutory auditing of accounts may not be entrusted to the board of statutory auditors and must be assigned to a statutory auditor or auditing firm enrolled in the dedicated register.

10.58 The statutory audit assignment lasts nine years for audit firms and seven for statutory auditors and may not be renewed or reissued unless at least four years have elapsed since the date of termination of the previous assignment.

SETTING UP A LOCAL MANAGEMENT COMPANY/INVESTMENT MANAGER

10.59 The professional practice of collective asset management is reserved to Italian Asset Managers, EU management companies and EU AIFMs.

EU Management Companies/EU AIFMs – Passporting of collective asset management services

10.60 Domestic law does not require an Italian local manager, and under the UCITS and AIFM Directives, EU management companies/EU AIFMs may perform the same collective asset management services in Italy for which they have been authorised in their home member state of origin on a freedom to provide services basis or by way of establishment. (Pursuant to Article 41*bis* and 41*ter* of the CFL).

10.61 In this regard, EU management companies/EU AIFMs which intend to manage Italian UCITS or Italian AIFs:

- must be authorised in the home state for the management of funds with the same characteristics as those they intend to set up and manage in Italy;

- must have agreed to provide the custodian with access to the information necessary for the performance of its duties.

10.62 In accordance with the UCITS and AIFM Directives, the EU management company/EU AIFM shall follow the relevant passporting procedure, according to which the Bank of Italy must be notified by the competent authority of the EU member state of the EU management company/EU AIFM (see Title VI, Chapter IV, of the Collective Asset Management Regulation).

SETTING UP A LOCAL MANAGEMENT COMPANY/INVESTMENT MANAGER

10.63 As for the specificities of the Italian domestic market, the Italian regulatory framework allows, in addition to the 'traditional' self-managed Italian Asset Managers, the establishment of:

(a) **Externally managed SICAVs/SICAFs**: The difference compared to the traditional 'self-managed' model, resides in the fact that the management of a SICAV's or SICAF's portfolio does not constitute a mere delegation of portfolio management services under Article 78 and ss. of Commission Delegated Regulation (EU) no. 231/2013 (**Regulation no. 231/2013**), but incorporates a true statutory designation. Indeed, SICAV's or SICAF's bylaws must entrust the management of the entire (and not part of) assets to an external manager. Such a manager must be authorised to provide asset management services (SGR, EU AIFM and an EU management company) and shall comply with capital, organisational and control requirements ordinarily set for self-managed asset managers;

(b) **Sub-threshold SGRs/SICAVs/SICAFs (sub-threshold AIFMs)**: Provisions on sub-threshold AIFMs apply to asset managers which exclusively carry out collective asset management services with regard to Reserved AIFs having AUM below the following thresholds:

    - below €100 million, including any assets acquired through the use of leverage; and

    - below €500 million where the relevant portfolio of AIFs are unleveraged and have no redemption rights exercisable during a period of five years following the day of initial investment in each AIF.

10.64 In addition, sub-threshold AIFMs may also be established as AIFs within the scope of Regulations (EU) no. 345/2013 (**EuVECA Regulation**) and no. 346/2013 (**EuSEF Regulation**).

10.65 Please find below a brief schedule summarising different pros and cons of this investment scheme:

<table>
<tr><th>Pros</th><th>Cons</th></tr>
<tr><td>Sub-threshold AIFMs are not required to comply, inter alia, with the provisions concerning:
• strategies for the exercise of voting rights provided by Article 37 of Regulation (EU) no. 231/2013;
• organisational and prudential requirements on remuneration policies and practices;
• prior application to the Bank of Italy/Consob for outsourcing of essential or important business functions.
In addition, sub-threshold AIFMs may centralise, in one independent control function, second and third level control functions (compliance, audit and risk management).</td><td>Sub-threshold AIFMs do not benefit from the provisions on the so-called European passport provided under Chapter VI of the AIFMD.
Therefore, sub-threshold AIFMs may not market Italian Reserved AIFs through the passporting procedure described above (the units/shares may still be subscribed on a genuine unsolicited approach or through national private placement regimes, optionally provided for by the AIFMD).
On the other hand, considering that EuVECA and EuSEF Regulations established a 'European passport' for managers intending to cross border market such AIFs in the EU, the above-mentioned marketing restrictions do not apply to EuVECA and EuSEF AIFs.</td></tr>
</table>

10.66 Below is a summary of the main peculiarities of the relevant authorisation procedures:

10.67 As a preliminary remark, even if the fund rules or by-laws of Italian Reserved AIFs are not subject to the approval procedure of the Bank of Italy, the same are in any case subject to the following authorisation procedures for the set-up of the relevant vehicle. Indeed, SICAVs/SICAFs which qualify as an Italian Reserved AIF are subject to the authorisation procedure for the set-up of an Italian Asset Manager.

Authorisation procedure – Self-managed Italian Asset Managers and sub-threshold AIFMs

10.68 Under Italian laws, the Bank of Italy, after consulting Consob, authorises self-managed Italian Asset Managers and sub-threshold AIFMs to provide collective asset management services, within ***90 days*** from the date of receipt of the complete application, where the following conditions are fulfilled:

(a) the legal form adopted is that of an Italian Joint Stock Company (*società per azioni – S.p.A.)*. The establishment of the S.p.A. is made by way of execution of a deed of incorporation before an Italian notary public. The deed of incorporation (*Atto Costitutivo*) also incorporates the by-laws (*Statuto*) of the company;

(b) the registered office and the head office of the company are in Italy;

(c) the paid-up capital is not less than that established on a general basis by the Bank of Italy:

- for self-managed Italian Asset Managers, €1 million (€500,000 for SGRs which intend to manage exclusively close-ended Reserved AIFs or for Reserved SICAFs);
- for sub-threshold AIFMs, €50,000;

(d) the representatives of the Company (board of directors, general manager, statutory auditors) fulfil the requirements (in terms of integrity, professionalism and independence) set by applicable laws (ie Article 13 of the CFL). Responsibility for verifying the fulfilment of such requirements and the probative completeness of supporting documentation falls to the company's board of directors. In such case, a certified copy of the minutes of the board meeting during which the integrity requirements have been verified shall be annexed to the application together with all the documentation grounding such evaluation;

(e) the qualified shareholders fulfil the requirements (in terms of integrity, competence and fairness) and meet the criteria laid down by Article 14 of the CFL;

(f) the structure of the group of which the Company is part is not prejudicial to the effective supervision of the SIM; and

(g) a programme of initial operations and a description of the organisational structure have been submitted together with the instrument of incorporation and the articles of association.

Authorisation procedure – Externally managed SICAVs/SICAFs

10.69 The Bank of Italy, after consultation with Consob, authorises the establishment of externally managed SICAVs and SICAFs within **90 days**. The authorisation shall be granted where the conditions under points (a), (b), (d) and (e) above set for the application of self-managed Italian Asset Managers and sub-threshold AIFMs are fulfilled and:

(a) the paid-up capital is not less than €50,000;

(b) the articles of association contemplate:

- for SICAVs, the exclusive purpose is collective investment of the capital obtained by the offer of its own shares to the public; for SICAFs, the exclusive purpose is the collective investment of the capital obtained by the offer to the public of its own shares and of the financial instruments of its equity holdings indicated in the said articles;
- the entire assets are entrusted to an external asset manager and the designated management company is identified;

(c) the stipulation of an agreement between the manager, if other than an SGR, and the custodian, which ensures this latter access to the information necessary for the performance of its duties, as contemplated by Article 41-bis (2-bis) of the CFL.

10.70 As for both the authorisation procedures under paragraphs **10.68** and **10.69**, please note that the 90-day term is not mandatory and that Italian Authorities, during the procedure, may request further information from the applicant company, at any time, thus extending the duration of the procedure.

10.71 In our experience, the Bank of Italy authorises the applicant company after five/six months from the filing of the application.

10.72 The authorisation shall be denied where verification of the conditions indicated above shows that sound and prudent management is not ensured.

OTHER KEY SERVICE PROVIDERS

10.73 For outsourcing, Italian Asset Managers, authorised pursuant to the UCITS and AIFM Directives, must comply with the provisions set by Article 75 and follow Regulation no. 231/2013. In particular, the same shall comply, inter alia, with the following general principles:

(1) the delegation structure does not allow for the circumvention of the AIFM's responsibilities or liability and the obligations of the AIFM towards the AIF and its investors are not altered as a result of the delegation;

(2) the asset managers ensure that the delegate carries out the delegated functions effectively and in compliance with applicable laws and regulations and must contractually establish methods and procedures for reviewing on an ongoing basis. In particular, the asset manager shall contractually ensure its instruction and termination rights, its rights of information, and its right to inspections and access to books and premises.

10.74 Additional requirements are set with regards to the delegation of portfolio management or risk management, which may be delegated exclusively to:

(a) EU management companies;

(b) investment firms authorised under Directive 2014/65/EU (**MiFID**) to perform portfolio management;

(c) credit institutions authorised under Directive 2006/48/EC having the authorisation to perform portfolio management under MiFID;

(d) self-managed AIFMs;

(e) third country entities authorised/registered for the purpose of asset management and effectively supervised by a competent authority in those non-EU countries. In such a scenario, the delegation is conditional upon the existence of a written arrangement between Italian Authorities of the

AIFM and the supervisory authorities of the non-EU undertaking to which delegation is conferred (please refer to Article 78(3) of Regulation no. 231/2013).

10.75 As for the peculiarities of the Italian framework, Article 50 of the Bank of Italy-Consob Joint Regulation of 29 October 2007, provides that Italian Asset Managers, who intend to outsource essential business, services or functions shall inform the Bank of Italy and Consob, providing the information listed under Annex no. 1 of the aforesaid Joint Regulation. Within 30 days from the date of receipt of the notice, the Bank of Italy and Consob may initiate an administrative ban procedure which ends within the following 60 days. As anticipated, such procedure does not apply to sub-threshold AIFMs.

Custodian

10.76 In accordance with Article 47 of the CFL, the custodian mandate may be conferred on authorised banks in Italy, Italian branches of EU banks, investment companies and Italian branches of EU investment companies. The custodian fulfils the obligations of custody of the entrusted financial instruments, verification of ownership, and also the obligation to keep registers of other assets. Unless entrusted to other subjects, it also holds the available liquidity of the UCIs.

10.77 The custodian may carry out other activities for the asset manager, including the calculation of the net asset value for UCITS, without prejudice to the application of the provisions on outsourcing pursuant to Regulation (EU) no. 231/2013.

TAX REGIME

10.78 Pursuant to Article 26-*quinquies* of Presidential Decree no. 600/73, income received by investors who have invested in an Italian fund (other than a real-estate AIF) are subject to a 26% final withholding tax. However, a derogation from the application of the single withholding tax is provided with reference to income deriving from:

(a) bonds and other public debt securities as well as bonds issued by the foreign states included in the 'white list', a 12.5% rate applies;

(b) foreign investors resident in states allowing an adequate exchange of information with Italy or institutional investors established therein which are exempted from the withholding tax;

(c) long-term savings plans (*Piani di Risparmio a lungo termine* – PIR), which are exempted from taxation. In order to obtain such facilitation, there are constraints on:

- the composition of the PIR's assets: (i) an amount equal to at least 70% of the PIR's assets must be invested in financial instruments (bonds or shares, un-listed or listed on regulated markets or on MTFs) issued or concluded with companies resident in Italy, or in EU member states or the European Economic Area states with a permanent establishment in Italy; out of this 70%, at least 30% of the PIR's assets must be invested in financial instruments issued by companies other than those listed in the FTSE MIB index of the Italian Stock Exchange or in equivalent indices of other regulated markets; (ii) concentration limit towards a single issuer/company is equal to 10%;

- the holding period of investment in the PIR fund must be at least five years;
- investment sums, each individual may not invest more than €30,000 per year in the PIR and within a total limit of €150,000.

10.79 In addition, please note that recently, Law Decree no. 50 of 11 April 2017, intervened on the issue of 'carried interest', thereby providing the conditions to be met in order to classify carried interest as income from capital/other income (and hence be subject to the above regime) rather than from employment/self-employment (which is taxed at a higher marginal rate – up to 43%).

Tax Treaties

10.80 The position of the Italian Ministry of Finance is that foreign funds do not fall within the scope of the treaties against double taxation. By contrast, according to the Ministry of Finance Italian funds are entitled to treaty benefits.

LOCAL STOCK EXCHANGE

10.81 The main local stock exchange is operated by Borsa Italiana S.p.A. which in June 2007 merged with the London Stock Exchange.

10.82 ETFplus is the market dedicated to the negotiations of exchange traded funds (ETFs), structured ETFs and exchange traded commodities (ETCs)/exchange traded notes (ETNs) and, since 1 December 2014, open-ended funds. In order to facilitate investors in the picking process, the market is composed of five segments (ETF index, structured ETF, actively managed ETF, ETC/ETN and open-ended UCI).

10.83 Following the harmonisation carried out by AIFMD, the investment vehicles market (MIV) has been devoted to both Italian and foreign corporate or contractual investment AIFs, open to retail investors or reserved for professional investors.

CONFIDENTIALITY LAWS

10.84 The confidentially law regarding investors' data is Legislative Decree no. 196/2003 (the Privacy Law).

10.85 The rules contained in the Privacy Law have to be complied with by the societa' di gestione del risparmio (SGR) (investment management company) with regard to all personal data acquired. In the context of an SGR, the type of data subject to the Privacy Law will relate to suppliers and clients.

10.86 The Privacy Law provides for the SGR to inform the physical persons whose data is owned by the same company with regard to the data's use. Data can then only be used after receiving the relevant approval of the people concerned.

ANTI-MONEY LAUNDERING LAWS

10.87 Except for investors identified by the fund as 'professional investors', anti-money laundering provisions require, inter alia, the insertion of all investors' data in a register (so-called *Archivio Unico Informatico*) and periodical (monthly) reporting to the UCI of all transactions (eg subscriptions and redemptions) in amounts higher than €12,500.

10.88 The Italian anti-money laundering regime has recently been reformed following the implementation of Directive (EU) 2015/849 on the prevention of the use of the financial system for the purposes of money laundering or terrorist financing (the Fourth Anti-Money Laundering Directive).

CONCLUDING REMARKS: WHAT ARE THE JURISDICTION'S UNIQUE SELLING POINTS?

10.89

- As for the strengths of the Italian market, one must note that Italian supervisory authorities are much more reliable and quicker than other European Supervisory Authorities.
- The authorisation process is reasonably short (about five/six months). Regulatory authorities, show an ever-increasing technical knowledge.
- Italy is an appealing country for fund distribution, because of Italian investors' net-worth eligibility for investments in fund units/shares.
- Rules on credit funds overcome the restrictions on activity for the granting of loans to the public in favour of banks and financial intermediaries under Article 106 of the Italian Consolidated Banking Law.

CHAPTER 11

JERSEY

GENERAL DESCRIPTION OF THE JURISDICTION

11.01 Jersey is a leading global centre for the establishment of funds and is at the forefront of international developments that have attracted international sponsors, fund managers, advisors and professional investors. One of the key features of Jersey's fund industry is the flexibility and range of structures and corresponding regulatory and commercial approaches, in addition to a full range of fund vehicles from private funds through to retail offerings and alternative investment funds.

11.02 Jersey (also referred to as the **Island**) is the largest of the Channel Islands and is located approximately 14 miles from France and approximately 77 miles from England. The Island has a population of over 100,000 people, its principal town being St. Helier. Jersey shares the same time zone as London. The Island enjoys first class air and sea links with the UK, as well as direct air links to many major European cities. Telecommunications links are excellent and highly resilient, with Jersey benefiting from fibre-optic submarine cables to the UK and France, world class data centres and an active digital/fintech community.

11.03 Whilst the UK represents the interests of the Island in certain matters of foreign policy, in negotiating international treaties, it must have regard to the separate municipal jurisdiction of Jersey and must consult with the Island before seeking to extend the jurisdiction of such international treaties to it. Jersey's authorities have exclusive competence to legislate on matters concerning their own internal governance and taxation.

11.04 Jersey is neither a member nor an associate member of the European Union. The Island's relationship with the EU is governed by Protocol 3 on the Channel Islands and the Isle of Man to the Treaty of Accession of 1972. The effect of this protocol is that the Island falls within the common customs area and the common external tariff, but is not required to comply with EU directives and is free to maintain an independent fiscal policy. The Island's government has increasingly developed relationships with EU member states as a 'third country' based around such areas as standard on the Alternative Investment Fund Managers Directive (**AIFMD**) and therefore anticipates retaining a position of continuity with regard to Brexit negotiations.

KEY MANDATORY REQUIREMENTS

General

11.05

- Persons who perform defined functions for collective investment funds in, or from within, Jersey must be authorised by the Jersey Financial Services Commission (the **JFSC**).
- Persons who carry out financial services business activities in, or from within, Jersey must obtain relevant licences, unless exempt.
- Jersey-based businesses holding investment business or other financial service business licences must comply with codes of practice.
- Jersey-based service providers who outsource activities should comply with the JFSC's outsourcing policy.
- All financial services and investment businesses are subject to Jersey's anti-money laundering legislation and 'know your customer' regulations.
- Jersey has a well-developed 'opt in' regime for the marketing of funds into the European Union (**EU**)/European Economic Area (**EEA**) in accordance with the private placement provisions of the AIFMD. For those funds not marketing into the EU/EEA, these rules do not apply.

RECENT DEVELOPMENTS

11.06 As of April 2017, Jersey has introduced a new regime for private funds, simplifying the regulatory regime, and enabling greater speed and flexibility in the Island's private funds area.

11.07 Following the implementation of the AIFMD in July 2013, regulations and codes apply in Jersey to alternative investment fund managers (**AIFMs**) actively marketing funds in the EEA. Funds marketing outside the EEA are unaffected as long as they do not have an EEA AIFM.

11.08 The Organisation for Economic Co-Operation and Development (the **OECD**) has been actively engaged in working towards exchange of information on a global scale and has published a global Common Reporting Standard for multicultural exchange of information pursuant to which many governments, including Jersey, have now signed multilateral agreements. A common implementing timetable saw the first exchanges of information in 2017 with further countries committed to implement the new global standard by 2018.

11.09 Jersey also received a fully compliant rating with the standards on international tax transparency from the OECD in November 2017.

THE REGULATION OF INVESTMENT BUSINESS

11.10 The responsibility for the regulation of Jersey's financial services industry lies with the JFSC. The JFSC is aligned with the standards of the third anti-money laundering directive and was the first offshore finance centre to become a full signatory to the IOSCO Multilateral Treaty, an international benchmark for international cooperation between regulators.

INVESTORS

11.11 Jersey is a leading funds domicile with over 50 years' experience as an international finance centre. At the end of September 2017, the overall net asset value of funds under administration in Jersey stood at US$265 billion. From an investor prespective, Jersey has an excellent reputation as an attractive funds jurisdiction due to its fiscal neutrality, robust, yet flexible regulatory framework with a strong focus on corporate governance and high quality of service providers.

SETTING UP A FUND

11.12 The regulatory regime in Jersey has developed a number of different products to cater for market needs and the expectation of investors in relation to the establishment of alternative investment funds. An example of this is the development of unregulated fund products that are targeted either at investors who can demonstrate sufficient wealth to cope with an unregulated fund product or that are listed in a regulated exchange.

11.13 The statutory and regulatory framework in Jersey has increasingly attracted funds that seek investment from high-net-worth individuals and other sophisticated and institutional investors rather than funds aiming to raise money through retail channels, though there are regulatory categories that facilitate the registration of all types of funds.

Jersey Private Funds

11.14 Following the popularity and widespread use of the pre-existing 'very private', private placement and the Control of Borrowing (Jersey) Order (COBO) only fund products, the JFSC launched its new, consolidated, Jersey Private Fund (**JPF**) regime in April 2017 to replace the three existing fund products. The new JPF regime provides a simplified fast-track regulatory authorisation process for the establishment of private investment funds, as well as providing certainty in respect of eligibility conditions. Existing fund products may be converted to JPF but are not required to do so. If they do not convert, they will continue to remain subject to their existing regulatory regime.

11.15 Key Features of a JPF:

- a JPF may only be offered to 'Professional Investors' or 'Eligible Investors' as outlined by the Jersey Private Fund Guide (**Guide**);
- a JPF is suitable for funds making offers to 50 or fewer Professional Investors or Eligible Investors where a cost-effective and non-intrusive regulatory environment is sought;
- a JPF can be closed or open-ended and can take a variety of legal forms (including a non-Jersey vehicle);
- the timescale for authorising a JPF is 48 hours from receipt by the JFSC of a complete application;
- a JPF must not be listed;
- whilst there is no absolute requirement for:
  - a JPF which is a company, to have any Jersey resident directors; or
  - a JPF which is a unit trust or partnership, to have a Jersey resident trustee or general partner, or Jersey resident directors of the trustee or general partner,

  at least one Jersey resident director would normally be required;
- a JPF is not required to have an offer document; however, if marketed into the EEA it must comply with the applicable sections of the Jersey AIF Code and may require an offer document;
- unless required by its constitutional documents, there is no need to produce audited accounts of a JPF;
- a JPF must appoint a Jersey-based, 'full substance' designated service provider (**DSP**) (ie usually its administrator), whose principal obligations will be to apply for JFSC consent, update the JFSC in respect of information supplied and support the JPF with its anti-money laundering obligations; and
- the activity of the JPF is subject to the JFSC's Sound Business Practice Policy which oversees investment by Jersey vehicles in certain 'high-risk' areas.

AUTHORISATION PROCEDURE

11.16 In order to establish a JPF, an application must be made to the JFSC by the DSP containing the following:

- details of the JPF including: its name, registered address, minimum investment amounts (if applicable), the 'relevant consent' being applied for, its investment policy, the name and function of each Jersey-based service provider, any regulatory exemptions being relied on by Jersey-based service providers (if applicable), and confirmation as to whether an auditor will be appointed; and

- confirmation that: all investors will be Professional Investors or Eligible Inventors, that the number of offers and the number of investors shall not exceed 50 (applying the guidelines in the Guide), and that the Jersey DSP will complete all client due diligence (**CDD**) checks before the launch of the JPF and will ensure compliance with all anti-money laundering (**AML**) requirements on an ongoing basis.

Expert Funds

11.17 The Jersey Expert Fund (**Expert Fund**) provides a streamlined authorisation process for Jersey collective investment funds targeting Expert Investors.

11.18 Key features of an Expert Fund:

- an Expert Fund may only be offered to Expert Investors, on the basis of an offer document setting out all material information. Expert Investors are deemed to be able to evaluate the risks of investing in an Expert Fund and to bear the economic consequences should the investment fail, and are therefore also deemed to require less regulatory protection in relation to the manner in which the Expert Fund is structured;
- to be an Expert Fund, the fund must have obtained a certificate under the Collective Investment Funds (Jersey) Law 1988 (**CIF Law**);
- the fund must comply with the Jersey Expert Fund Guide (**EFG**) published by the JFSC;
- following the implementation of the AIFMD in July 2013, regulations and codes apply in Jersey to AIFMs actively marketing funds in the EEA;
- the fund company, general partner or trustee must have at least two Jersey resident directors with appropriate expertise and the fund itself must be a Jersey company or have a Jersey general partner (if it is a Jersey limited partnership) or a Jersey trustee or manager (if a unit trust);
- each investor must sign an investment warning and fall within one of the categories set out in the EFG to be an 'expert investor';
- the investment adviser investment manager, which may be an entity based outside of Jersey, must satisfy the requirements as set out in the EFG;
- an Expert Fund must treat one of its service providers (typically a Jersey administrator but can be an investment manager) as a monitoring functionary with at least two Jersey resident directors with appropriate experience and registered to provide fund services business in Jersey. They will be required to monitor the compliance of the investment adviser with any investment or borrowing restrictions set out in the offer document;
- an Expert Fund must appoint an auditor;
- if the fund is open-ended, then custodial arrangements must be sourced from a separate custodian or trustee with staff and a physical presence in Jersey (although this can be waived in certain circumstances); and

- there are no restrictions imposed upon the level of borrowing or gearing adopted by an Expert Fund, provided that the approach to borrowing or gearing is clearly disclosed in the offer document.

11.19 Authorisation Process for an Expert Fund:

- In order to establish an Expert Fund, a standard application form must be completed, signed on behalf of the Expert Fund and the relevant Jersey fund service provider and filed with the JFSC, together with copies of the offer document, fees and a declaration certifying that the Expert Fund complies with the requirements of the EFG. The JFSC relies on the declaration in order to authorise the Expert Fund on an expedited basis.

11.20 The authorisation process will conclude with the issue of a Fund Certificate in relation to the Expert Fund and the registration under the Financial Services (Jersey) Law (FS Law) of any fund service providers not yet registered.

Unregulated Eligible Investor Funds

11.21 An unregulated Eligible Investor Fund (**EIF**) is a scheme or arrangement established in Jersey and in which only 'eligible investors' may invest. Such funds are exempted from regulation as 'collective investment funds' in Jersey by virtue of an enabling order made under the CIF Law, namely the Collective Investment Funds (Unregulated Funds) (Jersey) Order 2008 (as amended) (referred to as the **Unregulated Funds Order**).

11.22 Key features of an Eligible Investor Fund:

- a Jersey EIF may be offered to any number of Eligible Investors;
- an EIF includes an entity who makes a minimum initial investment or commitment of US$1million;
- an EIF may be structured as open- or closed- ended;
- it may be listed but only on exchanges or markets that permit transfer restrictions to ensure that only Eligible Investors may acquire the securities or interests;
- regardless of the number of potential investors to whom the fund is offered, a Fund Certificate is required in relation to a Jersey EIF and Jersey EIFs must comply with the Certified Funds Code;
- each of the Jersey fund service providers must be registered under the FS Law and comply with the Code of Practice for fund services business issued by the JFSC (**FSB Code**);
- regulated funds that have already been established in Jersey are not permitted to convert to unregulated funds; and
- other than a general partner of a Jersey limited partnership or the Jersey corporate trustee or manager of a unit trust and the registered office provider (generally a regulated administrator), there is no requirement for Jersey service

providers to be appointed as functionaries to an unregulated fund and these may be selected on a global basis to provide the best service to fund structures.

11.23 Authorisation process for a Jersey EIF:

- In order to establish a Jersey EIF, a standard application form must be completed, signed on behalf of the Jersey EIF and the relevant Jersey fund service provider and filed with the JFSC, together with a copy of the stated documentation, fees, a certificate certifying that the Jersey EIF offer document complies with the content requirements of the Jersey Eligible Investor Fund Guide and details (name, date of birth and address) of all the principal persons of the investment manager.

11.24 The authorisation process will conclude with the issue of a Fund Certificate in relation to the Jersey EIF and the registration under the FS Law of any fund service providers not yet registered.

Open-Ended Unclassified Funds

11.25 The CIF Law distinguishes between 'recognised funds' (which is a regime for retail funds outside the scope of this book) and 'unclassified funds'. Broadly, the term 'unclassified funds' includes all regulated funds which are not Recognised Funds.

11.26 Key features of an open-ended unclassified fund:

- an unclassified fund may have a corporate structure (including cells), or be a unit trust or limited partnership;
- to the extent that a fund is to be offered to more than 50 investors or is to be listed and the fund is not able to fall under the expedited regulatory approach offered under either the EFG or the Listed Fund Guide (**LFG**) published by the JFSC, a collective investment fund may be regulated as an unclassified fund. This will include compliance by the promoter of the fund with the JFSC's promoter policy;
- the application of the regulatory guidelines to an unclassified fund will primarily depend upon the minimum investment level of the fund and whether the fund is open-ended or closed-ended. An 'open-ended' fund is generally one that is open for redemptions and subscriptions at the option of the investor;
- if the fund is to be open-ended, the JFSC's Open-Ended Unclassified Collective Investment Funds Guide will apply, which sets out the documentary and structural requirements in relation to the fund, suggests investment and borrowing restrictions for different categories of fund and is particularly aimed at retail funds marketed to unsophisticated investors. The JFSC will also have regard to the Collective Investment Funds (Certified Funds – Prospectuses) (*Jersey*) Order 2012 in defining what is an acceptable standard of information in the offering document in relation to a 'collective investment fund' that is an open-ended company or open-ended unit trust;

- no investment or borrowing restrictions are prescribed for closed-ended unclassified funds. However, the JFSC will, for a retail fund, have regard to the guide as a benchmark and, as a condition to the registration certificate granted to the fund under the CIF Law, will require that any change in the investment or borrowing restrictions receives prior written consent from the JFSC;
- an open-ended fund will require a Jersey-resident manager and custodian;
- for a closed-ended fund, no separate custodian is required;
- the fund will be required to comply with the Fund Code; and
- all Jersey fund service providers to an unclassified fund must be registered in Jersey under the FSJ Law and will have to comply with the FSB Codes and Licensing Policy as referred to above.

Listed Funds

11.27 A Listed Fund is a closed-ended Jersey company which falls within the definition of a collective investment fund for the purposes of the CIF Law and is listed on a stock exchange or market recognised by the JFSC. There are two types of vehicles available for a listed product – a fund established under the CIF Law and governed by the LFG and an unregulated exchange-traded fund established in accordance with the Unregulated Funds Order.

11.28 Key features of a listed fund:

- it must be a closed-ended Jersey company;
- it must be listed on a stock exchange recognised by the JFSC;
- regardless of the number of potential investors to whom the fund is offered, a Fund Certificate is required in relation to a Listed Fund;
- Listed Funds must comply with the Certified Funds Code which sets out a regulatory framework of fundamental principles and practical guidance for all Certified Funds;
- each of the Jersey fund service providers must be registered under the FS Law and comply with the FSB Code;
- a Listed Fund which will be marketed in the EEA and its Fund Service Providers must comply with the applicable sections of the AIF Code;
- the Listed Fund must have a Jersey-based manager or administrator that will conduct due diligence on the investment manager and monitor its actions;
- the investment manager must be appropriately qualified in accordance with published criteria (principally it must be established and regulated in an approved jurisdiction);
- independent directors must form the majority of the board of directors of the Listed Fund and there must be at least two Jersey resident directors;

- directors and certain other officers of Listed Funds and the Listed Fund's fund service providers are required to submit personal questionnaires and to meet the JFSC's assessment of them as fit and proper;
- adequate arrangements must be made for the safe custody of the property of the fund. In the case of a hedge fund, the need for a custodian will be satisfied by the appointment of a prime broker with a credit rating of A1/P1;
- flexibility is maintained, as the JFSC will discuss any variations from the requirements of the Jersey Listed Fund Guide on a case-by-case basis; and
- a Listed Fund must be audited.

11.29 Authorisation process for a Listed Fund:

- In order to establish a Listed Fund, a standard application form is completed and filed with the JFSC, together with the relevant fees, a copy of the offer document and a declaration certifying that the Listed Fund complies with the requirements of the Jersey Listed Fund Guide. The authorisation process will conclude with the issue of a Fund Certificate in relation to the Listed Fund and the registration under the FS Law of any fund service providers not yet registered.

FEES

11.30 The Jersey Financial Services Commission's fee for an application of a certificate in relation to a Collective Investment Fund is £2,165.

11.31 For Jersey Private Funds, a fee of £1,070 is payable to the JFSC in respect of an application for a COBO consent for a JPF, with an annual fee of £500 also payable (pro-rated for the year in which the JPF is established). If the JPF is to be marketed in the EEA, a separate fee of £1,275 is payable in respect of the application for an AIF certificate, plus a further fee of £1,275 where the manager is required to register for AIF service business (**AIFSB**).

11.32 Generally, no statutory fees are payable in relation to an Unregulated Fund, other than the fees payable on the incorporation of a Jersey company or establishment of a limited partnership, if applicable. However, if a Jersey fund services business only provides services to Unregulated Funds, it will be required to pay an annual fee.

Annual Fees

11.33 Annual fees are payable in relation to a fund which holds a Fund Certificate. The fee amount depends on the total number of pools of assets in the fund at the time the fee is payable. This ranges from £1,405 if there is only one pool of assets to £35,535 if there are 200 or more pools of assets.

11.34 Statutory fees are also payable by Jersey fund service providers. A fee of £2,675 is payable for a fund service provider's application for registration under the FS Law. The annual fees payable by a fund service provider also depends upon the number of pools of assets in all the collective investment funds in relation to which it is a fund service provider. This ranges from £4,460 to £42,150.

STRUCTURE

Jersey Unit Trust

11.35 A Jersey Property Unit Trust (**JPUT**) is a specific type of Jersey trust which is commonly used to acquire and hold interests in UK real estate. Unlike a company, a JPUT is not a separate legal entity. The assets of the JPUT are held by its trustee on trust for the unitholders of the JPUT. The unitholders hold units in the JPUT, similar to shareholders holding shares in a company.

11.36 As the JPUT is a trust, the trustee will be the legal owner of the assets of the JPUT whereas the unitholders will be the beneficial owners of those assets. This is different from the position with a company, where shareholders have no direct ownership interest in the company's assets.

Companies

11.37 Companies are incorporated under the provisions of the Companies (Jersey) Law 1991 (the **Companies Law**). The liability of shareholders may be limited by shares or by guarantee or a combination of shares and guarantee, or it may be unlimited. The form usually chosen for investment funds is a company limited by shares. Fund companies, which are established as open-ended so that investors have the right to realise their investment in the company, will normally issue redeemable shares to facilitate this. Under the Companies Law, companies are not required to have an authorised share capital and may choose to have the power to issue an unlimited number of shares (subject in some circumstances to having authority from its shareholders to do so) with either a par value or no-par value.

11.38 In addition to the traditional type of limited liability company, the Companies Law also permits the incorporation of protected cell companies which are particularly well suited for use as umbrella funds and incorporated cell companies.

11.39 Incorporated cell companies are similar to protected cell companies, but go a stage further in that each cell is a separate company in its own right with its own constitution and capital structure.

11.40 All companies formed under Jersey law have a separate legal personality and are capable of suing and being sued in their own name. Management and control is vested in a board of directors although, particularly in the case of open-ended companies, it is often the case that investment management will be delegated to a management company.

Limited Partnerships

11.41 Limited partnerships, which are now the favoured vehicles for closed-ended private equity funds, are established under the provisions of the Limited Partnerships (Jersey) Law, 1994 (as amended). A limited partnership is created by a written partnership agreement and cannot come into existence until it has been registered in the register of limited liability partnerships maintained by the Registrar of Companies at the Jersey Registry.

11.42 A limited partnership consists of one or more general partners who are admitted to the partnership as general partners in accordance with the partnership agreement and who are jointly and severally liable for all debts of the partnership without limitation; and one or more limited partners who are admitted to the partnership as limited partners. Among the features which make the Jersey limited partnership attractive to fund promoters are the following:

- There is no limit on the number of limited partners who may be members of a limited partnership who benefit from well established 'safe harbour' provisions.
- A person may be both a general partner and a limited partner, and a body corporate or a partnership may be a general partner or a limited partner.
- The general partner is not required to be resident in Jersey.
- Although the partnership is registered in a public register which is open to inspection, the names of the limited partners do not appear on it.
- A limited partnership can distribute both capital and profits without formality, provided that the partnership is solvent before and after the distribution.

In 2011, Jersey introduced two additional types of limited partnerships: the 'separate limited partnership' and the 'incorporated limited partnership'. These two new limited partnerships offer a degree of separate legal personality and complement the range of existing partnerships that are already available in Jersey.

SETTING UP A LOCAL MANAGEMENT COMPANY/INVESTMENT MANAGER

11.43 The legal vehicle used for the investment manager or adviser to a fund will vary, depending on the form of the fund, but it is likely to be:

- a separate company (in the case of a corporate fund);
- a general partner (in the case of a limited partnership); or
- a trustee or separate management company (in the case of a unit trust).

11.44 There is a familiarity with structures such as limited partnerships acting as general partners and Jersey separate/incorporated limited partnerships which are usually used in certain structures.

11.45 Self-managed funds are also increasingly common in the case of certified funds as, pursuant to a law development in 2015, they are primarily regulated through their fund as opposed to manager regulation.

11.46 Investment managers for Jersey funds are often located in the jurisdiction where the promoter of the fund is based, although they may be based in Jersey. An increasing number of investment managers have relocated to, or established a presence in, Jersey and the tax and regulatory authorities have been supportive of these businesses.

11.47 Alternative asset promoters often establish a special purpose investment manager in Jersey to act for one or more funds, including to ensure that 'management and control' of the fund remains offshore. With the assistance of a recognised local administrator, this is generally a fast and straightforward process.

11.48 Investment management activities will fall within the definition of financial services business for the purposes of the Financial Services (Jersey) Law 1998 (**FSJL**). There are a number of factors relevant to whether an investment business registration is required, including whether any exemptions are available, such as the 'Professional Investor Regulated Scheme' exemption that depends on a number of acknowledgments in the case of professional investor structures.

11.49 To establish an investment management company in Jersey, an application would need to be made under the FSJL unless the activities of the investment manager fell outside the scope of the FSJL regime or an exemption could be identified. Applications usually take between four to six weeks to be processed (unless the application is made in conjunction with a Jersey fund establishment and/or the investment manager is to be a managed entity in which case the timeframe may be expedited) and a locally-based resource is required.

OTHER KEY SERVICE PROVIDERS

11.50 Other than a general partner of a Jersey limited partnership or the Jersey corporate trustee or manager of a unit trust and the registered office provider (generally a regulated administrator), there is no requirement for the Jersey service providers to be appointed as functionaries to an unregulated fund or private fund and these may be selected on a global basis to provide the best service to fund structures.

TAX REGIME

11.51 Taxation in Jersey is the responsibility of the Comptroller of Income Tax under the Income Tax (Jersey) Law 1961, as amended and under the Goods and Services Tax (Jersey) Law 2007. Jersey does not levy its own taxes on an investment scheme based in the Island, or on the investors in such a scheme. There is no capital gains tax, capital transfer tax, wealth tax, estate or inheritance tax payable in respect of the issue or realisation of investments in an investment scheme, whether that scheme is structured as an investment company, a unit trust or a limited partnership. Nor is any corporation tax, profits tax or withholding tax payable in relation to such a scheme. Jersey is free from all exchange control restrictions.

11.52 There is no stamp duty payable on share or unit transfers in an investment scheme (other than certain probate duties on the death of an individual investor), and no taxes by reference to a company's authorised or issued share capital.

11.53 The general rate of Jersey corporate income tax is 0% subject to the limited exceptions set out below:

- certain specified domestic Jersey utility companies shall be chargeable to Jersey income tax at a rate of 20% (comprising the Jersey gas, water, electricity, postal and telecoms utilities);
- income derived from leasing or ownership of Jersey land will continue to be chargeable to Jersey income tax at a rate of 20%; and
- certain 'financial services companies' shall be chargeable to Jersey income tax at a rate of 10%.

11.54 For these purposes, 'financial services companies' are Jersey companies that are regulated in Jersey as banks; as fund administrators or custodians; or are registered to carry out trust company business or investment business. Such administrators, custodians or registered persons will only be chargeable to Jersey income tax at the 10% rate if they carry on that business through a permanent establishment in Jersey.

11.55 Permanent establishment entails a physical presence in Jersey or a place of management of the company. The fact that the directors of a company regularly meet in Jersey will not, of itself, make their meeting place a permanent establishment. Nor will the exercise of clerical functions such as invoicing operations, management and administration services or the entering into of contracts in respect of a company's international business (to include, for example, swap financing and loan funding agreements) at the address of the company's registered office amount to carrying on business through a permanent establishment in Jersey for these purposes.

Base Erosion and Profit Shifting (BEPS)

11.56 Jersey has engaged with BEPS working parties and consultations to assess the OECD's October 2015 BEPS Action Plans, as well as scrutinise the EU Commission's 'BEPS Directive'. Jersey is already effectively a BEPS-compliant jurisdiction, due to Jersey's finance sector model and regulatory framework which prevents the island being exploited significantly for BEPS and ensures equivalent outcomes to those that both the OECD and EU Commission are seeking to secure. In addition, Jersey has taken the following action:

- Jersey became a BEPS Associate and a member of the BEPS Inclusive Framework from its inauguration in 2016.
- Jersey signed the BEPS Multilateral Instrument in June 2017 which aims to implement tax treaty-related measures to combat BEPS.
- Jersey has signed up to the Multilateral Competent Authority Agreement (**MCCA**) to assist with the sharing of relevant information in relation to Country by Country Reporting (**CbCR**) (Action 13), as well as broadly adopting the OECD's CbCR implementation package, to facilitate its implementation of this BEPS minimum standard, and has already put in place the relevant implementing regulations for CbCR.

LOCAL STOCK EXCHANGE

11.57 The International Securities Exchange (TISE) (formerly the Channel Island Securities Exchange prior to a rebrand completed in March 2017) is headquartered in Guernsey with offices also in Jersey and the Isle of Man.

11.58 The TISE provides a platform for the listing and electronic trading of a wide range of products, including trading companies, specialist debt, investment vehicles, special purpose acquisition companies and extractive industries. Provision is also made for secondary listings where a primary listing already exists on another exchange.

11.59 The TISE is an Affiliate Member of the International Organisation of Securities Commissions (**IOSCO**) and an Affiliate Member of the World Federation of Exchanges (**WFE**). The UK tax authority, Her Majesty's Revenue & Customs (**HMRC**), deems TISE to be a Recognised Stock Exchange for the purposes of investment by Self-Invested Personal Pensions (**SIPPs**) and Individual Savings Accounts (**ISAs**). HMRC's recognition also means that products listed on the TISE may be able to avail of the Quoted Eurobond Exemption (**QEE**). TISE is officially recognised by the German Federal Financial Supervisory Authority, BaFin, and the Australian Stock Exchange (**ASX**).

CONFIDENTIALITY LAWS

11.60 Jersey has no banking secrecy laws and follows the English common law model as regards the duty of confidentiality owed by a bank or other financial institution to its customers. The Royal Court of Jersey has held that banking confidentiality arises as a matter of an express or implied contractual obligation. The duty of non-disclosure is not absolute, but is qualified and will not apply, for example, where disclosure is required under compulsion of law or where disclosure is in the public interest.

11.61 In particular, Jersey's anti-money laundering legislation imposes a duty of disclosure by either requiring that suspicious transactions are reported or by providing that the making of such report will act as a defence, if the institution is charged with assisting another to retain the benefit of criminal conduct. A financial services business may be made the subject of a disclosure order under the Island's anti-money laundering, prevention of fraud or income tax legislation, and otherwise in accordance with an order of the Royal Court made pursuant to its jurisdiction in proceedings before it.

11.62 Jersey has in place data protection legislation in the form of the Data Protection (Jersey) Law 2005, intended to uphold an individual's right to privacy by ensuring that processing and use of their personal information follows a set of enforceable standards. The law applies, for example, to the treatment of personal data held by Jersey-based administrators. Jersey regulation to reflect the European-based General Data Protection Regulation will be implemented in 2018.

ANTI-MONEY LAUNDERING LAWS

11.63 Jersey has in place a number of statutory and regulatory measures to help prevent money laundering and the financing of terrorism, including:

- the Proceeds of Crime (Jersey) Law 1999, as amended, an 'all crimes' anti-money laundering law which applies to all persons and businesses, and which contains provisions under which assets that have been found to originate from criminal activities may be seized and confiscated and custodial sentences of up to 14 years may be imposed;
- subordinate legislation imposing additional requirements on financial services businesses to combat money laundering, including 'know your customer', reporting and record-keeping requirements; and
- the Criminal Justice (International Co-operation) (Jersey) Law 2001 to enable Jersey to cooperate with other countries in criminal investigations and proceedings.

11.64 The Island's anti-money laundering regime is recognised by the Financial Action Task Force as being in compliance with its 40 recommendations.

11.65 Jersey also co-operates in cross-border investigations. The Criminal Justice (International Cooperation) (Jersey) Law 2001 allows evidence gathered in Jersey to be used in foreign courts. This statute gives police expanded search and seizure powers and encourages co-operation with foreign investigators in financial crimes. Jersey has also signed memoranda of understanding with Germany, France and the US, giving international investigators greater access to the Island's financial records. In addition, the Corruption (Jersey) Law 2006 enables Jersey to become party to the 1999 Council of Europe Convention on Corruption and the 1997 OECD Convention on Combating Bribery of Foreign Officials in International Business Transactions.

CONCLUDING REMARKS: WHAT ARE THE JURISDICTION'S UNIQUE SELLING POINTS?

11.66 Jersey is widely regarded as a well-established stable, secure and trusted jurisdiction for the management and administration of a variety of fund structures. It offers a robust yet practical and flexible regulatory environment, with the highest quality service providers undertaking increasingly specialised services for leading alternative fund structures and their managers.

CHAPTER 12

LUXEMBOURG

GENERAL DESCRIPTION OF THE JURISDICTION

12.01 The constitutional monarchy which is the Grand Duchy of Luxembourg is a small country surrounded by France, Belgium and Germany. It has a land area of approximately 1,000 square miles and a population of around 580,000. Luxembourg's legal system is based on civil law.

12.02 The national language is Luxembourgish. French and German are also widely used in administrative matters. English is also commonly spoken. The capital and financial centre is Luxembourg City. Luxembourg is one hour ahead of GMT and six hours ahead of EST. Luxembourg adopted the European single currency, the euro, on 1 January 2002. There are no exchange controls.

12.03 Luxembourg's principal businesses include asset management (especially private banking), investment fund management, administration and custody, and other financial services.

12.04 The European Union Court of Justice, the Court of Auditors, the European Investment Bank and various other EU institutions such as the Secretariat of the European Parliament and other departments of the European Commission are situated in Luxembourg.

12.05 Additionally, Luxembourg benefits from EU and Organisation for Economic Co-operation and Development (**OECD**) membership, which may have marketing advantages.

KEY MANDATORY REQUIREMENTS

12.06

- No directly regulated fund can be established in Luxembourg without the prior consent of the Luxembourg regulator (the *Commission de Surveillance du Secteur Financier* or **CSSF**). No such consent will thus be required for a reserved alternative investment fund (**RAIF**) or for unregulated partnerships.
- The net assets of undertakings for collective investment (**UCIs**) must reach a minimum provided for by law (currently €1.25 million or equivalent in another currency) within twelve months (six months for Undertakings for Collective Investment in Transferable Securities (**UCITS**)) from the date the fund was authorised. For investment companies in risk capital, the minimum is set at €1 million or equivalent in another currency.

- A UCI must appoint a depositary having its registered office in Luxembourg, or established in Luxembourg if its registered office is in another member state of the European Union (EU member state).
- The central administration of any UCI or SICAR must be located in Luxembourg.
- There is a simplified listing procedure for the listing of Luxembourg funds on the Luxembourg Stock Exchange.
- Stringent anti-money laundering rules apply, and the acceptance of subscription monies from prospective investors is subject to the principle of 'know your customer'.
- Professional secrecy is set by statute.
- Luxembourg asset managers and management companies are subject to a specific approval procedure in Luxembourg.

RECENT DEVELOPMENTS

Limited Partnerships

12.07 When the Alternative Investment Fund Managers Directive (**AIFMD**) was transposed into Luxembourg law by the law of 12 July 2013 (**AIFM Law**), the Luxembourg government took the opportunity to reform the limited partnership regime, from both a corporate and fiscal perspective. The reform aimed at making Luxembourg limited partnerships more attractive structures for fund managers – in particular, for private equity fund managers. Today limited partnerships are used as fund vehicles for both regulated and non-regulated private investment funds which implement a wide range of investment strategies. Different types of partnerships exist, including one which does not have legal personality.

RAIFs

12.08 Following the introduction and implementation of AIFMD and in order to avoid a double layer of regulation (ie regulation both at the level of the investment fund and at the level of the alternative investment fund manager) Luxembourg introduced, by means of the law of 23 July 2016, the Reserved Alternative Investment Funds (**RAIFs**) regime. The RAIF is regulated only indirectly through its alternative investment fund manager (**AIFM**) (due to the requirement for the RAIF to be managed by an authorised AIFM), which significantly reduces the time to market. As a consequence, the RAIF (via its AIFM) benefits from the European passport granted by the AIFMD for marketing to professional investors in the EEA.

THE REGULATION OF INVESTMENT BUSINESS

12.09 The CSSF is the supervisory authority of the Luxembourg financial sector. It supervises, regulates, authorises, informs and, where appropriate, carries out on-site inspections and issues sanctions. It is responsible for promoting transparency, simplicity and fairness in the markets of financial products and services and for the enforcement of laws on financial consumer protection and on the fight against money laundering and terrorist financing.

12.10 The CSSF represents Luxembourg in the area of European and international regulatory supervision. It cooperates with the Luxembourg central bank (*Banque Centrale du Luxembourg)*, the European supervisory authorities (ESMA, EBA, EIOPA) and the other supervisory authorities at the international level.

INVESTORS

12.11 Luxembourg is a leading financial centre and a global location for all types of investors and investment funds. Luxembourg is the largest European fund domicile and second largest fund centre in the world. The success of Luxembourg is attributed to its business-enabling environment. A number of key factors make Luxembourg an attractive jurisdiction, including:

- A flexible and innovative regulatory framework.
- The responsiveness of the Luxembourg government, legislative body, and CSSF to practitioners' needs.
- Experienced and business-oriented professional service providers.
- The ability to achieve tax neutrality for products by considering direct and indirect taxation implications at fund and investor level.
- An attractive range of investment fund solutions.
- A political and social stable environment.
- A strong economy.
- An international and multilingual workforce.
- The central location at the political and geographical heart of Europe with easy access to other financial centres.

SETTING UP A FUND

Legal regime

12.12 Private funds (regulated directly or through their AIFM) can be established in Luxembourg under various legal regimes:

(a) Part II of the amended law of 17 December 2010 (**Part II Funds**);

(b) the amended law of 13 February 2007 on specialised investment funds (**SIFs**);

(c) the amended law of 15 June 2004 on *sociétés d'investissement en capital à risque* (investment companies in risk capital, **SICARs**);

(d) the law of 23 July 2016 on RAIFs.

In addition to the regulated fund regimes described above, fund vehicles for private funds may be structured as unregulated funds. For a variety of reasons, these funds would typically be structured as partnerships as described at **12.13** below.

12.13 Private funds can also be set up as non-regulated funds, usually using one of the legal forms of limited partnerships (see **12.07–12.08** above). These partnerships are formed under the amended law of 10 August 1915 on commercial companies and may, depending on the circumstances, be subject to the AIFMD and/or benefit from the de minimis exemptions under the AIFMD and the AIFM Law. Unregulated funds are not subject to the subscription tax which applies to most of the regulated funds directly or indirectly.

Part II Funds

12.14 Part II Funds are funds that have as principal object the investment in assets not qualifying as eligible assets within the meaning of Part I of the law of 17 December 2010 (ie UCITS eligible assets), as well as funds that could qualify as UCITS but are excluded from Part I of the law of 17 December 2010 either because of their investment policy or because of the rules applicable to the distribution of their shares.

12.15 Part II Funds have increased flexibility (as compared to UCITS) as regards the type of assets they can invest in, the investment strategies they can employ, the diversification rules they are subject to and the liquidity they can offer to investors. Historically Part II Funds have been used for real estate funds, hedge funds or funds of funds.

12.16 Part II Funds necessarily qualify as alternative investment funds (**AIFs**) under the AIFMD, which means that, without prejudice to the de minimis exemptions, they have to appoint an authorised external AIFM, or themselves become authorised as AIFM (internally managed AIFs).

12.17 Part II Funds benefit from the EU passport under the AIFMD regime. In Luxembourg, Part II Funds can be marketed to any type of investors, including retail investors.

SIFs

12.18 The SIF regime offers a more flexible framework for private funds than Part II Funds. SIFs may be marketed to a wider range of investors and provide increased flexibility in terms of permitted investments and investment restrictions.

12.19 The primary objective of a SIF must be the collective investment of funds raised from its investors applying the principle of risk diversification. The SIF Law provides that an investor in a SIF must qualify as a 'well-informed investor' within the meaning of the statutory definition. This category includes institutional and professional investors, and also investors who have made a written declaration confirming their status as well-informed investors and who either invest at least €125,000 (or equivalent) in a single SIF or in a sub-fund of an umbrella SIF, or who have been appropriately assessed by a credit institution (as defined by Directive 2006/48/EC), an investment firm (as defined by Directive 2004/39/EC) or a UCITS management company (as defined by Directive 2009/65/EC), which has certified the investor's ability to understand the risks associated with investing in a SIF. This is a significant provision enabling SIFs to target private individuals (such as high net worth individuals).

SICARs

12.20 SICARs operate under a regime which is tailor-made for private equity/ venture capital investments, including tax treatment which differs from that applicable to Part II Funds and SIFs. The concept of risk capital is set forth in the SICAR Law and provides that investment in risk capital means the direct or indirect contribution of assets to entities in expectation of their launch, development or listing on a stock exchange. In a similar manner as SIFs, SICARs are reserved to well-informed investors and can under certain conditions benefit from the AIFMD passport.

RAIFs

12.21 The RAIF regime is based on the SIF and SICAR regimes, with the important exception that the RAIF is not subject to authorisation or supervision as an investment fund, which makes it an attractive vehicle from a time-to-market perspective. As mentioned above at **12.08**, the RAIF must, however, designate an authorised AIFM, thus benefiting from the AIFMD passport as well as from the protection of the AIFMD framework. RAIFs are reserved to well-informed investors.

STRUCTURE

12.22 Most of the time, Luxembourg directly or indirectly regulated private funds qualifying as UCIs would generally be established using the following three main types of legal structure subject to what is specified hereafter:

(1) ***Fonds Commun de Placement* (FCP)**, which is similar to an open or closed-ended unit trust. An FCP does not have a separate legal identity. It is an unincorporated co-proprietorship of its assets, managed in the interest of its unitholders by a Luxembourg management company *(société de gestion)* in accordance with the management regulations which are generally signed by the management company and the depositary. The FCP is in principle tax transparent. A SICAR must be established in a corporate form and cannot be organised as an FCP.

(2) ***Société d'Investissement à Capital Variable*** **(SICAV)**, an open-ended or closed-ended investment company whose capital is variable and is always equal to the value of the net assets of the fund. Investors in such a fund are shareholders or limited partners (depending on legal form used) and have the usual shareholder rights or partners rights as specified in the partnership agreement. Private funds that are established as a SICAV are also subject to the Law of 1915 on commercial companies (save to the extent that the 2010 Law, the SIF Law or the RAIF Law (as the case may be) derogates from it).

(3) ***Société d'Investissement à Capital Fixe*** **(SICAF)**, usually a closed-ended investment company, where the capital is not adjusted automatically to match the net worth of the fund (ie, fixed capital funds).

For both SICAVs and SICAFs, the fund vehicle may take corporate or partnership forms as described at **13.25** below.

12.23 For a SICAV, SICAF and the management company of an FCP, depending on the type of entity, usually at least one shareholders'/partners' meeting would need to be held in Luxembourg each year.

12.24 Directors' meetings need not necessarily be held in Luxembourg, although holding meetings abroad may have adverse tax consequences. The directors need not be Luxembourg residents. It is, however, common to have at least one local director.

12.25 A SICAV or SICAF may be established under different corporate forms, but also as a limited partnership with one or more general partners who have unlimited and joint and several liability for the obligations of the partnership and one or more limited partners whose liability is limited.

12.26 The choice between the available structures depends among other things on the objective of the fund in terms of investment and marketing, the flexibility sought and on control and tax considerations.

Umbrella funds

12.27 A Part II Fund, SIF, SICAR and RAIF can also be organised as an umbrella fund. This type of fund is structured as a single entity with one or more compartments or sub-funds which may each operate with a distinct investment objective, specific terms, etc.

12.28 The relevant laws provide that, unless otherwise provided in the fund documentation, there is generally no cross-liability among sub-funds of the same umbrella fund due to ring-fencing, meaning that the rights of unitholders and creditors concerning a sub-fund or which have arisen in connection with the creation, operation or liquidation of a sub-fund are limited to the assets of that sub-fund. As a consequence, the assets of each sub-fund only answer for the liabilities, debts and obligations of that specific sub-fund. Every sub-fund is considered to be a separate entity and the umbrella fund constitutes a single legal entity.

FEES

12.29 On the filing of an application for a private fund subject to the approval and direct supervision of the CSSF, a CSSF filing fee must be paid. For a stand-alone fund, the CSSF charges a flat filing fee of €4,000 and €8,000 for an umbrella fund. Thereafter the CSSF will charge an annual fee amounting to €4,000 for a stand-alone fund and to €8,000 for an umbrella fund with 1 to 5 sub-funds (€15,000 from 6 to 20 sub-funds, €24,000 from 21 to 50 sub-funds and €35,000 for more than 50 sub-funds)

SUPERVISION

12.30 All regulated private funds established in Luxembourg are subject to the approval, supervision and control of the CSSF. In order to obtain the latter's approval, the fund must file an application with the CSSF which, inter alia, includes:

- draft constitutional documents;
- draft offering document;
- any draft agreements between the fund and third parties (including, for example, the depositary and the central administration agent);
- status under AIFMD;
- confirmation letter from the independent auditor;
- details of the investment manager(s) and directors of the fund (or of the management company of the FCP or of the general partner in case of a partnership structure).

12.31 These documents are normally submitted to the CSSF with the assistance of a Luxembourg law firm.

12.32 The offering document must contain such information as is necessary to enable investors and their investment advisors to make an informed judgment regarding their investment. It must also disclose such additional information as is necessary to provide fair and full information to investors (eg risk factors).

12.33 Once the fund has been authorised, it will be subject to permanent supervision and control by the CSSF. The CSSF reviews financial reports and annual and semi-annual financial statements (if any) as well as any changes in the constitutional documents, offering document, material contracts, or the operation or organisation of the fund.

INVESTMENT RESTRICTIONS

12.34 There are no restrictions in terms of eligible assets for Part II Funds, SIFs and RAIFs, meaning that they can follow any type of investment strategy (including hedge funds, real estate funds, private equity funds, venture capital funds, commodities funds, infrastructure funds, loan origination funds, fund of funds, microfinance funds or debt funds).

12.35 The investment restrictions applicable to Part II Funds are not set by law but in CSSF circulars (eg IML Circular 91/75 containing general investment restrictions and rules applicable to venture capital funds, future and options funds and real estate funds, and CSSF Circular 02/80 setting forth specific rules applicable in particular to hedge funds and funds of hedge funds). In terms of risk diversification, Part II Funds may not invest, in principle, more than 20% of their assets in one single issuer.

12.36 For SIFs and RAIFs, the law provides that they must be managed in compliance with the principle of risk spreading. CSSF Circular 07/309 provides that a SIF may not, in principle, invest more than 30% of its assets or commitments to subscribe securities of the same type issued by the same issuer. Furthermore, uncovered sales may not result in the SIF holding a short position in securities of the same type issued by the same issuer and representing more than 30% of its assets.

12.37 The CSSF may grant derogations from the above guidelines in some cases or, depending on the specific investment policy of the SIF, impose additional investment restrictions. For RAIFs, the governing body of the RAIF has the responsibility to assess the level of risk spreading deemed appropriate for the RAIF's portfolio.

12.38 SICARs are not required to operate under the principle of risk-spreading, but are limited in terms of eligible assets.

ACCOUNTS/AUDIT REQUIREMENTS

12.39 An audited annual report must be made available free of charge to shareholders or unitholders and sent to the CSSF. The CSSF requires funds to complete annual reports, the form and contents of which must comply with applicable law. The annual report must be published within six months of the financial year-end. For Part II Funds unaudited semi-annual reports are also required; they must be published within three months of the period-end and filed with the CSSF.

12.40 The accounting information included in the annual report of a Luxembourg fund must be audited by a Luxembourg-authorised auditor. The auditor's report must certify that the accounting information presents a true and fair view of the financial position of the fund. Annual reports of investment companies must be filed at the Registrar of Companies (*Registre de Commerce et des Sociétés*) in English, French, German or Luxembourgish.

SETTING UP A LOCAL MANAGEMENT COMPANY/INVESTMENT MANAGER

12.41 All Luxembourg AIFs (non UCITS funds which raise capital from a number of investors, with a view to investing it in accordance with a defined investment policy for the benefit of those investors) must appoint an authorised AIFM, unless they are internally managed or authorised as an AIFM under the AIFM Law or opt to be under the AIFMD thresholds regime. The following will therefore focus on the setting up of an AIFM, and will therefore not cover 'non-AIFM' management companies or 'MIFID' asset managers.

Authorisation process

12.42 Any Luxembourg company intending to act as AIFM shall be authorised by the CSSF beforehand. The application file for authorisation shall include, as a minimum requirement, the information listed in the 'Application questionnaire for the set-up of a fully licensed alternative investment fund manager', which can be downloaded on the CSSF website.

12.43 The information to be provided will include, in particular, a description of:

(1) The direct and indirect ownership structure: the AIFM must inform the CSSF of the identities of the shareholders, whether direct or indirect, natural or legal persons, that hold qualifying participating interests (ie, the holding, directly or indirectly, of at least 10% of the capital or of the voting rights or which enable them to exert significant influence on the management of the asset manager), together with the amount thereof.

(2) The capitalisation of the management company: Luxembourg AIFMs are required to meet the AIFMD minimum capital requirements. The minimum capital requirement is the highest of (a) €125,000 plus 0.02% of assets under management over €250 million; and (b) one quarter of fixed annual overheads.

(3) Professional standing and experience and rules of conduct: the members of the administrative, managerial and supervisory bodies of the AIFM, as well as its shareholders, must produce evidence of their professional standing (which will be assessed on the basis of police records and of any evidence tending to show that the persons concerned are of good repute and offering every guarantee of irreproachable conduct).

(4) The division of the areas of responsibility of the conducting persons (a minimum of two conducting persons is required) with a description of their experience in their respective areas of responsibility.

(5) Central administration and organisation: it is necessary to demonstrate that the central administration and the registered office of the AIFM are in Luxembourg. The applicant must dispose of a solid system of internal governance, including in particular a clear organisational structure with a well-defined, transparent and coherent division of the responsibilities, effective processes of detection, of management, of control and of declaration of risks to which it is or could be exposed, adequate mechanisms of internal

control, including sound administrative and accounting procedures, as well as mechanisms of control and security for information processing systems.

(6) The program of activities.

(7) Provisional three-year budget of the AIFM.

(8) Draft articles of association of the AIFM.

(9) Description of the administrative, accounting and IT infrastructure of the AIFM, including a functional organisation chart which indicates the number of persons working for the AIFM.

(10) Name of the *réviseur d'entreprises agréé* (approved statutory auditor).

(11) Details of the persons responsible for the functions of compliance, internal audit, risk management, anti-money laundering procedures.

(12) Description of the risk management process applied by the AIFM to the AIFs managed.

SUPERVISION

12.44 AIFMs are subject to the supervision of the CSSF.

12.45 The CSSF has the right to request from the AIFM all information useful for the execution of its tasks. It may inspect the books, accounts, registers and all other deeds and documents of the AIFM. The CSSF will receive the audit reports, long-form reports and written observations issued by the external auditor of the AIFM. If the AIFM wishes to change external auditors, it may do so only after having obtained a written authorisation from the CSSF. The CSSF may request an external auditor to perform an audit of one or several specific aspect(s) of the business and the functioning of the AIFM. The external auditor is required by law to notify the CSSF without delay of certain situations of which he becomes aware during the course of his audit, such as a serious breach of the provisions of the law or of any of the regulations.

CSSF Fees

12.46 The CSSF charges a flat fee of €15,000 for the examination of the authorisation request. Thereafter the CSSF will charge an annual fee amounting to €35,000.

OTHER KEY SERVICE PROVIDERS

12.47 The Luxembourg financial sector comprises internationally-recognised legal, tax and accounting experts with particular expertise in investment funds. The sector is supported by over 100 financial institutions legally entitled to conduct all types of banking activities. Luxembourg financial institutions have been involved in collective investment business for over 30 years and are well equipped to provide the requisite services.

Depositary

12.48 All directly or indirectly regulated private funds established in Luxembourg must appoint a depositary.

12.49 The Financial Sector Law provides for a new licensing regime for depositaries servicing AIFs that are mainly invested in assets other than financial instruments that can be held in safe custody, so long as the AIFs do not allow their investors to request the redemption of their shares/units for at least five years following investment. These depositaries, which need not to be authorised as a credit institution or an investment firm, will need to be approved and subject to the prudential supervision of the CSSF.

12.50 Depositaries servicing AIFs within the scope of the AIFMD will need to provide cash monitoring, safekeeping and oversight duties in accordance with the AIFM Law.

12.51 The depositary may delegate the above-mentioned safekeeping functions under certain conditions.

Central administration

12.52 The central administration of any Luxembourg directly or indirectly regulated private fund qualifying as UCI or SICAR must be located in Luxembourg. CSSF Circular 91/75, as amended by CSSF Circular 05/177, sets out what is required in terms of this central administration, as follows:

(a) accounts must be compiled and accounting documents must be available in Luxembourg;

(b) the subscription and redemption of shares or units must be carried out in Luxembourg;

(c) the register of shareholders or unitholders must be kept in Luxembourg;

(d) the prospectus, financial reports and other documents intended for investors must be prepared in co-operation with the central administration in Luxembourg;

(e) correspondence with, and dispatch of, documents intended for shareholders or unitholders must be carried out from Luxembourg and under the responsibility of the central administration in Luxembourg; and

(f) the confirmed and released net asset value must be in Luxembourg.

TAX REGIME

Part II Funds, SIFs and RAIFs

12.53 Luxembourg directly or indirectly regulated private funds (except RAIFs investing only in securities representing risk capital; see **12.57** below) are exempt from corporate income taxes and net wealth tax but are subject to an annual subscription tax. No withholding tax is levied on payments by such Luxembourg private funds to their investors.

12.54 Subscription tax is an annual tax, payable quarterly and assessed on the total net asset value on the last valuation day of each quarter.

12.55 The rates of the annual subscription tax include the following:

- standard rate 0.05%: for funds governed by Part II of the Law of 17 December 2010;
- standard rate 0.01%: for SIFs and RAIFs;
- cash and monetary funds/sub-funds: 0.01%, except that SIFs, RAIFs/ institutional sub-funds or institutional classes of units of such type of funds/ sub-funds are exempt;
- institutional sub-funds or institutional classes of units of funds governed by Part II of the Law of 17 December 2010: 0.01%; and
- fund of funds: rates as mentioned above apply, but assets represented by investments in funds that are themselves subject to the annual subscription tax are exempt.

12.56 The following are also exempt from the subscription tax:

- Part II Funds, SIFs and RAIFs or their sub-funds or classes the securities or partnership interests of which are reserved for (i) institutions for occupational retirement provision, or similar investment vehicles, set up on one or several employers' initiative for the benefit of their employees and (ii) companies of one or several employers investing the funds they own, in order to provide their employees with retirement benefits;
- Part II Funds, SIFs or RAIFs or their sub-funds or classes whose main objective is the investment in microfinance institutions; and
- Exchange traded Funds.

SICARs

12.57 SICARs and RAIFs investing only in securities representing risk capital set up as a joint-stock company (*société de capitaux*) are fiscally opaque and liable to Luxembourg corporation taxes at the combined rate of 26.01% in Luxembourg-City for 2018. They are also subject to an annual minimum net wealth tax.

12.58 However, they benefit from a special tax exemption on income derived from transferable securities (*valeurs mobilières*), as well as from capital gains realised upon the disposal of these securities. Capital losses realised upon the disposal of transferable securities are not tax deductible. Indeed, as a general principle, expenses related to exempt income are not tax deductible. No withholding tax is levied on distributions made by a SICAR to its investors.

12.59 A SICAR organised as a partnership (*société de personnes*) and in particular a limited partnership ((common limited partnership (**SCS**) or special limited partnership (**SCSp**)) is transparent for Luxembourg income tax and net wealth tax purposes. A SICAR organised as an SCS/SCSp is thus itself not subject to income tax or net wealth tax in Luxembourg.

Limited Partnerships

12.60 An AIF adopting the form of an SCS/SCSp acting as an investment vehicle is fully transparent without being subject to municipal business tax as long as its general partner does not hold more than 5% of the partnership interest, without the SCS/SCSp carrying out commercial activities. Furthermore, on 9 January 2015, the Luxembourg tax authorities published tax circular LIR 14/14 which clarifies the situation in which a SCS/SCSp could be considered as carrying on trade or business. The circular also clarifies that a SCS/SCSp that is an alternative investment fund is deemed not to carry out a commercial activity. Therefore, an unregulated SCS/SCSp could be subject to municipal business tax if it represents a business undertaking, ie, if it carries out commercial activities or is deemed to be commercially tainted.

Access to double tax treaties

Part II Funds, SIFs and RAIFs

12.61 The Luxembourg tax administration has provided guidance in a circular of the director of the tax administration (circular L.G. – A. 61 of 8 December 2017), which includes a list of the double tax treaties from which a Luxembourg corporate private fund (except RAIFs or SICARs investing only in securities representing risk capital) can benefit. As of the date of writing of this chapter, corporate regulated private funds have access to more than 50 double tax treaties (out of an overall total of 81). Pursuant to the circular, 21 double tax treaties are not accessible by Luxembourg corporate regulated private funds as of this date. For the remaining double tax treaties, treaty access is uncertain or subject to certain formalities, but not necessarily excluded.

SICARs and RAIFs investing only in securities representing risk capital

12.62 SICARs and RAIFs investing only in securities representing risk capital organised as a joint-stock company should generally benefit from the double tax treaties entered into by Luxembourg (at least from a Luxembourg tax perspective), as they are fully liable to Luxembourg corporation taxes, despite the objective exemption of income and capital gains derived from transferable securities. The Luxembourg tax authorities are therefore prepared to issue, on demand, residence certificates for SICARs. However, treaty benefit should be analysed on a case-by-case basis for each double tax treaty. Indeed, it should be noted that certain jurisdictions decline treaty access to the SICAR, given that it benefits from an extensive objective tax exemption, which could effectively reduce the taxable base to zero.

12.63 SICARs and RAIFs investing only in securities representing risk capital organised as a common limited partnership SCS or a special limited partnership (SCSp) are in principle transparent for the purposes of the Luxembourg corporation taxes. They should thus not have access to the double tax treaties entered into by Luxembourg, unless a relevant double tax treaty provides that partnerships may benefit from the double tax treaties. The partners of a SICAR organised as an SCS/SCSp may, however, themselves claim treaty protection in accordance with their local tax laws and the relevant double tax treaties.

OECD's BEPS Action Points

12.64 In 2013 the OECD published its report on addressing Base Erosion and Profit Shifting (**BEPS**) and its action plan on BEPS. The aim of the report and the action plan is to address and reduce aggressive international tax planning. The OECD released its final recommendations on various action points in October 2015. The OECD announced that more than 100 jurisdictions concluded negotiations on 24 November 2016 on a multilateral instrument that will amend their respective double tax treaties (more than 2,000 double tax treaties worldwide) in order to implement the tax treaty-related BEPS recommendations. On 7 June 2017, the multilateral instrument was signed, in total, by 68 jurisdictions, including Luxembourg, and will enter into force after five countries have ratified it. The multilateral instrument will then enter into effect for a specific tax treaty after all parties to that treaty have ratified the multilateral instrument.

12.65 In the context of private funds, the most significant areas are likely to include: (i) Hybrids – Action 2 – as this may impact on the efficiency of financing instruments used by private funds to repatriate profits to their investors, (ii) Interest Deductions – Action 4 – as the limitation of interest deductions on debt financing may potentially increase the tax leakage on certain leveraged acquisition structures, (iii) Treaty Abuse – Action 6 – as this may impact on the ability of fund holding structures to benefit from double tax treaties and (iv) Permanent Establishment – Action 7 – as this may imply that advisory services rendered to private funds may be treated as giving rise to a taxable presence for those entities in the jurisdiction from which the advice was provided.

LOCAL STOCK EXCHANGE

12.66 The Luxembourg Stock Exchange (the **LSE**) operates two markets: a regulated market referred to as 'Bourse de Luxembourg' and a multilateral trading facility referred to as the 'Euro MTF' in accordance with the MiFID Directive.

12.67 The regulated market offers an EU passport to issuers who are subject to the requirements of Directive 2003/71/EC on the prospectus to be published when securities are offered to the public or admitted to trading and amending Directive 2001/34/EC (as amended) (the **Prospectus Directive**) and Directive 2004/109/EC of the European Parliament and of the Council of 15 December 2004 on the harmonisation of transparency requirements in relation to information about issuers whose securities are admitted to trading on a regulated market and amending Directive 2001/34/EC (as amended) (the **Transparency Directive**).

12.68 The Euro MTF is a platform which is outside of the scope of the Prospectus Directive and the Transparency Directive and is a market not included on the list of regulated markets published by the European Commission.

12.69 The regulated market is supervised by the CSSF which approves prospectuses relating to the admission to trading on a regulated market of financial assets falling under the scope of the Prospectus Directive.

12.70 The LSE approves the prospectuses relating to the admission to trading on a regulated market of securities which are outside the scope of the Prospectus Directive or to the admission of securities to a market not included on the list of regulated markets published by the European Commission such as the Euro MTF.

12.71 Any Luxembourg private fund wishing to have its shares or units listed on one of the markets operated by the LSE (ie the regulated market or the Euro MTF) may apply for such a listing.

CONFIDENTIALITY LAWS

12.72 Luxembourg professional secrecy and its specific application to the banking and financial community, ie banking secrecy, do not apply to investment funds as such, except in tax matters. Luxembourg investment funds merely have an obligation to maintain confidentiality, which gives rise, where applicable, to civil liability.

12.73 Professional secrecy rules apply only to directors, members of the management and supervisory bodies, conducting persons, employees and other persons at the service of credit institutions and professionals of the financial sector governed by the laws of Luxembourg. Hence, it applies to most professionals who provide services to Luxembourg investment funds.

12.74 To properly perform its management and administration, but also to conduct an effective marketing policy, Luxembourg investment funds and their service providers hold, store and process personal information of shareholders. In this context, investment funds have to comply with the provisions of the Luxembourg law of 2 August 2002 on the protection of personal data, as amended. Personal information may include names, contact details (including postal or e-mail address), banking details, invested amount and holdings in the fund.

12.75 It is important to note that European Regulation 2016/1279 on data protection will replace Directive 95/46/EC and reform data protection rules in the European Union, introducing several key changes directly applicable to all member states from 25 May 2018.

ANTI-MONEY LAUNDERING LAWS

12.76 Luxembourg investment funds and their service providers are subject to the anti-money laundering and counter terrorism financing (**AML**) laws and regulations of Luxembourg. These laws are derived from the AML Directive 2005/60/EC. In accordance with these laws and regulations, obligations are imposed on all professionals of the financial sector in order to prevent undertakings for collective investment from occurrences of money laundering and financing of terrorism. As a result of such provisions, the registrar and transfer agent of a Luxembourg fund must ascertain the identity of the subscriber in accordance with Luxembourg laws and regulations, and may require subscribers to provide any document it deems necessary to effect such identification.

12.77 Luxembourg is currently in the process of implementing the provisions of the fourth AML Directive 2015/849.

CONCLUDING REMARKS: WHAT ARE THE JURISDICTION'S UNIQUE SELLING POINTS?

12.78 Luxembourg is Europe's leading cross-border investment funds domicile, both for UCITS and AIFs. With all the available types of investment funds, the significant modernisation of the limited partnership vehicles and the recent introduction of the RAIF regime, Luxembourg offers asset managers a unique fund structuring toolbox in a politically, socially and economically stable environment and is frequently chosen as the location for the launch of investment funds and investment fund platforms across a broad spectrum of investment strategies.

CHAPTER 13

MALTA

GENERAL DESCRIPTION OF THE JURISDICTION

13.01 Malta and its two sister islands are situated in the Mediterranean, south of Sicily and north-east of Africa, mid-way between Gibraltar and the Suez Canal. Malta is one hour ahead of GMT and six hours ahead of EST. Malta has a land area of 200 square miles and its population is approximately 400,000. The capital and financial centre is Valletta. The official languages are Maltese and English, but Italian is also widely spoken. English is the language used in business transactions and is fluently spoken by almost all Maltese nationals.

13.02 Malta is a former British colony which became a republic in 1974. Malta's legislature includes the President and a 65-seat House of Representatives elected under universal franchise from 13 constituencies.

13.03 Malta's legal system is based on Roman civil law, with a substantial overlay of English common and statutory law. The Republic has also aligned its laws with the applicable rules of the European Union in view of its accession to the EU on 1 May 2004.

13.04 On 1 January 2008, Malta replaced its currency with the euro. Exchange control has been liberalised with the coming in to force of the External Transactions Act 2003, which has replaced the Exchange Control Act 1972. The new Act removed all exchange control restrictions which were previously imposed by the Exchange Control Act. Consequently, investments by Maltese residents, and by collective investment schemes (**CIS**), are not restricted in any way and do not require approval from the Central Bank of Malta. Recently, the Central Bank of Malta has issued circulars and standard forms which require Maltese resident investors to notify it for statistical purposes (no approval is required in this sense) of any direct investment in companies located abroad and of any foreign currency portfolio investment.

13.05 Banking, investments, accounting, custodial and legal services in Malta are of a high standard and widely available. The presence of 69 financial institutions, over 146 investment services licence holders (the majority being fund management companies), 27 fund administrators, 61 insurance companies including captive (re)insurers and protected cell companies, 11 insurance managers and 48 pension schemes and funds evidence Malta's strong reputation as a top funds jurisdiction.

13.06 These institutions are supplemented by local management, financial and corporate service companies, which include over 10,000 professionals and employees.

KEY MANDATORY REQUIREMENTS

13.07

- With the exception of Notified Alternative Investment Funds (**NAIFs**), the approval of, and licensing by, the Malta Financial Services Authority (**MFSA**) is required before a fund can be established in Malta.
- A promoter who is new to the MFSA must be able to show competence, integrity and reasonable past experience in the kind of investment service which he/she will be conducting in, or from within, Malta for him/her to be granted a licence by the MFSA to provide that particular service.
- Any service provider who is providing management and custody services to a Malta-licensed scheme must be licensed to provide such services by the MFSA or must be licensed as an investment manager or custodian in another jurisdiction with the same or a higher level of regulation. The jurisdictions which are considered by the MFSA to have the same or a higher level of regulation are all the EU, European Economic Area (**EEA**) states and any other country with whom Malta has signed a multilateral or bilateral memorandum of understanding covering the area of financial services.
- Holders of investment services licences are subject to certain minimum financial resources requirements. This does not apply to collective investment schemes (**CIS**).
- The acceptance of subscription monies from prospective investors is subject to international standard 'know your customer' regulations and the procedures required by Malta's Prevention of Money Laundering Act 1994, as amended and the regulations issued thereunder. This Act and the regulations are in line with all the European Union's Directives on money laundering (including the fourth anti-money laundering directive) and the Financial Action Task Force's (**FATF**) Recommendations.

RECENT DEVELOPMENTS

13.08 Following the implementation of the Alternative Investment Fund Managers Directive of 2011 (**AIFMD**) the MFSA created new types of funds available to EU alternative investment fund managers (**AFIMs**), namely the 'Alternative Investment Fund' (**AIF**) and the NAIF.

13.09 Furthermore, on 1 April 2016, the MFSA published a Circular to the Financial Services Industry on the Consolidation of the Maltese Fund Frameworks, in which it was announced that the funds frameworks would be consolidated and reduced.

13.10 Existing funds licensed under the previous fund regime will continue to be regulated by their respective regime, however all new applicants will operate under the proposed consolidated regime outlined below.

Current Fund Regimes

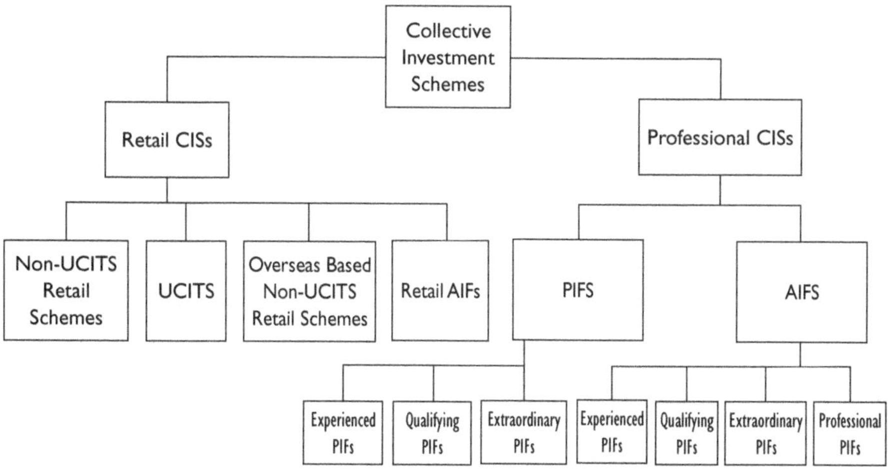

Revised Fund Regimes

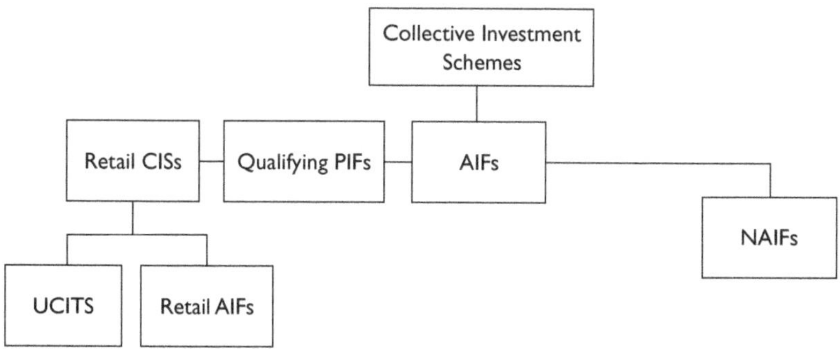

THE REGULATION OF INVESTMENT BUSINESS

13.11 The MFSA regulates the financial services sector in Malta and acts as the single main regulator.

13.12 The MFSA is readily available for face to face meetings with existing and potential fund promoters and is seen as an approachable regulator.

13.13 The Central Bank of Malta is the responsible body for the compilation of financial statistics in Malta.

INVESTORS

13.14 Various factors make Malta an attractive jurisdiction for both professional and retail investors. Amongst these factors is the fact that Malta benefits from a single regulator, which provides a one stop shop for promoters and investors, widely available and cost-efficient service providers, favourable tax treatment, and passporting rights in relation to professional investors. As an EU member Malta adheres to all the applicable EU Directives, giving comfort to potential and current investors.

SETTING UP A FUND

13.15 Maltese funds may take the form of any of the following:

- A Private Limited Liability Company/A Public Limited Liability Company;
- An investment company with variable share capital (open-ended) (SICAV);
- An investment company with fixed share capital (closed ended) (INVCO);
- A Limited Partnership;
- A Unit Trust;
- A Foundation;
- A Contractual Fund.

13.16 Mutual funds can be established as companies, foundations, mere contractual arrangements, unit trusts or partnerships; however, unit trusts and limited partnerships have rarely been used. The Companies Act 1995 (**CA**) provides for detailed regulations of CIS, which take the form of a limited partnership whereas the Trusts and Trustees Act caters for unit trusts. Funds generally fall within the definition of CIS, and are, therefore, regulated under the Investment Services Act (**ISA**). Some funds (including NAIFs and EU AIFs managed by an EU AIFM that has exercised its marketing right under the AIFMD or AIFs whose AIFM has completed the appropriate registration for private placement in Malta) are exempt from licensing under applicable regulations. Funds may either be open-ended or closed-ended and can be self-managed (if they have a corporate structure) or externally managed.

Open-ended mutual funds

13.17 Open-ended mutual funds are formed as companies or, alternatively, as partnerships by registration under the CA. Applications to license the fund as a CIS are made to the MFSA. The company's proposed name can be reserved with the Registrar of Companies up to three months prior to incorporation. An open-ended mutual fund must obtain the MFSA's 'no objection' before it can be incorporated.

13.18 Mutual fund companies must file the memorandum and articles of association and the draft prospectus as well as the appropriate fee, when making a licensing application.

SICAVS

13.19 The most popular forms of Maltese investment vehicles are corporate variable capital funds (**SICAV**), usually established as open-ended funds. SICAVs can also be established as umbrella funds. A SICAV which is established as an umbrella fund is allowed to have the assets and liabilities of each of the sub-funds forming part of the umbrella structure treated as a patrimony separate from the assets and liabilities of each other sub-fund of the same SICAV. Accordingly, the liabilities incurred in respect of each sub-fund must be paid out of the assets forming part of its patrimony. If these assets are insufficient to satisfy creditors' claims, then such creditors shall have no claim or right of action against the other assets of the SICAV. This is typically known as segregation of assets and liabilities.

13.20 The CA regulates SICAVs by re-stating certain rules which are normally applicable in the context of a limited liability corporate structure (in particular, those relating to share capital and distribution of profits), in order to render such rules more appropriate for investment vehicles. Several other rules in the CA are also disapplied in a SICAV structure. The objects of a SICAV have to be limited to the collective investment of its funds in moveable or immoveable property, with the aim of spreading risk and giving the shareholders the benefit of management of its funds. The variability of the SICAV's capital allows for significant flexibility in shareholder operations.

13.21 A Maltese company must have the following:

- a minimum of one director, who need not be resident in Malta;
- a company secretary; and
- independent directors, in the case of a company listed on the Malta Stock Exchange (**MSE**) or another recognised investment exchange.

13.22 A Maltese company must also have a registered office in Malta and keep its corporate records and the register of officers and directors at the registered office. The company's financial records should be kept in Malta for regulatory compliance reasons.

13.23 A company's memorandum and articles of association will be kept on the public file maintained by the Registrar of Companies. The names of the company's officers are available to the public. The register of shareholders for a mutual fund company is not public, although any member and officer has access to the register of members.

Unit trusts — Maltese law

13.24 A unit trust is a contractual agreement entered into between the management company and the trustee. The trust deed sets out, inter alia, unitholders' rights, the duties, appointment and removal of the manager and trustee, investment and borrowing powers and restrictions, and the methods of administration, termination and winding-up of the affairs of the trust. Unit trusts must seek licensing under the ISA as a CIS.

13.25 Following the enactment of the Trusts and Trustees Act at the beginning of 2005, a unit trust which is governed by Maltese law can have both Maltese resident and foreign investors.

13.26 Trustees which carry on business in Malta would need to seek approval from the MFSA.

Unit trusts — foreign law

13.27 Foreign law trusts are recognised in Malta under the Trusts and Trustees Act. It is, therefore, possible to set up an investment fund as a foreign law trust.

NAV of locally-based CISs	
December 2015	€10,252 million
September 2016	€9,801 million
March 2017	€9,598 million

Data supplied by the MFSA

Limited partnerships

13.28 Limited partnerships are governed by the CA. The partnership agreement must state the nature of the business to be carried out by the partnership. The partnership must maintain a registered office in Malta, where it must keep a register of limited partners. General partners' surnames may appear in the name of the partnership. However, if a limited partner's name appears in the name of the partnership, that partner will be deemed to be a general partner and will lose the benefit of limited liability.

13.29 There are two forms: the unlimited partnership *(en nom collectif)* and the limited partnership (or *partnership en nom commandite).* The CA provides for detailed rules applicable to CISs which are set up as limited partnerships. So far, the partnership structure has not been popular with fund managers due to the perceived inadequacies in the legal framework. These inadequacies have been satisfactorily addressed a couple of years ago by certain changes to the CA, which provide another structure which is appropriate for CISs.

Foundations

13.30 Funds may also be constituted as foundations; a foundation must be constituted by a founder for: (i) the fulfilment of a specific purpose (ii) the benefit of a named person or class of persons, and whose assets are administered by a designated person. Foundations are granted legal personality and when used for collective investment purposes have a limitless life.

Contractual Funds

13.31 A CIS can be established through a deed of constitution between the investment manager and the custodian. Funds established in this way will not benefit from legal personality.

Closed-ended funds

13.32 Closed-ended funds are incorporated as investment companies by registration under the CA. The MFSA must be satisfied as to the investment management experience of the promoters of the fund.

13.33 The general information relating to any company incorporation above will also apply to closed-ended funds. A closed-ended fund could take the form of a normal trading company, which would be subject to all the rules and restrictions which normally apply to limited liability companies under the CA or could also be an investment company with fixed share capital (**INVCO**), to which particular rules on distribution and capitalisation of profits apply. There are particular requirements which apply to INVCOs, such as the requirement that they invest in securities, distribute 85% of their income and are listed on the MSE. A closed-ended fund may also be set up as a SICAV, a variable capital company, if a redemption process is integrated in advance into the structure and regulated in detail in the memorandum and articles of the company.

13.34 Types of funds under the current practice of the MFSA, CISs are classified either as retail schemes (which could be UCITS or non-UCITS) or as professional investor funds (PIFs), AIFs or as NAIFs. The processing of applications for licensing of mutual funds varies, depending on whether the company intends to carry on 'retail' or 'professional investor' activities. Retail funds are subject to a more detailed review of the investment objective and restrictions, which results in a longer licensing process. Furthermore, the due diligence exercised on the manager, custodian and advisers is more thorough. Retail schemes are not appropriate for hedge and other alternative fund products or there are requirements for diversification and limits on leverage.

Funds (including sub-funds) domiciled in Malta (2014–2016)

	2014	2015	2016
AIFs	11	54	86
PIFs	507	458	460
UCITS	64	82	91
NAIFs			2
Retail Non-UCITS	12	12	9
Total locally based CISs	594	606	646
Foreign Based	16	12	12
Recognised Private CIS	5	8	8
Total CIS	**615**	**626**	**666**

Data supplied by the MFSA

PIFs

13.35 The PIF structure was designed for fast-track regulatory approval of funds aimed at investors sophisticated enough to do their own due diligence. A PIF is a non-retail fund which can be private or public in nature. PIFs are regulated by a rule book issued by the MFSA, which caters specifically for the authorisation and ongoing compliance requirements of PIFs. PIFs are suitable for use as hedge funds and other alternative funds and may be constituted as a multiclass fund or umbrella fund.

Eligible Investors

13.36 Only 'qualifying investors' may invest in PIFs. In order to qualify as a 'qualifying investor', an investor must certify that he/she conforms to certain criteria.[1]

1 These criteria are that the investor invests a minimum of €100,000 or its currency equivalent in the PIF/AIF/NAIFs which investment may not be reduced below this minimum amount at any time by way of a partial redemption; and declares in writing to the fund manager and the PIF/AIF/NAIF that it is aware of and accepts the risks associated with the proposed investment; and satisfies at least one of the following:

- (i) a body corporate which has net assets in excess of €750,000 or which is part of a group which has net assets in excess of €750,000 or, in each case, the currency equivalent thereof;
- (ii) an unincorporated body of persons or association which has net assets in excess of €750,000 or the currency equivalent;
- (iii) a trust where the net value of the trust's assets is in excess of €750,000 or the currency equivalent; an individual whose net worth or joint net worth with that of the person's spouse, exceeds €750,000 or the currency equivalent; or a senior employee or director of a service provider to the PIF/AIF/NAIF.

13.37 Unitholders who are 'qualifying investors' must maintain, at all times, a minimum investment amount of €100,000 or its equivalent in the PIF. The total amount of the investment may not fall below this amount, unless such a reduction is a result of a fall in the PIF's net asset value. Provided that the aforementioned thresholds are complied with at all times, then additional investments of any amount may be made.

Authorisation procedure

13.38 The application for licensing of a PIF is normally processed within one to three months of submission of full documentation, provided that the PIF satisfies the MFSA's requirements and has its service providers (ie, the manager, the custodian/prime broker and the administrator) licensed as such in Malta or in a country which the MFSA considers to be a recognised jurisdiction. The MFSA may, where certain criteria are met, also accept service providers which may not be established and regulated in a Recognised Jurisdiction.[2]

13.39 If these criteria are not satisfied, an 'in principle' approval can be requested at a preliminary stage on an appropriate form. An 'in principle' approval would be granted if the MFSA is satisfied of the regulatory regime to which the fund's investment manager is subject.

13.40 PIFs must issue an offering document, but this will not need to contain all the normal details of a prospectus for a retail fund. The offering document must provide sufficient details to enable a prospective investor to come to an informed decision, and should include all material information as at the date of the document.

13.41 PIFs are subject to a one-off application fee of €2,000. The scheme's licence fee amounts to a further €2,000 which is payable on issue of the licence and annually thereafter.

13.42 PIFs may also elect to be self-managed, in which case it must have an initial capital of €125,000.

Investment restrictions

13.43 No significant restrictions are imposed on the investment powers of PIFs, other than when investing in immovable property (maximum leverage of 50%). The lack of investment restrictions makes PIFs appropriate hedge funds

2 This is permitted:
i) where the Service Provider is the subsidiary of a firm that is regulated in a Recognised Jurisdiction, that retains control of its subsidiary and undertakes to provide all the necessary information to the MFSA; or
ii) where the MFSA considers that the Service Provider is subject to regulation to an equal or comparable level in the jurisdiction concerned.

and other alternative fund vehicles. PIFs are also exempt from the risk spreading requirement.

Accounts

13.44 Limited liability companies (such as SICAVs and INVCOs) and limited partnerships incorporated in Malta as CISs, must submit annual accounts to the Registry of Companies reflecting the state of affairs of the particular entity as on its accounting reference date, which must comply with International Accounting Standards.

13.45 Unit trusts are not required to file any accounts nor any annual return at the Registry.

13.46 A PIF listed on the MSE must, inter alia, be incorporated or otherwise established in Malta or such other jurisdiction as is recognised by the listing authority, and have a licence from the MFSA. It will, therefore, have to comply with the MFSA requirements relating to PIFs, with the Listing Rules issued by the listing authority and with the MSE bye-laws.

13.47 The application for licensing with the MFSA runs in parallel with the application for listing, since the MFSA is also the listing authority, so the process is normally well coordinated.

13.48 There is an initial non-refundable fee of €1,200 in respect of an application made by a CIS, and an annual listing fee of a further €1,200. Where the applicant applies to list multiple sub-funds, the following amounts apply in respect of the annual fees (exclusive of 18% VAT):

No. of sub-funds	Fee per class (€)
First 5	1,200 per sub-fund
6 – 10	1,000 per sub-fund
11 – 15	700 per sub-fund
16 and over	500 per sub-fund

13.49 If the scheme already has a primary listing on another recognised and regulated exchange, the initial and annual fees are reduced to 50% of the rate which is normally applicable to primary listings.

AIFs

13.50 An AIF is a CIS which is available to EU AIFMs. AIFs are regulated according to EU standards and are therefore designed for full-scope EU AIFMs seeking a regulated type of fund (other than a UCITS fund). AIFs may also be used by self-managed AIFs which exceed the AuM Thresholds.

Eligible Investors

13.51 An AIF (with the exception of Retail AIFs) may be subscribed to by Professional Investors (as defined under annex II of MiFID) and by Qualifying Investors, as defined above, whereby the minimum investment must be €100,000 or the equivalent.

13.52 A 'Professional Investor' is 'an investor who possesses the experience, knowledge and expertise to make its own investment decisions and properly assess the risks that it incurs.'

13.53 In order to qualify as Professional Investor, the entity should fall into one of the following categories:

(i) Credit Institutions.

(ii) Investment Firms.

(iii) Other authorised or regulated financial institutions.

(iv) Insurance Companies.

(v) Collective Investment Schemes and management companies of such Schemes.

(vi) Pension funds and management companies of such funds.

(vii) Commodity and commodity derivatives dealers.

(viii) Locals.

(ix) Other institutional investors.

13.54 Professional investors which do not fall under any of the above may also be treated as professional investors upon request and subject to fulfilling certain conditions.

Authorisation procedure

13.55 The MFSA would require the following documents in support of an application for a CIS licence for an AIF:

(a) Application Form – to be signed by applicant;

(b) Checklist confirming the contents of the Offering Documents;

(c) Corresponding application fee;

(d) Draft Offering Memorandum and Offering Supplement/s;

(e) Draft Memorandum and Articles of Association;

(f) Resolutions of the Governing Body of the AIF;

(g) Minutes of the first board meeting of the AIF;

(h) a near final draft of the Management, Administration and Depositary Agreements to be entered into by the AIF.

13.56 Additional documents may need to be provided on a case by case basis.

13.57 The application form and the supporting documentation will be reviewed by the MFSA who will revert with their comments within 10 to 15 business days from the submission of a complete application pack. Once the MFSA concludes its review, it will issue its 'in-principal approval' for the issuance of the licence. This 'in-principal approval' is valid for three months within which period the applicant must finalise any outstanding matters. If any pre-licensing licensing conditions are not resolved within the three months, the 'in-principal approval' shall cease which would mean that a fresh application together with the corresponding fee would need to be re-submitted.

Supervision

13.58 An AIF must appoint an AIFM, a Custodian, (Depositary), an Auditor, a Compliance Officer and a Money Laundering Reporting Officer (**MLRO**).

13.59 A corporate form AIF must have at least three directors, one of whom is required to be independent. Unless the AIF is self managed, there are no residency requirements for the directors.

Fees

13.60 AIFs are subject to a one-off application fee of €2,000 per scheme and €1,000 per sub-fund. The scheme's licence fee amounts to a further €2,000 and €600 per sub-fund which is payable on issue of the licence and annually thereafter.

Accounts/audit requirements

13.61 The AIFM on behalf of the AIF shall appoint an auditor approved by the MFSA. The Auditor shall be a person empowered to audit accounts in terms of Directive 2006/43/EC of the European Parliament and of the Council of 17 May 2006 on statutory audits of annual accounts and consolidated accounts.

13.62 The AIF must obtain an engagement letter from the Auditor clearly identifying the services to be offered by the Auditor and the Auditor's fees.

13.63 The AIF shall make available to its auditor the information and explanations he/she needs to discharge his/her responsibilities as an auditor and in order to meet the MFSA's requirements.

NAIFs

13.64 EU AIFMs have the option of setting up a NAIF, which is a special class of AIF which is exempt from the licensing requirement established by the ISA in respect of CIS.

13.65 The setting up of NAIFs is regulated by the provisions of the Investment Services Act (List of Notified AIFs) Regulations, 2016. NAIFs are not authorised by the MFSA and in order to set up a NAIF its existence must merely be notified to the MFSA.

13.66 NAIFs are available to Professional Investors Qualifying Investors (as defined above).

Authorisation Procedure

13.67 The NAIF regime seeks to address time to market issues which fund managers meet when setting up regulated vehicles. In fact, NAIFs established in Malta by an EU AIFM, are subject to a fast track registration process of 10 working days from the date of submission of a complete notification pack with the MFSA.

13.68 The MFSA relies on the regulated status of the AIFM, established in Malta or in the EU/EEA, to ensure compliance with the applicable law and to monitor the fitness and properness of the NAIF's service providers. All the NAIFs established in Malta will be listed on the MFSA's website.

Continuing Obligations

13.69 The AIFM is responsible for selecting the service providers of the NAIF and must ensure that each service provider is competent, qualified and capable of providing the services in respect of which it is engaged. The NAIF may appoint service providers as it deems necessary. However, it is obliged to appoint an AIFM, an Administrator, a Depositary and an Auditor.

Investment Restrictions

13.70 NAIFs are generally not subject to any investment restrictions other than those which may be established by the AIFM and set out in the offering documents. However, a NAIF can only be established in respect of AIFs investing in financial instruments. Although this includes private equity funds, this requirement excludes real estate funds and lending funds (unless investing in financial instruments).

Fees

13.71 A fee of €2,000 for the NAIF and €1,000 per sub-fund is payable to the MFSA in respect of the initial registration of the NAIF in the Notified AIF List of the MFSA. Thereafter, an annual fee of €2,000 for the NAIF and €600 per sub-fund is payable on each anniversary of the date of inclusion of the NAIF in the List of Notified.

Accounts/Audit Requirements

13.72 The NAIF must also appoint an Auditor approved by the MFSA. The NAIF must make available to the appointed Auditor, the information and explanations it requires to discharge its responsibilities as an auditor and in order to meet the MFSA's requirements.

SETTING UP A LOCAL MANAGEMENT COMPANY/INVESTMENT MANAGER

13.73 A CIS may either be externally managed, or if it adopts a corporate structure, be authorised as a self-managed fund.

13.74 Where a CIS is self-managed, the general requirement would be to have at least one locally resident director, to establish an investment committee, additionally AIFs and NAIFs must also need to have hierarchically segregated risk and valuation functions.

Incorporation

13.75 The recommended corporate structure for an investment manager who intends to obtain a licence to operate in Malta, is that of a private limited liability company incorporated under the CA. Under the CA, the company must have its registered office in Malta (where it would keep its corporate records and the register of officers and directors), submit annual accounts to the Registry of Companies, hold annual general meetings (not necessarily in Malta) and file annual returns. The company's memorandum and articles of association must be filed at the Registry of Companies and will be available to the public.

13.76 The objects clause of the memorandum and articles of an investment management company must state that the company will be acting as an investment adviser/manager to professional investor funds and other non-retail collective investment schemes, which are available only to professional or experienced investors.

13.77 Registry fees are payable only upon registration. The registration fee is calculated on the authorised share capital of the company. The minimum amount is of approximately €245, rising to a maximum of approximately €1,400 on a share capital of around €3m.

AUTHORISATION PROCEDURE

13.78 The AIFMD regulates the licensing of AIFMs and Malta was one of the first countries in the EU to publish AIFMD implementing measures and the AIFMD has been transposed into national law under the Investment Services Act 1994 (**ISA**). AIFMs are authorised by the MFSA in terms of the (**ISA** to provide the service of collective portfolio management under the ISA. The concept of 'management of AIFs' is comprised of the core activities of portfolio management and risk management, with the AIFM licence covering both these activities.

13.79 The AIFM may also perform additional functions in the course of the management of AIFs including administration (legal and fund management accounting, customer inquiries, valuation and pricing including tax returns, regulatory compliance monitoring, maintenance of unit/shareholder register, distribution of income, unit/shares issues and redemptions, contract settlements, recording keeping), marketing and other services specifically related to the assets of an AIF.

13.80 The MFSA may also authorise an AIFM, subject to certain conditions, to provide certain additional investment services permitted under MiFID including discretionary portfolio management, investment advice, safekeeping and administration of fund units and the receipt and transmission of orders in relation to financial instruments.

13.81 The AIFM may also be authorised as a UCITS management company.

13.82 In view of the above, an AIFM will be required to apply with the MFSA for a Category 2 Investment Services Licence.

AIFMs

13.83 Full Scope AIFMs are subject to the provisions of the AIFMD, as implemented, under the provisions of which an AIFM must appoint a single independent depositary, being an eligible entity, for each AIF it manages mainly responsible for cash monitoring, oversight in respect of assets and transactions of the AIF and custody and safe-keeping of assets. AIFMs and prime brokers are prohibited from acting as depositaries, however, such prohibition is lifted in the case of prime brokers where measures have been taken to functionally and hierarchically separate the two functions and where no potential conflicts of interest arise.

13.84 The Board of Directors of AIFMs should be made up of at least three Members (one of whom should be resident in Malta).

13.85 The MFSA requires meetings of the Board of Directors to be held at least four times a year, with three out of four meetings being physically held in Malta.

13.86 The AIFM's head office is to be located in Malta and could either make use of shared office space or have its own offices. Either way, it is essential that such office space is equipped with, an independent telephone line, an internet connection and filing space.

13.87 An AIFM is also expected to appoint a person to act as the Money Laundering Reporting Officer (**MLRO**).

13.88 In addition to general operating conditions, AIFMs are also subject to specific requirements in terms of remuneration, conflicts of interest, risk management and liquidity management.

13.89 The MFSA Rules for Investment Services Providers lay down further conditions for a management company of a CIS. These conditions regulate conflicts of interest between the scheme and its manager, the independence of the manager from the custodian, the use of the fund's assets by the manager, the appointment by the manager of auditors for the scheme, the control which the manager can exercise over the scheme's operations, box dealings, advertisements and exchange control requirements. It is not required for the majority of the board of directors of a SICAV to be independent from the SICAV's investment manager. However, one must keep in mind that if the SICAV is to be listed on the MSE, the Listing Rules currently require the presence of a majority of independent directors.

13.90 The MFSA's Investment Services Guidelines require an investment manager to have funds of at least €125,000, while the investment manager is also subject to ongoing rules on its liquid capital. The guidelines lay down the criteria which would have to be used for the calculation of the company's financial resources.

Submitting the licence application

13.91 The MFSA will carry out a due diligence exercise on the entities and/or individuals to be involved in the company's structure and its operations. The applicant will have to submit, inter alia, a business profile, its constitutional documents, a financial resources statement, its latest audited accounts, copies of insurance policies (if any), and the projected profit and loss account and balance sheet for three years following the granting of the licence.

13.92 There is an initial non-refundable application fee of €5,000 in respect of an application for a Category 2 Investment Services Licence made by an investment management company. The investment manager would also have to pay an annual fee of €4,500.

13.93 The AIFM will be required to submit certain information on its promoters, its prospective directors, its internal organisation and the AIF/s that it intends to manage.

13.94 The MFSA will generally:

- consider the nature of the services to be offered by a AIFM and the persons to whom such services will be marketed;
- look into the experience and track record of all parties who will be involved in the provision of the management services, including investment committee members and portfolio managers; and
- ascertain that the qualifying shareholders, Compliance Officer, Money Laundering Reporting Officer, Directors and Senior Managers of the AIFM are of good standing and satisfy the 'fit and proper' test.

13.95 MFSA Rules provide that an investment services business should effectively be directed or managed by at least two individuals in satisfaction of the 'dual control' principle. Such persons must be of sufficiently good repute and sufficiently experienced – to the satisfaction of the MFSA – so as to ensure the sound and prudent operations of the AIFM.

Supervisory Fees

13.96 An application for a Category 2 Investment Services Licence must be accompanied by a non-refundable Application Fee of €5,000. Once licensed, the AIFM will be required to pay to the MFSA a Licence Issue Fee of €4,500. Thereafter the AIFM will be required to pay to the MFSA an Annual Supervisory Fee (due on the anniversary of the issue of the Licence) of:

- for revenue up to €250,000: a Supervisory Fee of €4,500; and
- further tranches of revenue €250,000 (up to €5,000,000): add a Supervisory Fee of €400 per tranche or part thereof.

Accounts/Audit requirements

13.97 The investment manager is bound to submit annual and interim financial statements to the MFSA. These returns should provide details of the licence holder's profits and losses, assets and liabilities, expenses, adjustments, liquid capital, funds under management, and details on client bank accounts and assets, and on own account trades. The MFSA's rules now require these financial statements to be prepared in accordance with International Accounting Standards.

13.98 The licensed investment manager will also be regulated by the MFSA on a continuing basis, and on-site inspections are occasionally carried out by

MFSA officials. Indeed, licensed investment managers are bound to comply with a number of ongoing obligations partly reflecting the Markets in Financial Instruments Directive which has been fully transposed and implemented in Malta by the MFSA.

De Minimis AIFMs

13.99 The AIFMD has led to the introduction of a number of specific requirements relative to AIFMs responsible for portfolio and risk management. Apart from the '"full AIFM' regime described above, a lighter (de minimis) regime is available for AIFMs which, whether directly or indirectly, manage portfolios of AIFs whose assets under management collectively do not exceed the following amounts:

- €100 million; or
- €500 million in the case of AIFMs that manage only unleveraged AIFs that do not have redemption rights exercisable during a period of five years following the date of the initial investment in each AIF concerned.

13.100 A de minimis AIFM will be exempt from complying with the provisions of the AIFMD with the exception of certain reporting requirements to the MFSA.[3]

13.101 Where the conditions prescribed above are no longer met, the de minimis licence holder shall inform the MFSA and apply for an extension to its de minimis Category 2 Licence to a full AIFM Category 2 Licence.

13.102 Nonetheless, an AIFM that could be classified as de minimis may 'opt in' under the AIFMD and choose to be subject to all the obligations prescribed therein. In doing so, it would be able acquire the AIFMD passport, which is otherwise not available to de minimis AIFMs.

OTHER KEY SERVICE PROVIDERS

13.103 AIFs and NAIFs must have a depositary which is either resident in Malta or a credit institution established in an EU state, whereas PIFs are exempt from the requirement to appoint a Maltese custodian and may appoint a custodian established outside Malta.

13.104 Custodians established in Malta must hold a Category 4a Licence. In certain circumstances, a fund may appoint a custodian which has a Category 4b

3 These reporting requirements cover the investment strategies of the AIFs under management; the main instruments in which the AIFs under management are trading; and the principal exposures and most important concentration of the AIFs under management.

Licence. A Maltese custodian may delegate safekeeping to a global custodian or to a sub-custodian.

13.105 Local or foreign prime brokers may be appointed. Where the prime broker also has a safekeeping role (as if permitted for PIFs), the MFSA will require evidence that the prime broker is reputable and regulated in its country of residence.

TAX REGIME

Tax at the fund level

Income tax and capital gains

13.106 Maltese tax legislation taxes income and certain capital gains unless they are otherwise exempt from tax. Like of all other mutual funds licensed in Malta which invest more than 15% of their assets outside Malta, PIFs licensed in Malta are exempt from tax on their income or capital gains (excluding any income derived from immovable property situated in Malta).

Tax at the investor level

Income tax and capital gains

13.107 A non-Maltese resident investing in a fund licensed in Malta will not be subject to income tax in Malta on any gains derived from the transfer of any units in a CIS that is not a property company.

Stamp duty

13.108 The transfer of shares in a Maltese company is normally subject to stamp duty in Malta. However, where the transfer of the shares/units is in a PIF which is licensed under the ISA, the transfer would be exempt from stamp duty in Malta.

Double tax treaties

13.109 Malta has signed comprehensive double tax treaties with the following 72 countries: Albania, Australia, Austria, Azerbaijan, Bahrain, Barbados, Belgium, Bulgaria, Canada, China, Croatia, Cyprus, the Czech Republic, Denmark, Egypt, Estonia, Finland, France, Georgia, Germany, Greece, Guernsey, Hong Kong, Hungary, Iceland, India, Ireland, Isle of Man, Israel, Italy, Jersey, Jordan, Republic of Korea, Kuwait, Latvia, Lebanon, Libya, Lichtenstein, Lithuania, Luxembourg, Malaysia, Mauritius, Mexico, Moldova, Montenegro, Morocco, the Netherlands, Norway, Pakistan, Poland, Portugal, Qatar, Russia, Romania, San Marino, Saudi Arabia, Serbia, Singapore, Slovakia, Slovenia, South Africa,

Spain, Sweden, Switzerland, Syria, , Tunisia, Turkey, UAE, Uruguay, Vietnam, UK and the US.

BEPS AND EXCHANGE OF INFORMATION

13.110 Malta's tax system is fully compatible with the Organisation for Economic Co-operation and Development (**OECD**) principles. Malta is a Base Erosion and Profit Shifting (BEPS) associate and has signified its commitment to support the OECD efforts to combat Base Erosion and Profit Shifting in international tax structures.

13.111 Malta has over the years participated actively in all of the international tax transparency initiatives, and was an early adopter of all EU directives and other international agreements aimed at improving transparency between EU and other countries on tax matters.

13.112 Malta will also fully transpose into its legislation those elements of the EU's recently adopted Anti-Tax Avoidance Directive (itself implementing some of the OECD BEPS recommendations) which do not already form part of Malta's tax legislation.

LOCAL STOCK EXCHANGE

13.113 The MSE is a member of the World Federation of Exchanges, the Federation of European Securities Exchanges and the International Organisation of Securities Commissions. Entities listed on the MSE are subject to the MSE's bye-laws and to the Listing Rules of the MFSA, which is the listing authority responsible for the regulation of all investment exchanges which may be set up in Malta. Promoters of investment exchanges who want to use Malta as a base must obtain recognition from the MFSA, as listing authority, prior to commencing operations in Malta. To date, the MSE is the only 'recognised investment exchange' operating in Malta.

13.114 The MSE currently lists a number of local securities and more than 250 international funds.

13.115 A new applicant for listing on the MSE must be sponsored by a locally-approved sponsoring broker. The sponsoring broker will then act as the principal channel of communication with the MSE and with the listing authority. An applicant for listing must submit an application and issue a prospectus complying with the Listing Rules.

ANTI-MONEY LAUNDERING LAWS

13.116 Maltese legislation on the prevention of money laundering is in line with the EU Directives and the FATF's Recommendations. Indeed, Maltese anti-money laundering legislation also reflects the provisions of the EU's Fourth Directive on Anti-money Laundering Directive. The MFSA, the Central Bank and the MSE have issued guidelines to financial operators.

13.117 Furthermore, on 16 December 2013 Malta and the US signed an Intergovernmental Agreement to improve international tax compliance and to implement the US Foreign Account Tax Compliance Act (**FATCA**) which was transposed into Maltese legislation by the Exchange of Information (United States of America) (FATCA) Order of 2014.

CONCLUDING REMARKS: WHAT ARE THE JURISDICTION'S UNIQUE SELLING POINTS?

13.118 Malta is ranked as a top EU funds domicile due to its tailored fund regime, efficient and accessible regulator, lower costs as compared to other EU countries, as well as the availability of effective services including legal services and corporate service providers.

CHAPTER 14

SINGAPORE

GENERAL DESCRIPTION OF THE JURISDICTION

14.01 Singapore is an independent city-state located at the tip of the Malayan peninsula in South East Asia. Its time zone is GMT plus eight hours. Its legal system is based on English common law, although a considerable body of law (particularly on financial services regulation) is now set out in statute form. Its currency is the Singapore dollar (**SGD**). There is no exchange control in Singapore.

14.02 Singapore is a member of the United Nations (**UN**), and through its government agencies, actively participates in all leading international regulatory organisations, including the Basel Committee for Banking Supervision, the International Association of Insurance Supervisors, the International Organisation of Securities Commissions, and the Financial Action Task Force.

14.03 Singapore's financial services sector is regulated by the Monetary Authority of Singapore (**MAS**), a unitary regulatory agency established by an Act of the Singapore Parliament. The MAS is conferred powers to regulate the different sectors of the financial services industry through sector-specific legislation, including the Banking Act (Chapter 19, Singapore Statutes), the Insurance Act (Chapter 142, Singapore Statutes), Securities and Futures Act (Chapter 289, Singapore Statutes) (**SFA**) and the Financial Advisers Act (Chapter 110, Singapore Statutes) (**FAA**). The regulation by the MAS of financial services is to a very high standard and Singapore enjoys the reputation of being one of the world's leading financial centres.

KEY MANDATORY REQUIREMENTS

14.04

- Singapore law on intermediary licensing distinguishes between the activity of fund management and the activity of marketing a fund. The former is regulated under Part IV of the SFA while the latter is regulated under the FAA. There is a limited degree of overlap in coverage between the two regimes, which is resolved via exemptions. To the extent that an intermediary intends to engage in one or both activities in Singapore, it is important to obtain legal advice as to the applicable regulatory position.
- The SFA also contains, in Part XIII, separate rules regulating the offering of certain classes of investments (including funds) to persons in

Singapore. The default rule is that a prospectus (compliant with prescribed requirements) is needed, and in the case of a fund that constitutes a collective investment scheme under the SFA, the fund has to be registered with MAS through a process known as authorisation (for locally constituted funds) or recognition (for foreign funds). Exemptions from either or both of these requirements are available, subject to compliance with relevant conditions.

- Both the SFA and the FAA can have extra-territorial application, and it is important to ensure that activity conducted abroad but aimed or directed at the Singapore market does not fall foul of the SFA and FAA requirements.

RECENT DEVELOPMENTS

14.05 In January 2017, the Singapore Parliament passed the Securities and Futures (Amendment) Act 2017, which once implemented will effect significant amendments to the SFA, including a substantial change to the terminology currently in use. Among other things, amendments will be made to the following:

(a) what constitutes a collective investment scheme and what constitute securities;

(b) what constitutes the activity of fund management, and the replacement of the term dealing in securities with the new term dealing in capital markets products;

(c) the statutory definitions of an institutional investor and of an accredited investor.

14.06 It is likely that the amendments will take effect sometime in the course of 2018. What follows below is an account of the law prior to the coming into effect of the Securities and Futures (Amendment) Act 2017.

14.07 In March 2017, MAS also issued a consultation paper announcing proposals to introduce into Singapore law a new corporate structure, to be called the Singapore Variable Capital Company (**S-VACC**), that is specifically designed for collective investment schemes. The S-VACC structure is modelled on similar structures in other jurisdictions such as Luxembourg and will have separate and segregated cells so as to accommodate umbrella fund structures. The proposal is presently at the public consultation stage and it is unclear when formal legislation will be introduced in the Singapore Parliament.

THE REGULATION OF INVESTMENT BUSINESS

14.08 As mentioned earlier, the MAS is a consolidated financial services regulator responsible for all sectors of the financial services industry. It also serves as the central bank of Singapore.

14.09 The regulatory framework for the regulation of the Singapore capital markets is established by the SFA and the FAA. A common terminology is adopted across both of these statutes. In Singapore, the term collective investment scheme is used to describe a fund that is within the scope of the SFA and FAA. While the term collective investment scheme had traditionally contemplated only open-ended structures, since 1 July 2013 however, most classes of close-ended funds are now also considered to be collective investment schemes.

14.10 The SFA is a complex piece of legislation made up of distinct parts, each providing for the regulation of different aspects of the Singapore capital markets. Part IV of the SFA provides for the licensing and regulation by MAS of intermediaries, including those engaged in the activities of dealing in securities, and providing fund management services. Part XIII of the SFA independently regulates the offering in Singapore of various types of investments (including collective investment schemes).

14.11 The FAA is a related piece of legislation that provides for licensing and regulation by MAS of financial advisory services, which is an expression referring largely to activities that involve the giving of investment related advice, including as a distinct sub-category, the marketing of collective investment schemes.

INVESTORS

14.12 For the purposes of the Singapore regulatory framework for funds and fund management, the law recognises three relevant categories of investors – institutional investors, accredited investors, and retail investors.

14.13 The term institutional investor, as defined in the SFA and FAA, refers mainly to financial institutions operating in Singapore, as well as certain entities and agencies related to the Singapore government. Notably the term does not include foreign financial institutions that do not have a presence locally.

14.14 The term accredited investor, as defined in the SFA and FAA, refers to persons (individuals or corporations) that meet a specified wealth or income threshold. Currently the thresholds are, in the case of individuals, net assets exceeding SGD2 million or annual income of at least SGD300,000; and, in the case of corporations, net assets exceeding SGD10 million. Similar thresholds are provided for in subsidiary legislation in the case of other structures, such as a partnership or a trust.

14.15 It should be noted that in some contexts, the Singapore regulatory regime also recognises a fourth category of expert investors. This refers to persons whose businesses involve the acquisition and disposal of securities and other capital markets products. This category is, however, not of direct relevance here, as the term expert investor is not used within the context of the regulatory framework for funds and fund management.

14.16 The term retail investor is not defined in the SFA or FAA, but the term is generally understood in local usage to refer to investors who are neither institutional investors nor accredited investors.

14.17 In general, licensing and other regulatory requirements under Part IV of the SFA and under the FAA are less stringent where the intermediary serves only institutional investors and accredited investors, but not retail investors. Likewise, the fund registration and disclosure requirements under Part XIII of the SFA are generally less stringent where a fund is offered only to institutional or accredited investors rather than retail investors.

SETTING UP A FUND

14.18 A Singapore collective investment scheme may be organised in various forms recognised under Singapore law, including:

- As a company incorporated under the Companies Act (Chapter 50, Singapore Statutes);
- As a limited liability partnership under the Limited Liability Partnerships Act (Chapter 163A, Singapore Statutes);
- As a limited partnership under the Limited Partnerships Act (Chapter 163B, Singapore Statutes);
- As a business trust under the Business Trusts Act (Chapter 31A, Singapore Statutes);
- As a unit trust.

14.19 Incorporating a company in Singapore is a swift process. However, there are drawbacks associated with structuring a collective investment scheme in the form of a Singapore incorporated company – primarily in connection with restrictions in the mode and manner of returning capital to investors. Limited partnerships have a structure generally appropriate for a collective investment scheme. There is also specific provision in the Limited Partnership Act to safeguard the privacy of investors who hold interests in a collective investment scheme structured as a limited partnership. However, a limited partnership is not recognised as a legal person under Singapore law and as such, tax treaty relief may not be available. The structure of a limited liability partnership is commonly used only by professional services firms transitioning out from the common law partnership structure. In practice, almost all collective investment schemes constituted in Singapore are structured as unit trusts. A unit trust is a fund constituted by a trust deed and where the fund assets are owned by a trustee but managed by a third-party fund manager. As mentioned above, Singapore is likely to introduce a new variable capital company structure, specifically for collective investment schemes.

14.20 Aside from the legal form of the collective investment scheme, there are additional requirements under the SFA that must be observed before units in the scheme can be offered in Singapore. Under Division 2 of Part XIII of the SFA, a collective investment scheme must be authorised or recognised by MAS before its units may be offered to persons in Singapore, unless an exemption is available. Authorisation under section 286 is the process for a scheme constituted in Singapore. Recognition under section 287 is the process for a scheme constituted outside Singapore.

14.21 An application for authorisation of a locally constituted scheme under section 286 of the SFA involves submitting to MAS information in a prescribed form under the Securities and Futures (Offer of Investments) (Collective Investment Schemes) Regulations 2005. The application fee payable is SGD1,200. In the case of an umbrella fund, the application fees are charged on a per sub-fund basis.

14.22 In the case of a collective investment scheme constituted as a unit trust, MAS must be satisfied that:

(a) there is a manager, who is appropriately licensed or authorised by exemption to conduct fund management services;

(b) there is a trustee for the scheme approved under section 289 of the SFA;

(c) there is a trust deed in respect of the scheme entered into between the manager and the trustee that complies with prescribed requirements; and

(d) the scheme, the manager and the trustee comply with the SFA and the Code for Collective Investment Schemes.

14.23 The trustee for a collective investment scheme must be a public company that is approved by MAS under section 289 of the SFA. A fee of SGD500 is payable for an application by a public company for MAS approval to act as a trustee for collective investment schemes. After approval, an approved trustee is required to pay a fee of SGD2,000 for the year it is approved and for each year it continues to be so approved.

14.24 The Code on Collective Investment Schemes (**the Code**) is a non-statutory code issued by MAS pursuant to the SFA that spells out the best practices on the management, operation and marketing of schemes which managers and approved trustees are expected to observe. While a failure to comply will not of itself render a person liable to criminal proceedings, such failure may be relied upon by any party in legal proceedings as tending to establish or negate any liability in question in such proceedings.

14.25 Accounting, audit and reporting requirements for authorised collective investment schemes are detailed in the Code, as are the rules on valuation of scheme units.

14.26 There are various appendices in the Code that specify the investment restrictions and other requirements applicable to different types of collective investment schemes. Appendix 3 specifically applies to a hedge fund, which the Code defines as a scheme that aims to achieve a high return through the use of advanced investment strategies that could include use of illiquid financial instruments, leverage or short selling, and investment into alternative asset classes. In practice however, hedge funds tend to be available in Singapore only to non-retail investors and are registered with MAS as restricted schemes via CISNet, in reliance on the exemption in section 305 of the SFA (which will be discussed below).

14.27 Apart from authorisation/recognition requirements, where there is an offering in Singapore of units of a collective investment scheme, Division 2 of Part XIII of the SFA also requires that such an offering must be accompanied by a disclosure document called a prospectus and by a product highlights sheet, each compliant with prescribed requirements and to be lodged or registered with MAS. A fee of SGD1,000 is payable for lodgement of a prospectus. The fee is on a per prospectus basis, regardless of the number of sub-funds covered in the prospectus.

14.28 Depending on the circumstances of a particular offering, Division 2 of Part XIII of the SFA provides various exemptions from the requirement for authorisation/recognition requirement and/or the requirement for lodgement of the prospectus and product highlights sheet. In practice, the exemptions most commonly relied upon in Singapore are as follows:

(a) the private placement exemption in section 302C of the SFA – where units in the scheme are offered only to no more than 50 persons over any period of 12 months. This exemption dispenses with the requirement for the scheme to be authorised/recognised, as well as with the requirement for the scheme to be accompanied by a prospectus and product highlights sheet. There are however elaborate ancillary rules governing how one is to adhere to the 50 offerees limit.

(b) the institutional investor exemption in section 304 of the SFA – where units in the scheme are offered only to persons who qualify as institutional investors. This exemption also dispenses with the requirement for the scheme to be authorised/recognised, as well as with the requirement for the scheme to be accompanied by a prospectus and product highlights sheet.

(c) the accredited investor/relevant person exemption in section 305 of the SFA – where units in the scheme are offered only to persons who qualify as accredited investors, certain persons in a comparable position, or where the units in the scheme are offered on terms that the minimum consideration be (currently) SGD200,000. This exemption does not dispense with the requirement for authorisation/recognition nor the requirement for a prospectus and product highlights sheet. Instead, the requirement for authorisation/recognition requirement is replaced with a simplified notification process via an online platform operated by MAS known as CISNet. And in lieu of a prospectus and product highlights sheet, a copy of the information memorandum (containing certain basic prescribed disclosures) is required to be lodged with MAS as part of the notification process through CISNet. Such schemes, not being available to retail investors, are generally referred to within the regulatory terminology as restricted schemes.

14.29 The above exemptions are subject to other conditions, including various resale restrictions.

SETTING UP AN INVESTMENT MANAGEMENT COMPANY

14.30 The activity of fund management is subject to regulation under Part IV of the SFA. The intermediary licensing system under Part IV of the SFA is a modular one in that a person would ordinarily need to hold a capital markets services licence issued by MAS to carry on, as a business, any one or more regulated activities (of which there are presently nine categories, including fund management).

14.31 The term fund management is defined as undertaking on behalf of a customer (whether on a discretionary authority granted by the customer or otherwise):

(a) the management of a portfolio of securities or futures contracts; or

(b) foreign exchange trading or leveraged foreign exchange trading for the purpose of managing the customer's funds

14.32 The activity of fund management however does not include management of a real estate investment trust as this is a separately licensable activity. A real estate investment trust is a particular type of collective investment scheme that is constituted as a trust, that invests primarily in real estate and real estate-related assets (as specified by MAS in the Code) and whose units are listed on a securities exchange.

14.33 Given that the statutory definition of fund management emphasises the provision of management services to a separate customer, it is not strictly required for a fund to engage a third-party manager. In theory, a fund that is constituted as a company (unusual as this may be in the Singapore context) may manage its own corporate assets without contravening the licensing requirements relating to fund management services. However, care would be advisable. MAS has stated that it looks to substance over form. Where a company is organised as a fund (with the investment management function in the hands of one or more persons who are distinct from the shareholders providing the investment capital), there is still a risk that the MAS may nevertheless regard the arrangement as fund management.

14.34 Singapore is recognised as a leading asset management centre in Asia and the Singapore Finance Ministry has in place a number of measures (primarily in the form of tax incentives) to encourage entities to base their fund management operations within Singapore. It is common that the funds themselves would be domiciled elsewhere but are managed from Singapore.

14.35 The regulatory regime for fund managers in Singapore exists in four distinct tiers, with a new tier of licensed venture capital fund managers being introduced in October 2017.

14.36 The first tier comprises non-retail fund manager companies, who are registered with MAS to operate on an exempt basis. MAS refers to this tier of managers as RFMCs. RFMCs are limited to serving no more than 30 qualified investors and managing no more than SGD250 million of assets. Qualified investors are a sub-species of non-retail investors and no more than 15 of these 30 qualified investors can be collective investment schemes.

14.37 The next tier also comprises non-retail fund management companies. However, fund managers in this tier are licensed by MAS but the terms of their capital markets services licence also limit them to serving only non-retail investors (ie institutional and accredited investors). MAS refers to this tier of managers as AI LFMCs. Unlike RFMCs, there are no constraints on the number of investors who may be served by an AI LMFC. Nor is there a cap on the amount of assets which an AI LFMC can manage.

14.38 The next tier is of licensed fund management companies whose capital markets services licence permits them to serve all types of investors, including retail investors. MAS refers to this tier of managers as Retail LFMCs.

14.39 In October 2017, MAS introduced a further tier of licensed fund management companies but whose capital markets services licence would limit them to managing venture capital funds. MAS refers to this tier of fund managers as VCFMs. To qualify, the venture capital fund must be one that invests at least 80% of its committed capital in securities that are directly issued by unlisted business ventures that have been incorporated for no more than 10 years. The fund units must also not be continuously available for subscription and cannot be redeemed at the discretion of the investor. Furthermore, the venture capital fund can only be offered to institutional investors and to accredited investors (or, in the case of investors outside Singapore, to investors who are in a class equivalent to accredited investors). VCFMs are only subject to a minimal set of compliance requirements and are generally not required to comply with staff competency requirements, capital requirements and ongoing business conduct requirements, each of which might otherwise apply.

14.40 The fee for applying for a capital markets services licence for fund management is SGD1,000 (in the case of Retail LFMCs, AI LFMCs and VCFMs). No fees are currently payable for an application for RFMC status. Retail LFMCs, AI LFMCs and VCFMs have to pay an annual fee of SGD4,000 once they are granted a capital markets service licence for fund management, while RFMCs have to pay an annual fee of SGD1,000 once granted RMFC status.

14.41 For Retail LFMCs, AI LFMCs and RFMCs, the applicant must be a company incorporated in Singapore with two directors, and a permanent physical office in Singapore. To meet Companies Act requirements, in practice, at least one of the directors of the company would have to be resident in Singapore. There must be a minimum number of professional staff meeting the competency requirements specified in MAS guidelines. Amongst other conditions, the fund management company must also satisfy MAS that its shareholders, directors and representatives are fit and proper, based on the Guidelines on the Fit and Proper Criteria issued by MAS. For VCFMs, MAS has waived requirements for minimum professional staffing and for the professional staff to meet competency requirements. It is only necessary for the VCFM to have two directors (of which one is to be resident in Singapore) and for its shareholders, directors and representatives to meet the Fit and Proper Criteria.

14.42 The base capital requirements vary across the different tiers – SGD250,000 for RFMCs, SGD500,000 for AI LFMCs, and SGD1,000,000 for Retail LFMCs. AI LFMCs and Retail LFMCs, being licensed under the SFA, are further required to abide by the risk based capital requirements in the Securities and Futures (Financial and Margin Requirements) Regulations. VCFMs are not subject to any requirements as to base capital nor as to risk capital.

14.43 Individuals employed by an AI LFMC or a Retail LFMC to carry out the activity of fund management on behalf of their principals are also subject to individual regulation under the SFA. Such individuals are referred to as representatives and must be registered with MAS under the MAS Representative Notification Framework (**RNF**). To qualify for registration under the RNF, the individuals would ordinarily have certain minimum educational qualifications and also to pass prescribed modules of the Capital Markets and Financial Advisory Services examinations. For each application for registration of a representative, a lodgement fee of SGD100 is payable and each representative must also pay an annual fee of SGD200. The RNF regime does not apply to representatives of RFMCs and VCFMs.

14.44 All fund managers (other than VCFMs) are also expected to have in place compliance arrangements commensurate with the nature, scale and complexity of their business, and appropriate risk management frameworks. Business activities must be subject to internal audit (again to be commensurate with the nature, scale and complexity of the business) and there must also be an external audit conducted annually. Naturally, it would be advisable for VCFMs to follow suit even though there are no binding requirements for them to do so.

14.45 Professional indemnity insurance is mandatory for a Retail LFMC and strongly encouraged for an AI LFMC and for an RFMC. As mentioned, there are no requirements for VCFMs.

14.46 On an ongoing basis, all fund managers (other than VCFMs) are required to ensure that the assets under their management are subject to independent custody either by a prime broker, a depository or bank suitably licensed or authorised to perform such a custodial function. Independent of the audit requirement, assets under management must also be subject to independent valuation and reporting. This requirement may be met by appointing a third party to perform the valuation or by having an in-house fund valuation team that is segregated from the investment management team. For VCFMs, MAS indicated that investors into the venture capital fund managed by the VCFM may negotiate their requirements with the VCFM.

14.47 The marketing of a fund within Singapore is a separate activity that comes under the purview of the FAA. Thus a fund manager must always check if it requires to obtain an authorisation by exemption under the FAA.

14.48 Apart from the above, regulated financial institutions (including all classes of fund managers) are generally required to comply with regulatory requirements issued by MAS from time to time, whether in the form of binding notices and directions, or in the form of non-binding guidelines. These would include those relating to risk management, outsourcing and measures to prevent money laundering and terrorist financing.

TAX REGIME

14.49 The corporate income tax rate in Singapore is presently 17%. Corporate tax operates on a single tier – with profits being taxed at the corporate level and subsequent dividend distribution are not subject to further tax.

14.50 Singapore has in place a variety of tax incentive measures to attract fund managers and funds to set up in Singapore. For fund managers, the Financial Sector Incentive (Fund Management Company) Scheme promotes the conduct of fund management in Singapore by offering concessionary tax rates in respect of certain qualifying income, provided that certain conditions are met. For funds, there are several schemes available to offer tax exemption for certain types of income and gains arising from certain types of investments. Most of the tax incentive schemes apply to income derived from funds managed in Singapore by an approved fund manager, and would be subject to different conditions according to the particular scheme. The tax incentive regimes available can change from time to time, and it would be advisable to consult specialist tax advisers at the appropriate time.

14.51 Singapore joined the OECD's Inclusive Framework for Implementing Measures against Base Erosion and Profit Sharing in 2016, and signed the Multilateral Convention to Implement Tax Treaty Related Measures to Prevent Base Erosion and Profit Sharing in June 2017.

14.52 Singapore also has a goods and service tax, which is levied on nearly all supplies of goods and services systems, including most forms of financial services. The current rate of tax is 7% although in certain circumstances, the law allows for a zero-rating of goods and services tax.

LOCAL STOCK EXCHANGE

14.53 Singapore Exchange Ltd operates two platforms – a securities exchange run by Singapore Exchange Securities Trading Ltd, and a futures exchange run by Securities Exchange Derivatives Trading Ltd. Apart from this, there is a third exchange, operated by ICE that trades in certain classes of energy, agriculture and financial futures.

CONFIDENTIALITY LAWS

14.54 Common law principles of confidentiality generally apply, although there is a stricter set of statutory confidentiality rules applicable to certain classes of financial institutions such as banks and merchant banks. In addition, there is the Personal Data Protection Act (Act 26 of 2012) which governs the handling of personal data (data about an individual who can be identified from that data or from that data and other information) by organisations generally.

14.55 In the case of a collective investment scheme constituted as a unit trust, there is no legal requirement for the trustee to maintain a publicly available register of unit holders. In the case of a scheme constituted as a limited partnership and whose assets are managed by a licensed fund manager, the Limited Partnership Regulations provide that the particulars of the limited partners filed with the Registry of Limited Partnerships are not open to inspection by the public.

ANTI-MONEY LAUNDERING LAWS

14.56 Singapore's anti-money laundering laws are not consolidated within a single statutory framework. The Corruption, Drug-Trafficking and Other Serious Crimes (Confiscation of Benefits) Act (Chapter 65A, Singapore Statutes) (**CDSA**) criminalises the offence of money-laundering and establishes a regime for the reporting of suspicious transactions. Under the CDSA, a person is required to file a suspicious transaction report if he knows or has reasonable grounds to believe that any property represents, is used or intended to be used in connection with any act that might constitute a Singapore money laundering predicate offence or an offence under a foreign law that corresponds to a Singapore money laundering predicate offence. Singapore adopts a list approach in defining what money laundering predicate offences are, and these are set out in the First and Second Schedules to the CDSA. The Terrorism (Suppression of Financing) Act (Chapter 325, Singapore Statutes) (**TSOFA**) gives effect to the International Convention for the Suppression of Financing of Terrorism and criminalises the financing of terrorism. Like the CDSA, it also establishes a reporting regime for alerting the authorities to suspected terrorism financing activities.

14.57 By contrast, 'know-your-customer' (**KYC**) requirements are generally imposed on a sector specific basis by regulatory agencies. Thus, in relation to financial institutions (including fund managers), MAS issues legally binding notices to different classes of financial institutions requiring them to undertake KYC measures when taking on a customer, and, after a customer is onboarded, to monitor the activity of customers on an ongoing basis. A risk-based approach is adopted, with customers presenting higher money-laundering or terrorism financing risks expected to be more closely scrutinised and monitored as opposed to other presenting lower risks. In the context of fund management, the term customer is defined to include, not only the fund from whom it holds the management mandate, and also each of the investors who invest into the fund.

CONCLUDING REMARKS: WHAT ARE THE JURISDICTION'S UNIQUE SELLING POINTS?

14.58 The key strengths of Singapore are its reputable legal and regulatory system, and the very low levels of corruption. These elements give it a distinct advantage over other Asian capitals.

CHAPTER 15

UNITED ARAB EMIRATES

GENERAL DESCRIPTION OF THE JURISDICTION

15.01 The United Arab Emirates (**UAE**) is a federation of seven emirates, namely: Dubai, Abu Dhabi, Ajman, Fujairah, Ras Al Khaimah, Sharjah, and Umm Al Quwain. It was formed in 1971, making it one of the youngest nations in the Middle East, with an estimated population of 9.4 million, of which a very high proportion are expatriates employed in a wide range of industries (circa 80%).

15.02 The legal system in the UAE is based on both civil code principles and on the Islamic Shari'a law. However, the application of Shari'a is generally limited to: (a) being used by courts as an interpretative aid where there is no express legislation governing a particular question; (b) religious, morality, and personal law matters, particularly involving Muslims (eg, inheritance, divorce, etc.); and (c) transactions which are intentionally expressed to be Shari'a-compliant (eg, Islamic finance transactions).

15.03 Save where contrary to UAE law (including Shari'a and public policy), the UAE recognises and allows for the concept of freedom of contract. This allows contractual counterparts to regulate their relationship as they choose.

15.04 Whilst Arabic is the first language, English is widely spoken and used in business.

Currency

15.05 The official currency of the UAE is the Emirati Dirham (AED, sometimes abbreviated Dhs), which is pegged to the US dollar at a rate of US$1.00 = AED 3.67. Interest rates (to the extent applicable) in the UAE tend to parallel those in the US.

15.06 There are no currency exchange controls and, save for restrictions on transactions involving Israeli counterparties or currency, no restrictions on the remittance of funds (save that the anti-money laundering laws in the UAE have been progressively tightened, which could have an impact on such matters – see **15.73** below).

Free Zones

15.07 The UAE contains various free zones, which are areas that have special tax, customs, and imports regimes, and are governed by their own framework of regulations (with the exception of UAE criminal law).

15.08 Two of these free zones, namely the Dubai International Financial Centre (**DIFC**) and the Abu Dhabi Global Financial Market (**ADGM** and, together with the DIFC, the **Financial Free Zones**), which were created (pursuant to Federal Law No. 8 of 2004 on the Establishment of Financial Free Zones) to encourage foreign investment and attract the international financial services industry, also have their own financial services regulators and court systems.

15.09 Consequently, from a financial regulatory perspective (and in broad terms) the UAE is divided into the Financial Free Zones on the one hand and the rest of the UAE (including all other free zones) on the other. All areas outside of the Financial Free Zones are colloquially (and in this chapter) referred to as 'onshore'.

15.10 The DIFC, which is located within the city of Dubai, is arguably the leading and best-known financial services hub in the Middle East (despite having only been established in 2004), with an active industry comprising local, regional and global asset management firms. There are currently more than 1,500 active companies operating in the DIFC with a combined workforce of more than 21,000 people (see also **15.17** below). The DIFC is a common law jurisdiction with its laws and regulations modelled on the best practices of the world's major financial jurisdictions (specifically the UK) and embody the best of international financial and commercial law.

15.11 The ADGM was founded in 2013 and is the first financial free zone in Abu Dhabi (the capital of the UAE). The laws and rules applicable in the ADGM are very similar to those of the DIFC and therefore are also equivalent to leading international standards. Despite its relative infancy, the ADGM is gaining traction amongst both local and global asset managers, a trend that is expected to continue as firms seek to access the considerable capital pools located in Abu Dhabi (such as the numerous sovereign wealth funds located there).

15.12 Asset management in the UAE is principally conducted out of the DIFC, Dubai (onshore), and the ADGM. However, given the relative dominance of the DIFC in the local market, this chapter is weighted more towards it than any of the others.

KEY MANDATORY REQUIREMENTS

15.13 As set out above, the UAE includes two Financial Free Zones, being the DIFC and the ADGM, which have their own laws and regulations in respect of the promotion of foreign funds in or from those Financial Free Zones. At present, there is no passporting amongst the UAE, the DIFC or the ADGM.

15.14 There is no express general private placement exemption for foreign funds in the UAE (except a private placement to government bodies and government-owned entities) and therefore a foreign promoter should engage a locally-licensed placement agent and obtain the prior approval of the Emirates Securities and Commodities Authority in respect of each investment fund to be promoted in the UAE (whether as a public or private offering). There is, however, a specific exemption in the UAE for private placements made on a reverse solicitation basis and also a widespread market practice of offering on a cross-border basis including into the DIFC and ADGM.

15.15 Any marketing of a foreign fund in the DIFC must be carried out by a firm duly licensed by the Dubai Financial Services Authority (**DFSA**) (an **Authorised Firm**). The Collective Investment Law, DIFC Law No. 2 of 2010, as amended (the **CIL**), provides that an Authorised Firm may only offer a foreign fund if:

(a) the foreign fund meets either (i) the criteria for a Designated Fund in a Recognised Jurisdiction (as defined in the DFSA's rulebook) or (ii) other criteria prescribed in the Collective Investment Rules;

(b) the Authorised Firm has a reasonable basis for recommending the foreign fund as suitable for the particular client to whom the offer is made; or

(c) the Foreign Fund is a type of fund that (i) has or intends to have 100 or fewer investors, (ii) is offered to persons only by way of a private placement, (iii) is offered to persons who meet the criteria to be classified as a Professional Client, and (iv) requires an initial subscription of at least $50,000 per investor.

15.16 Many foreign promotors are keen to promote funds throughout the Gulf region which consists of six countries (Bahrain, Kuwait, Oman, Qatar, Saudi Arabia, and the UAE), including various financial centres and free zones within each country, each with different rules and regulations regarding the promotion of foreign funds. At present, there is no passporting between any of the Gulf countries. This can make it somewhat of a complex process to promote in the Gulf region and it is critical that a foreign promoter obtains proper legal advice and carefully plans its promotional activities across the Gulf countries.

RECENT DEVELOPMENTS

2024 Strategy and Fund Managers Initiative

15.17 In 2014, the DIFC announced a 10-year growth strategy (2024 Strategy) with targets that include:

- increasing assets under management in the DIFC from US$10.4 billion (as of 2014) to US$250 billion;
- more than tripling the number of financial firms in the DIFC (from 362 as of the end of 2014); and
- increasing the size of the workforce in the DIFC from approximately 18,000 in 2014 to 50,000.

15.18 In light of the 2024 Strategy, both the DFSA and the DIFC Authority (Authority) were tasked with investigating and proposing strategies for boosting the number of fund managers and funds established in the DIFC.

15.19 In late 2016, the DFSA issued a Consultation Paper in order to seek feedback from market participants on proposals to amend (among other things) the base capital requirement for fund managers.

15.20 In formulating its proposals for the Consultation Paper, the DFSA benchmarked capital requirements against a number of established funds jurisdictions (including the BVI, the Cayman Islands, Ireland, Luxembourg, Malta, the UK, Guernsey, Hong Kong, Jersey and Singapore). As a result of such benchmarking, it was proposed that the base capital requirement be reduced from the US$500,000 it was previously set at (see '*Establishment and Logistics*' for further detail). Following positive feedback, the proposals were implemented by the Board of the DFSA, effective as of 1 February 2017.

15.21 To complement the DFSA's efforts, the Authority's Wealth and Asset Management Team announced the '*DIFC Fund Managers Initiative*' in January 2017. Pursuant to the Initiative, the Authority has reduced set-up costs for fund management firms looking to establish themselves and one or more of their funds in the DIFC. Effective 1 February 2017, such firms will not be required to pay the application fee otherwise payable to the Registrar of Companies upon incorporation nor, for the first two years, the commercial license fee (see **15.47** below for further detail). Furthermore, if the firm leases operating space within an Authority-owned building in the DIFC, its rent for the first two years will be reduced by 50%.

15.22 For non-retail fund managers, the above-mentioned changes together represent a reduction of at least US$450,000 in their initial outlay (before factoring in any additional savings available on rent or as part of the Authority's service provider outreach programme). The savings could be even higher for firms that would otherwise have established an offshore fund and fund manager coupled with a DIFC-based investment adviser or asset manager (which is a relatively common structure in the DIFC).

Value Added Tax

15.23 The UAE implemented value added tax at the rate of 5% on 1 January 2018. Such tax is chargeable on (amongst other things) fees payable for financial services (such as investment management fees) and consequently such firms are required to register with the Ministry of Finance for the sake of reporting and remitting such tax revenues.

THE REGULATION OF INVESTMENT BUSINESS

Introduction

15.24 As noted above, from a financial regulatory perspective the UAE is divided into the Financial Free Zones on the one hand and the rest of the UAE on the other. It is important to note that each of these jurisdictions (and their respective regulators) are independent of each other. Consequently, holding a licence in one of these jurisdictions does not automatically authorise its holder to perform, outside of the relevant jurisdiction, any activity that is permitted under such licence; a separate licence is required in each jurisdiction. The one exception to this is that the ADGM establishment law provides that an ADGM entity may conduct marketing activities within the Emirate of Abu Dhabi outside of the ADGM, although there remains some legal uncertainty around this.

UAE (onshore)

15.25 Onshore, financial services (other than banking activities) are regulated by the Emirates Securities and Commodities Authority (the **SCA**); for the sake of completeness: the licensing and regulation of banking activities is under the remit of the UAE Central Bank.

15.26 Any firm (whether based inside or outside the UAE, including in a free zone other than a Financial Free Zone) that intends to conduct investment management activities in the UAE must obtain a license from the SCA prior to conducting such activities. '*Investment management*' for such purposes is defined as the management of securities portfolios for the account of third parties, or the management of mutual funds in accordance with the investment objectives and policies defined in the investment management agreement between the investment manager and its client. There is an exemption with regard to financial portfolios owned by federal and local government entities.

DIFC

15.27 Financial services in the DIFC are regulated by the DFSA.

15.28 The Regulatory Law, DIFC Law No. 1 of 2004, as amended (the **Regulatory Law**) empowers the DFSA to (among other things) issue and administer supplementary rules and regulations for financial firms setting up and operating in the DIFC. Pursuant to this power, the DFSA has issued and maintains a rulebook with which firms must comply (the **DFSA Rules**).

15.29 The DFSA Rules are largely based upon the equivalent rubrics issued by financial regulators in other global financial centres (principally, the handbook issued by the Financial Conduct Authority of the UK) and, in the same vein as the source material, are divided into modules that address separate topics. Aside from the universally applicable modules (eg, the '*General*' module), the ones most relevant to asset managers are the '*Collective Investment Rules*' (the **CIR**), '*Prudential – Investment, Insurance Intermediation and Banking*', and (in the case of firms dealing with Shari'a-compliant products) the '*Islamic Finance Rules*' modules.

15.30 Generally speaking, DFSA licences are not categorised by industry or service (ie, there is no simple 'banking' or 'asset management' licence). Instead, each licence is granted for a bespoke combination of activities, meaning that applicants are required to identify every activity that will comprise their intended financial service. While this might appear unduly onerous at first glance, it has the advantage of allowing firms to be able to mix and match (or, indeed, discard) authorisations as suits their exact needs. One exception to this is the licence of '*Managing a Collective Investment Fund*' (ie, the permission required to act as a fund manager in or from the DIFC). This licence (which colloquially, but incorrectly, is referred to as a Category 3C licence) automatically allows the holder to also perform the following activities: Arranging Deals in Investments; Dealing in Investments as Principal; Dealing in Investments as Agent; Managing Assets; Providing Custody; and Providing Fund Administration – each of which is a facet of a fund manager's role and would otherwise need to be applied for separately. However, the upshot of this extensive authorisation is that the application process and ongoing regulatory obligations are commensurately more involved than is the case with other licences.

15.31 Consequently, asset management firms in the DIFC often look to structure their operations in a way that properly matches the services they will need to provide with an appropriate level of regulatory oversight.

ADGM

15.32 The Financial Services and Markets Regulations 2015 (**FSMR**) contain the regulatory framework for the ADGM and are supplemented by various rulebooks as well as indicative, non-binding guidance, issued by the Financial Services Regulatory Authority (the **FSRA**), the financial services regulator in the ADGM.

15.33 Under the FSMR, firms carrying on financial services business such as investment management in the ADGM are subject to licensing by both the ADGM (in terms of the obligation to hold a commercial licence) and the FSRA (in respect of the financial services licensing). The FSMR contain two key prohibitions, namely providing financial services without a licence or exemption, and making an authorised financial promotion.

15.34 The ADGM fund management regime (as encapsulated in the FSMR and '*Fund Rules*' issued by the FSRA thereunder) substantively mirrors the regime in the DIFC, which offers some level of consistency across the local market.

INVESTORS

UAE

15.35 Foreign investors are mainly drawn by the country's economic stability, low energy costs, tax-free environment for businesses, absence of limitations on repatriation of profits, and the government's openness towards a diversified economy. Dubai, which is the largest city in the country (ahead of Abu Dhabi, the capital), currently hosts a great number of expatriates living and working or owning companies and makes it the de facto local hub for international trade. As noted above, Abu Dhabi is the seat of power in the UAE and is home to most of the nation's sovereign wealth funds and oil companies.

Free zones

15.36 Dubai's free zones are also one of the UAE's strongest attractions for foreign investors as there are no restrictions on foreign ownership of companies (as there are outside the free zones). Conditions for doing business in free zones are highly attractive with tax concessions, having no restrictions on the repatriation of capital and profits, and freedom from currency restrictions and import duties.

15.37 Dubai is home to more than 20 free zones at present and the number is growing. Recently, the government has launched the Dubai Smart City Program which offers foreign investors a modern infrastructure for company registration services.

15.38 Free zones have been fundamental in developing Dubai's reputation as an attractive place to establish a business. Subject to certain exceptions, businesses wishing to set up in the free zones are required to establish places of business physically within the geographical boundaries of the particular free zone, which means international enterprises must put firm roots down in the region which, in turn, encourages sustainability and longevity in terms of commitment to the region.

SETTING UP A FUND

15.39 In common with other popular fund domiciles globally, the DIFC has created an attractive infrastructure for the asset management industry, including a zero rate of tax in the DIFC; a good network of double taxation treaties; no restrictions on foreign ownership; the ability to establish certain types of funds on an accelerated basis; and regulatory oversight by the DFSA. While only a small number of funds have been domiciled in the DIFC to date, the rate is increasing, and it is anticipated that this trend will continue.

15.40 The Collective Investment Law, DIFC Law No. 2 of 2010, as amended (the **CIL**), frames the creation and regulation of funds in the DIFC and sets out three types of DIFC-domiciled funds (**Domestic Funds**): '*Public Funds*'; '*Exempt Funds*'; and '*Qualified Investor Funds*'.

15.41 Public Funds are highly regulated funds that require the prior approval of the DFSA. There is no minimum subscription amount per investor, nor is there a limit on the number of investors. Investors in a Public Fund may be Professional Clients or Retail Clients (as defined under DIFC law – these definitions largely follow the standards that would be expected in other jurisdictions).

15.42 Exempt Funds are less regulated than Public Funds and do not require the prior approval of the DFSA. However, the fund manager of an Exempt Fund must notify the DFSA at least 14 days prior to the offer of interests in the fund. The minimum subscription amount in respect of an Exempt Fund is US$50,000 per investor, and the maximum number of investors is 100. Investors in an Exempt Fund must be Professional Clients.

15.43 Qualified Investor Funds (**QIFs**) were introduced in 2014. QIFs are the least regulated form of fund in the DIFC, being exempt from many of the regulations applicable to Public Funds and Exempt Funds. QIFs do not require the approval of the DFSA. However, the fund manager of a QIF must notify the DFSA at least 14 days prior to the offer of interests in the fund. The minimum subscription amount in a QIF is US$500,000 per investor and the maximum number of investors is 50. Investors in a QIF must be Professional Clients. The ability to offer less-regulated fund regimes, and to put the onus of compliance on the manager rather than, directly, a regulator, is a theme that other fund domiciles are also now adopting.

	Public Fund	Exempt Fund	QIF
Investor requirements	Professional Clients and Retail Clients	Professional Clients only	Professional Clients only
Manner of offering	Private placement and public offering	Private placement only	Private placement only
Maximum number of investors	N/A	100	50
Minimum subscription	N/A	US$ 50,000	US$ 500,000
Regulatory approval	Application to the DFSA	Notification to DFSA at least 14 days prior to offer	Notification to DFSA at least 14 days prior to offer
Prospectus requirement	Yes – detailed prescribed disclosure content	Yes – limited prescribed disclosure content	Very limited – information memorandum
Permitted to list on exchange	Yes	No	No

15.44 Given the 'light touch' approach of the DFSA with respect to QIFs and the relative speed in setting up QIFs, a number of regional managers have recently chosen to domicile funds in the DIFC as QIFs, rather than in other offshore or tax-free jurisdictions.

SETTING UP A LOCAL MANAGEMENT COMPANY/INVESTMENT MANAGER

Introduction

15.45 It is important to note at the outset that the terms '*fund manager*' and '*investment manager*', (which are, colloquially speaking, often used interchangeably and, in many jurisdictions, refer to the same role) have distinct meanings in the DIFC. According to the CIL and the DFSA Rules, a fund manager is the person that (i) establishes, manages, operates or winds up a fund and (ii) is legally accountable to the investors for the management of such fund (and any property held for or within it). By way of comparison, the term 'investment manager' (in the context of a fund) refers to a person who performs discretionary portfolio management services on behalf of a fund but is not necessarily legally accountable to investors (or otherwise responsible for the establishment, management, operation or winding-up of the fund). Furthermore, in the DIFC, a fund manager's licence must include a '*Managing a Collective Investment Fund*' permission whereas investment management activity may be carried out with a '*Managing Assets*' licence. This section focusses on fund managers. See '*Alternative Structures*' below for additional commentary on investment managers.

15.46 A Domestic Fund must be managed by a fund manager that is either (i) incorporated in the DIFC and licensed by the DFSA or (ii) incorporated and regulated in a DFSA-recognised jurisdiction, meets certain other criteria set out in the CIL and the CIR and is registered with the DFSA as an 'External Fund Manager'. Whilst the application process for becoming an External Fund Manager is, in theory, less involved than that for a firm established in the DIFC itself, this is not a particularly popular route and, to date, only one firm has been registered in this manner. It is worth noting that neither the ADGM, the UAE nor any of the traditional offshore financial centres (such as the Cayman Islands) is a DFSA-recognised jurisdiction.

Establishment and Logistics

15.47 The exact process for establishing a fund management business in the DIFC varies depending upon the legal structure chosen and the type of fund(s) to be managed by it. However, in essence, the process involves parallel applications being made to the DIFC Registrar of Companies (in order to incorporate the entity) and to the DFSA (in order to licence it). As a practical first step (and to facilitate the application process) early engagement with both the Business Development team of the DIFC Authority and the DFSA is encouraged.

15.48 The information and documentation to be submitted to the Registrar of Companies to incorporate a company limited by shares (ie, the most popular structure for fund management firms in the DIFC) includes: details and ID copies of the authorised signatories, directors, direct shareholders, and ultimate beneficial owners (see '*Confidentiality*' below for how such items are handled). Furthermore, the company's articles of association are required to be either physically signed in the presence of an official in the Registrar's office or, if signed outside of the UAE, notarised by the UAE embassy in the relevant country. Typically, an application fee of US$8,000 and a commercial licence fee of US$12,000 p.a. is payable in connection with such incorporation. However, as mentioned above, pursuant to the DIFC Fund Managers Initiative, these fees are waived for persons setting-up fund management firms. Additional fees (in the region of US$1,500) are also payable for the purposes of data processing and/or transmission. The incorporation process itself typically takes two to three working days.

15.49 Given that fund management is a regulated activity, the incorporation process for a fund manager cannot be completed without the DFSA's prior approval. The application process involves engaging with the DFSA (who will appoint a relationship manager for the purposes of both the application and ongoing relations). The DFSA application process seeks to test the fitness and propriety of the individuals and/or corporate group setting up the firm, as well as the adequacy of the proposed systems and controls of the firm. Matters inspected as part of the process include: strategy and rationale for establishing the DIFC (including target markets, details of existing and proposed clients and an analysis of likely market competition), organisational structure and corporate governance issues, proposed resources and control environment (including human capital, risk management and outsourcing arrangements) and financial projections for three years.

15.50 The DFSA typically aims to complete the review and licensing process within four months of the initial application. However, there is a fast track available for fund managers seeking to manage only QIFs – the DFSA aims to complete this process in four to six weeks, which is possible because the application relies heavily on self-certification of eligibility by the manager. Licensing fees range from US$5,000 for a fund manager of only QIFs (provided that they are not umbrella funds) to US$10,000 for managers of other types of funds (or more, if managing an umbrella fund with more than two sub-funds). Fund managers are also required to apply for an endorsement to control client assets, the fee for which is an additional US$5,000.

15.51 Generally speaking, any entity established in the DIFC must have a physical office location in the DIFC. Corporate entities must have a minimum of two directors; corporate directors are not permitted. Furthermore, any DFSA-licensed firm (including a fund manager) must have the following appointees as a bare minimum:

- senior executive officer (who must be a UAE resident);
- finance officer;

- compliance officer (who must be a UAE resident); and
- money laundering reporting officer (who must be a UAE resident).

15.52 It is possible to outsource the finance officer, compliance officer and money laundering reporting officer functions to third-party service providers, subject to such service providers being appropriately licensed and having adequate resources, systems and controls. Furthermore, the compliance officer and money laundering reporting officer roles are typically combined and performed by a single individual.

Capital requirements

15.53 As mentioned above the base capital requirement for fund managers has been reduced, effective as of 1 February 2017, from US$500,000 to:

- US$140,000, for managers of Public Funds; and
- US$70,000, for managers of Exempt Funds and/or QIFs.

15.54 However, as a condition to taking advantage of the reduced base capital requirement, the firm in question may not hold any permission other than Managing a Collective Investment Fund (ie, it may not perform any financial services other than fund management).

15.55 It is important note here that the base capital requirement forms only part of a DFSA-licensed firm's capital requirements. Essentially, a fund manager's actual capital requirement is determined by looking not only at the DFSA-prescribed base capital requirement (as referred to above), but also by looking at its annual audited expenditure and applying a set formula thereto (currently 13/52, provided the firm is not holding client assets itself). If such expenditure-based figure is higher than the base capital requirement, that will be taken to be the firm's capital requirement.

Alternative Structures

15.56 As explained above, there is a distinction in the DIFC between the roles of 'fund manager' and 'investment manager'. Given that an investment management permission appears to grant the same asset management powers as a fund management licence while minimising liability to investors, establishing a firm as an investment manager instead should not be a foregone conclusion. Crucially, the Managing Assets permission does not entitle the holder to perform all of the other activities automatically available to a fund manager – this means that, unless such activities are applied for separately, the firm's operations will necessarily be limited. Furthermore, the DFSA is likely to look very closely at any fund structure proposed by an investment management firm, in order to be satisfied that the firm will not itself be performing fund management activities and to ensure that there is another entity within the fund structure that meets the 'legal accountability to investors' aspect of a fund manager's role.

15.57 Another, and more popular, option is to set up an investment advisory firm, which typically involves applying for the Advising on Financial Products and Arranging Deals in Investments permissions (colloquially referred to as a Category 4 licence). In this scenario, the firm does not conduct any fund or portfolio management activities in or from the DIFC, but instead advises an offshore manager or (if applicable) the fund's board of directors in respect of the management of the fund and/or its assets. Furthermore, the authorisations referred to above also entitle the advisory firm to arrange, structure and negotiate investment opportunities for the fund, as well as to perform marketing and placement services on the fund's behalf. The investment advisory option has the benefit of a more rapid application process, a lower ongoing regulatory burden and a lower capital requirement. However, as is the case in other jurisdictions where such an approach is equally popular, it is important to: (i) give the offshore manager (or the fund's board, as applicable) real power to approve or reject the advisory firm's recommendations; and (ii) avoid having the same (or mostly the same) individuals in control of both the advisory firm and the offshore manager/ board. Otherwise, the DFSA is likely to determine that management is actually being conducted within the DIFC.

15.58 One final option worth noting is establishing a Representative Office – this is a branch of a foreign regulated entity that is registered with (and authorised by) the DFSA to perform marketing and placement activities in or from the DIFC. The key conditions to this permission are: (i) the activities to be performed by the Representative Office must be within the scope of the regulatory licence held by its head office; (ii) the Representative Office's activities cannot relate to DIFC entities (ie, only foreign funds may be marketed or placed by the Representative Office); and (iii) the funds being marketed must be being offered by an affiliate of the Representative Office (and its head office). While this may sound quite restrictive, it is nonetheless a model that has found some considerable interest, as there are currently almost 70 Representative Offices operating in the DIFC.

15.59 The above should serve to illustrate the importance of carefully considering which licence is actually required. While the prestige of a full-blown fund management licence is undeniably attractive, it may well be possible for a firm to secure a licence for the functions it truly wishes to perform in a more efficient manner than it otherwise believes. It is no coincidence that of all the asset management firms established in the DIFC, only 30 or so are fund managers, approximately 100 are investment managers and 300 or so are structured as investment advisers.

OTHER KEY SERVICE PROVIDERS

15.60 The CIR requires that the fund manager of each Domestic Fund delegates responsibility for the custody and safe keeping of such fund's property to a third-party service provider that meets the criteria to be an '*Eligible Custodian*'. Such criteria include (amongst other things) being a separate legal entity from the fund manager and being either a DFSA-licensed custodian or bank, licensed to provide custody services by another financial regulator within the UAE, a financial services regulator in a DFSA-recognised jurisdiction or a financial services regulator in a '*Zone 1*' jurisdiction (namely: Australia, Austria, Belgium, Canada, Denmark, Finland, France, Germany, Greece, Hong Kong, Iceland, Ireland, Italy, Japan, Luxembourg, Netherlands, Norway, Portugal, Singapore, Spain, Sweden, Switzerland, UK or US).

15.61 There is a general exemption from the requirement to appoint a third-party custodian in the case of real estate funds and private equity funds, provided that adequate alternative arrangements have been made for the custody and safe keeping of assets and certain other requirements set out in CIR are satisfied.

15.62 Separately, the CIL requires each Domestic Fund to appoint an auditor, who is registered with the DFSA. The function of the auditor is to conduct an audit of the fund's financial statements (in accordance with the requirements of the relevant standards published by the International Auditing and Assurance Standards Board) and produce an annual report on the fund's annual accounts in accordance with the requirements set out in the CIR.

15.63 The CIR also provide for a fund manager to be able to delegate its fund administration and investment management functions (respectively) to appropriately licensed service providers, whether in the DIFC, a DFSA-recognised jurisdiction or a Zone 1 jurisdiction. Whilst delegation of investment management responsibilities is not de rigueur in the DIFC, it is not unheard of. However, administrative functions (such as valuations, capital calls, and maintenance of books and records) are commonly delegated to third party fund administrators.

15.64 In the event that a fund manager delegates any activities or outsources any its functions, it remains ultimately liable to investors for any acts or omissions of the appointed service providers as if they were the acts or omissions of the fund manager itself.

LOCAL STOCK EXCHANGE

15.65 There are currently three stock exchanges in the UAE, including (a) the Dubai Financial Market (**DFM**) which is situated in Dubai, UAE and is regulated by the SCA; (b) the Abu Dhabi Exchange (**ADX**), which is situated in Abu Dhabi, UAE and is regulated by the SCA; and (c) NASDAQ Dubai which is situated in the DIFC and is regulated by the DFSA.

15.66 The Market Rules of the DIFC (and the listing criteria of Nasdaq Dubai) provide that the units of a foreign fund may only be listed be if (a) it is Designated Fund from a Recognised Jurisdiction (each as defined in the DFSA's rulebook);

or (b) it is a fund approved by the DFSA as a fund subject to equivalent regulation as that applying to a Public Fund (see above) and, in the case of a Foreign Fund which meets the criteria of a property fund, it is a closed-ended investment vehicle and 60% or more of the fund's assets comprise Real Property.

15.67 Both the DFM and ADX allow foreign funds to be listed. However, NASDAQ Dubai is the only exchange in the UAE to date with listed Real Estate Investment Trusts.

CONFIDENTIALITY LAWS

15.68 Whilst there are no federal data protection laws in the UAE, each of the Financial Free Zones have developed a body of legislation dealing with such matters within their respective jurisdictions.

15.69 Such laws are largely based upon (and are equivalent to) European legislation and focus predominantly on the protection of personal data relating to individuals. Consequently, there are consent requirements and rights of access given to such subjects similar to those applicable in other international financial centres.

15.70 In the DIFC, the rules are contained in the Data Protection Law, DIFC Law No. 1 of 2007 (as amended) and the Data Protection Regulations in force from time to time. Similar rules are found in the Data Protection Regulations 2015 of the ADGM.

15.71 Separately, both the DIFC and the ADGM have publicly accessible databases which identify not only the names and registered addresses of entities established within their respective jurisdictions but also (amongst other things) the identity of their directors and incorporating shareholders and the amount of their authorised and issued share capital. Access to corporate information in other parts of the United Arab Emirates (including other free zones) varies across the relevant registrars, but is generally more restricted than in the DIFC and the ADGM.

15.72 For the sake of completeness, it is worth noting that pursuant to the Penal Code of the UAE, which is encapsulated in Federal Law No.3 of 1987 and applies across the State, unauthorised publication of personal data (which is generally defined as relating to an individual's private or family life) is a criminal offence.

ANTI-MONEY LAUNDERING LAWS

15.73 The UAE has been progressively strengthening its anti-money laundering legislation in line with the OECD's Financial Action Task Force's Recommendations.

15.74 The anti-money laundering rules are split between federal law (principally Federal Law No. 4 of 2002 on Combating Money Laundering and Terrorist Financing, Federal Law No. 1 of 2004 on Combating Terrorism Offences and Federal Law No. 7 of 2014 on Combating Terrorist Crimes) and, in the case of the Financial Free Zones, the additional laws and regulations issued therein (being, in the case of the DIFC, Chapter 2 of Part 4 of the Regulatory Law and the '*Anti-Money Laundering, Counter-Terrorist Financing and Sanctions*' module of the DFSA Rules and, in the ADGM, the Anti-Money Laundering and Sanctions Rules and Guidance issued by the FSRA).

15.75 In essence, the legislation requires a risk-based approach to anti-money laundering, meaning that the exact due diligence requirements in respect of clients varies depending upon the exact circumstances. In practice, this means (particularly in the Financial Free Zones) that the level of disclosure required is often higher than that found in other international financial centres.

TAX REGIME

15.76 There is no federal corporate or income tax levied in the UAE (except on oil companies and foreign banks), whether in the mainland or within the free zones. Consequently, any income and/or capital gains generated and/or distributed by investment funds are free of any direct taxation in the UAE (whether at the level of the fund itself or in the hands of investors).

15.77 Furthermore, there are no exchange controls on the remittance of profits or repatriation of capital and there are virtually no restrictions on foreign trade.

15.78 However, as noted above, it is expected that VAT will be introduced across the UAE as of 1 January 2018 and will be payable in respect of all goods and services supplied within or from the UAE (subject to limited exceptions, such as core household items and education).

CONCLUDING REMARKS: WHAT ARE THE JURISDICTION'S UNIQUE SELLING POINTS?

15.79 Throughout the financial downturn and the recent slide in oil prices, the UAE has shown its resilience. It has proved that its economy operates outside of the oil and energy sectors, and that it has the infrastructure to maintain and grow its asset management industry. Also, the UAE appears to be isolated from the general geo-political instability that plagues the region, which makes it all the more attractive for foreign business.

15.80 Regional and international managers see the UAE as the logical centre for the asset management industry in the Middle East, with Dubai serving as the hub. The DIFC has capitalised on this success by progressively updating and simplifying its funds regime whilst maintaining the integrity and robustness of its regulatory framework. Abu Dhabi is seeking to emulate this success with the establishment of the ADGM – a natural competitor to the DIFC, given the similarity of its offering. Regardless of which of the Financial Free Zones ultimately wears the crown, the UAE is likely to remain, for the foreseeable future, the regional jurisdiction of choice for the international asset management industry.

CHAPTER 16

THE UNITED KINGDOM

GENERAL DESCRIPTION OF THE JURISDICTION

16.01 The United Kingdom (UK) is located in the north-eastern Atlantic Ocean off the coast of continental Europe and consists principally of the island of Great Britain and the northern part of the island of Ireland, in which it shares a land border with the Republic of Ireland.

16.02 It has an area of approximately 93,600 square miles (242,500 square kilometres) and a population of more than 65.6 million.

16.03 Its time zone is Greenwich Mean Time (GMT) and its currency is the pound sterling (GBP). English is its only official language, except in Wales where Welsh has equal standing within the public sector.

16.04 The legal systems in England, Wales and Northern Ireland are common law based, whereas in Scotland the legal system has a civil law base with a common law overlay.

16.05 The UK is a member of the Organisation for Economic Co-operation and Development (**OECD**) and the European Union (**EU**), although it is currently in the process of leaving the EU (*see* **16.07** et seq below).

KEY MANDATORY REQUIREMENTS

16.06

- Persons operating or managing investment funds in the UK will generally need to be authorised by UK Financial Conduct Authority (**FCA**) or be a passported branch of an appropriately regulated firm in the wider European Economic Area (**EEA**).
- The FCA's authorisation process for management entities is relatively long, but a number of UK service providers can provide temporary 'warehousing' arrangements to enable management activity to be commenced more quickly.
- Open-ended UK funds available for retail investment need to be authorised by the FCA either as UCITS Schemes under the EU UCITS Directive or as Non-UCITS Retail Schemes (**NURS**).
- An FCA authorised professional investor fund category (a Qualified Investor Scheme (**QIS**)) with more relaxed investment and borrowing restrictions is

available, but it tends to be used for specialist products aimed at the UK market and there has been limited take up of it.

- The UK's taxation of FCA authorised funds is relatively complex, but funds can benefit from the UK's wide range of double tax treaties. This complexity can make these funds more difficult to explain to non-UK investors, but for funds seeking to access double tax treaty networks FCA authorised funds and UK listed investment trusts can offer greater tax efficiency than their Luxembourg or Irish analogues.

- Non-FCA authorised UK fund structures are most often used for real estate, private credit and private equity funds primarily involving UK assets or which target mainly UK investors. UK London listed investment trusts are a long standing, respected and popular permanent capital investment fund structure. Most other non-FCA authorised funds managed from the UK are domiciled outside the UK.

- NURS, QIS and non-FCA authorised UK funds managed from the UK will require the manager to be regulated under the EU Alternative Investment Fund Managers Directive (**AIFMD**) or fall within an exemption.

- The UK has implemented the EU's Fourth Money Laundering Directive, with relatively onerous customer due diligence requirements for regulated firms.

RECENT DEVELOPMENTS

Brexit

16.07 On 23 June 2016, the UK voted to leave the EU and, on 29 March 2017, it formally commenced the exit process by serving notice of its intention to leave under Article 50 of the EU Treaty. Service of this notice started a two-year process for negotiating the terms of exit. If no terms of exit and no extension are agreed, the UK will simply exit the EU at the end of the two-year period on 29 March 2019.

16.08 The main impacts of Brexit on the management and marketing of funds in and from the UK will flow from the fact that – absent a special deal – the burdens and benefits of EU financial services legislation would cease to apply to the UK.

16.09 The burdens that could be foregone include the increased regulatory restrictions and requirements imposed by the EU, particularly in recent years. However, wholesale reform of the current UK financial services regulations seems unlikely, at least in the short term.

16.10 The main benefits to be lost are the 'passporting' rights under the EU financial services directives, including the EU Markets in Financial Instruments

Directive (**MiFID**), the UCITS Directive and AIFMD. These directives apply detailed regulatory requirements to EU firms, which, in return, are given rights to passport their products and services elsewhere in the EU. After Brexit, UK firms would become 'third country' firms as regards the EU, and cease to benefit from these passporting regimes. Similarly, firms in the remaining 27 EU member states could lose their passporting rights into the UK.

THE REGULATION OF INVESTMENT BUSINESS

16.11 Two financial services regulators are established under the Financial Services and Markets Act 2000 (**FSMA**): the FCA and the Prudential Regulation Authority (**PRA**).

16.12 The FCA is the principal regulator of investment business and investment funds. UK fund managers, other investment managers and distributors of funds will generally be authorised and regulated by the FCA. All UK regulated funds must be authorised by the FCA.

16.13 The PRA is the principal prudential regulator of banks, insurers and certain large investment firms. Many institutions that are regulated by the PRA for prudential purposes are also regulated by the FCA for conduct of business purposes. Most UK depositaries and custodians will be dual regulated by the PRA and FCA.

16.14 The UK Listing Authority (**UKLA**) is a division of the FCA and is responsible for maintaining the Official List of UK listed securities. The UKLA is therefore responsible for the listing of UK exchange traded funds (**ETFs**), listed closed ended investment companies (referred to as 'investment trusts') and other exchange traded products.

INVESTORS

16.15 The main target market of most FCA authorised funds is UK investors, notwithstanding the ability to passport those funds throughout the EEA. This is in part due to the relative complexity of the UK taxation regime (see **16.89** et seq below).

16.16 Most other funds managed from the UK tend not to be UK domiciled structures. This has been facilitated by the UK's historically permissive rules on marketing of unregulated collective investment schemes to professional and institutional investors in the UK.

16.17 Non-FCA authorised UK fund structures are most often used for real estate, private credit and private equity funds involving UK assets or which target mainly UK investors.

SETTING UP A FUND

16.18 Funds established and operated in the UK include both funds authorised by the FCA and funds that are not. Even for non-FCA authorised funds, the operator (including the fund itself if self-managed) will generally require FCA authorisation under the AIFMD, unless an exemption applies. FCA authorised funds must be open ended whereas non-FCA authorised UK funds may be open or closed ended.

FCA Authorised Funds

16.19 FCA authorised funds must take one of a range of regulatory structures and legal forms, which will drive the FCA requirements for its investment policies and restrictions and the range of persons to whom it can be marketed.

Regulatory Structures

16.20 Three principal regulatory structures are permitted for FCA authorised funds: UCITS Schemes, NURS and QIS.

16.21 UCITS Schemes and NURS may be marketed to the public in the UK, whereas QIS are subject to substantially the same marketing restrictions as an unregulated collective investment scheme (see **16.75** below).

16.22 UCITS Schemes will benefit from the UCITS Directive marketing passport and may be marketed to the public throughout the EEA. NURS and QIS are AIFs and may be marketed to professional investors throughout the EEA under the AIFMD marketing passport.

UCITS Schemes

16.23 UCITS Schemes are authorised under the EU UCITS Directive and the requirements of the UCITS Directive, as implemented in the UK, will apply in full.

16.24 As regards investment restrictions, the investments of a UCITS Scheme must consist solely of any or all of:

- transferable securities;
- money-market instruments;
- units in collective investment schemes;
- derivatives and forward transactions;
- deposits; and

- for an ICVC (as defined below) only, movable and immovable property essential for the direct pursuit of the fund's business.

16.25 Transferable securities must generally be listed and money-market instruments must be listed or be issued by a regulated financial institution. However, UCITS Schemes may invest up to 10% of NAV in aggregate in other transferable securities and money-market instruments.

16.26 Collective investment schemes must be other UCITS funds or meet certain UCITS equivalency requirements. In either case, the underlying fund must not invest more than 10% of its assets in other funds, which effectively prohibits UCITS Schemes from investing in funds of funds or feeder funds.

16.27 A UCITS Scheme may not short and may not borrow (other than on a temporary basis up to 10% of NAV). However, a UCITS Scheme may engage in synthetic shorting and leverage through investment in derivatives.

16.28 The underlying of any derivative must be a permitted investment for a UCITS Scheme or be a financial index satisfying certain criteria, an interest rate, foreign exchange rate or currency. The global exposure relating to derivatives and forwards held in a UCITS Scheme may not exceed the net value of the scheme property. Global exposure may be calculated either under the commitment approach or using a value at risk (VaR) methodology.

16.29 As regards liquidity, a UCITS Scheme must have at least two valuation points each month and pay redemptions within four business days of the relevant valuation point (or of the date the required title transfer documents are received, if later).

16.30 Limited gating (referred to as 'deferred redemption' in the FCA rules) is allowed, but only for daily dealing funds. Where requested redemptions exceed 10% of the fund's NAV (or some other reasonable proportion disclosed in the prospectus), redemptions may be deferred to the next valuation point.

Non-UCITS Retail Schemes (NURS)

16.31 NURS are UK retail funds and are subject to FCA rules that permit wider investment powers than a UCITS Scheme. NURS qualify as alternative investment funds (**AIFs**) for the purposes of the AIFMD.

16.32 Accordingly, the requirements applicable to a NURS will be a combination of the UK requirements implementing the AIFMD and specific FCA rules for NURS.

16.33 As regards investment restrictions, a NURS may invest, broadly speaking, in any of the investment types permitted for a UCITS Scheme, plus immovables (ie real property) and gold.

16.34 Many of the investment limits are somewhat more relaxed than for a UCITS Scheme. For example:

(1) transferrable securities and money-market instruments: the limit on unlisted and non-regulated issuer securities and instruments is increased from 10% to 20% of NAV in aggregate;

(2) collective investment schemes: a NURS that is not a FAIF (as defined below) may invest up to 20% of NAV in unregulated collective investment schemes, and the limit for an underlying fund's investment in collective investment schemes is increased from 10% to 15%;

(3) borrowing: a NURS may borrow up to 10% of NAV on a non-temporary basis.

16.35 A sub-type of NURS, called a Fund of Alternative Investment Funds (**FAIF**), permits 100% of the fund's NAV to be invested in unregulated collective investment schemes, but requires the Alternative Investment Fund Manager (**AIFM**) of the FAIF to carry out enhanced due diligence meeting criteria specified in the FCA rules on each of the alternative funds in which it invests. The FAIF rules still include a requirement that each underlying fund must be prohibited from investing more than 15% of its NAV in other funds, but this requirement can be applied at the level of a master fund where the underlying fund is a feeder.

16.36 A Property Authorised Investment Fund (**PAIF**) is a further sub-type of NURS which invests in real property and benefits from a particular UK tax treatment (see **16.89** et seq below).

16.37 As regards liquidity, a NURS is generally subject to the same FCA rules as a UCITS Scheme – ie it must have at least two valuation points each month and pay redemptions within four business days – except that a FAIF or a PAIF may operate 'limited redemption' arrangements under which dealing days may be limited to once every six months, provided that redemption proceeds are paid out no later than 185 days from the date of the receipt and acceptance of the redemption instruction.

16.38 The 'deferred redemption' rules for NURS are also relaxed, subject to the requirement that redemption proceeds are paid out no later than 185 days from the redemption instruction.

16.39 These extended limited redemption and deferred redemption arrangements must operate within the same 185-day period.

Qualified Investor Schemes (QIS)

16.40 Unlike a UCITS Scheme and a NURS, a QIS is not available for investment by the general public. Rather, ownership of its units is restricted to those categories of investor to which an FCA authorised firm is permitted under the FCA rules in COBS 4.12 to promote an unregulated collective investment scheme (see **16.75** below).

16.41 A QIS is subject to fewer investment restrictions than a UCITS Scheme or NURS.

16.42 Broadly speaking, a QIS may invest in:

- most categories of FCA regulated investment – the permitted investment categories include substantially all securities and derivatives;
- real property;
- precious metals; and
- commodity contracts traded on a UK Recognised Investment Exchange or Recognised Overseas Investment Exchange.

16.43 A QIS may invest in most collective investment schemes, provided that scheme is FCA authorised or recognised or it:

- operates in accordance with the principle of risk spreading;
- is the subject of an independent annual audit conducted in accordance with international standards;
- the calculation of its NAV and the maintenance of its accounting records are segregated from its investment management; and
- unless it is a master fund, is prohibited from investing more than 15% of its value in other funds.

16.44 In addition, a QIS' borrowings must not exceed 100% of NAV, and its total exposure relating to derivatives must not exceed its NAV.

16.45 As regards liquidity, the FCA rules do not specify any minimum dealing frequency for a QIS, only that the maximum period between dealing days will depend on the reasonable expectations of the target investor group and the particular investment objectives and policy of the fund.

NURS and QIS – Application of AIFMD

16.46 As NURS and QIS are AIFs, their management will be subject to the additional requirements of the AIFMD, unless their AIFM qualifies under the exemption for 'small' AIFMs.

16.47 Accordingly, NURS and QIS need to have an ACD/AFM that is regulated by the FCA either as a Full-scope UK AIFM or a Small authorised UK AIFM.

16.48 A Full-scope UK AIFM will, in addition to the FCA's rules for NURS or QIS, be subject to the UK's implementation of AIFMD, including as regards the appointment of a depositary, valuation, the use of leverage, delegation arrangements, the provision of information to investors, the contents of fund annual reports and regulatory reporting to the FCA.

16.49 By contrast, a Small authorised UK AIFM will generally be exempt from AIFMD requirements in managing the fund, except that the AIFM will be required to comply with part of the AIFMD requirements for regulatory reporting to the FCA (referred to as 'Annex IV' reporting).

16.50 To qualify as a Small authorised UK AIFM, the AIFM must meet one of the following thresholds in relation to the 'Total AUM' of the AIFs under management (where 'Total AUM' is calculated as the sum of the absolute values of each of the AIF's portfolio positions, with derivative positions converted into equivalent positions in the underlying):

- where Total AUM does not exceed €100 million, including assets acquired through leverage;
- where Total AUM does not exceed €500 million, but only where all AIFs managed by the AIFM are unleveraged and subject to a five-year lock up from initial investment.

16.51 Given the liquidity requirements of NURS and QIS, only the first €100 million threshold will be relevant.

16.52 Full-scope UK AIFMs will benefit from AIFMD passporting and may be marketed throughout the EEA to professional investors, and to retail investors where permitted in particular EEA states.

16.53 NURS and QIS managed by a Small authorised UK AIFM will not benefit from any passporting rights.

Legal Form of FCA Authorised Funds

16.54 All funds authorised by the FCA must have both an authorised fund manager (**AFM**) as its operator and a depositary and must take one of the following legal forms:

(1) corporate: The FCA's corporate fund structure is the Investment Company with Variable Capital (**ICVC**), sometimes known as an Open-Ended Investment Company (**OEIC**). The operator of an ICVC is its Authorised Corporate Director (**ACD**). The ACD is normally the only director of an ICVC, although further individual directors are permitted. An ICVC must have an ACD and may not be self-managed. An umbrella ICVC has segregated liability between its sub-funds.

(2) trust: The Authorised Unit Trust (**AUT**) is the oldest type of UK authorised fund. The depositary of an AUT serves as its Trustee and its appointed investment manager (referred to as its Manager) is the AFM.

(3) contractual: An ACS can be established either as:

- a Co-ownership Scheme, which is a new common contractual fund form established under FSMA;
- a Limited Partnership Scheme, which are limited partnerships registered under the Limited Partnerships Act 1907 (the '**1907 Act**'), but which may not be PFLPs (as defined in **16.65** below).

Unlike an ICVC or an AUT, ownership of units in an ACS is restricted to (i) persons who qualify as per se professional clients under MiFID (ie excluding 'elective' professional clients), (ii) large investors who invest at least £1 million and (iii) persons who already hold units in the ACS.

16.55 All fund types other than Limited Partnership Schemes may be established either as single schemes or as umbrella schemes with multiple sub-funds.

FCA Authorisation Process

16.56 The authorisation process is commenced by submission of an application form (different forms apply to an ICVC, AUT or ACS), together with the required supporting documents, including a draft prospectus and constitutional documents, and a filing fee. A certificate from a solicitor is required for the constitutional documents.

16.57 The filing fee will vary depending upon the type of fund and whether it will be an umbrella, and are currently as follows:

	single fund	umbrella
UCITS Scheme	£1,200	£2,400
NURS	£1,500	£3,000
QIS	£2,400	£4,800

16.58 The FCA's statutory time limits for determining a fund authorisation application depend upon the type of fund. For a NURS or QIS, the limit is six months of receipt of a complete application or 12 months from receipt of an incomplete application, and for a UCITS Scheme, two months of receipt. In practice, the FCA is often able to determine applications more quickly. Its informal targets are to process a NURS application within two months and a QIS application within one month.

Exchange Traded Funds

16.59 A UK domiciled ETF must be an ICVC authorised either as a UCITS Scheme or NURS. Most are listed on the Main Market of the London Stock Exchange.

16.60 Accordingly, the establishment of an ETF will involve three main applications:

- to the FCA for the authorisation of the ICVC (see **16.56** above);
- to the UKLA (which is part of the FCA) for admission to the Official List;
- to the London Stock Exchange (or other exchange) for admission to trading.

Non-FCA Authorised UK Funds

16.61 This category includes any UK open or closed-ended fund structure that is not authorised by the FCA.

16.62 Although the FCA does not authorise these funds, it will often nevertheless regulate them, directly or indirectly. For example, unregulated funds that are operated in the UK will need to have an FCA regulated AIFM, unless the fund falls within one of the available exemptions for group structures, family office funds, etc. Listed investment trusts will be regulated by the FCA both under AIFMD and in its role as the UKLA.

16.63 Subject to compliance with applicable requirements under the AIFMD, the listing rules and the fund's own constitutional documents, there are no specific investment restrictions or liquidity constraints on non-FCA authorised UK funds.

16.64 Similarly, there is no prescribed list of available non-FCA authorised UK fund structures, but the most common are limited partnerships and, for listed investment trusts, public limited companies (**PLCs**).

Limited Partnerships

16.65 Limited partnerships under the 1907 Act are used widely in the UK for private equity, venture capital and real estate funds and for family office structures. They must have at least one general partner and at least one limited partner, and must be registered under the 1907 Act in one of England and Wales, Scotland or Northern Ireland. An English limited partnership does not have independent legal personality distinct from that of its partners. A Scottish limited partnership does have legal personality distinct from that of its partners, and therefore can own assets in its own name, borrow money and grant security over those assets, enter into contracts on its own behalf, and sue and be sued as a separate legal entity.

16.66 As in most other jurisdictions, a general partner has unlimited liability for the debts or obligations of the limited partnership. The liability of a limited partner is limited to its capital contribution, however if it takes part in the management of the business of the limited partnership it is liable for all debts and obligations of the limited partnership (as if it were a general partner) incurred while doing so. Therefore the management responsibilities of the limited partnership are commonly retained by the general partner and delegated to an appropriately regulated management entity that is not liable on a statutory basis for the debts and obligations of the limited partnership.

16.67 The 1907 Act was amended on 6 April 2017 to introduce a new Private Fund Limited Partnership (**PFLP**) regime, which is an elective regime available for existing and new limited partnerships under the 1907 Act. A PFLP must be a collective investment scheme under FSMA (most conventional limited partnership investment vehicles should be collective investment schemes). The advantages of the PFLP regime include:

1. a safe harbour list of of non-exclusive activities that do not constitute taking part in the management of the limited partnership (which are common rights reserved for limited partner advisory committees in investment fund limited partnership agreements), such as participating in a decision to extend the life of a partnership, appointing a liquidator, and approving the partnership accounts or asset valuations;
2. limited partners in a PFLP are not required to make a capital contribution; and
3. reduced notification requirements on transfers of interests, and the nature and term of the partnership.

16.68 A person that manages a limited partnership in the UK that is an AIF is required to be regulated by the FCA either as a Full-scope UK AIFM or as a Small authorised UK AIFM (see **16.46** above).

Listed Investment Trusts

16.69 UK listed investment trusts, including real estate investment trusts (REITs) and venture capital trusts (VCTs), are listed closed-ended funds organised as PLCs the securities of which may be sold to the public in the UK. Most are listed on the London Stock Exchange's Main Market.

16.70 As closed-ended companies, they will not qualify as collective investment schemes and will not therefore be subject to the UK's UCIS promotion restriction (see **16.75** et seq below).

16.71 They will qualify as AIFs, and if managed in the UK will need to have an AIFM that is either as a Full-scope UK AIFM or as a Small authorised UK AIFM. Their initial offer will be subject to the AIFMD marketing restriction (see **16.75** et seq below), but the FCA takes the view that this restriction does not generally extend to secondary market trading.

16.72 The listing of a UK investment trust involves two main applications:

- to the UKLA for admission to the Official List, which will include approval of the prospectus (see **16.75** et seq below);
- to the London Stock Exchange (or other exchange) for admission to trading.

16.73 The FCA's Listing Rules require that the investment trust have a board of directors which is able to act independently of any investment manager appointed to manage its investments.

16.74 The London Stock Exchange's rules for Main Market listing include a 'free float' requirement that 25% of the shares be in public hands.

Marketing – AIFMD, the Unregulated CIS Promotion Restriction and the Approved Prospectus Requirement

16.75 There are three separate regulatory regimes that potentially can apply to the marketing/promotion of UK AIFs in the UK:

(1) The AIFMD marketing restriction: For a UK AIF managed by a Full-scope UK AIFM, the AIFM will need to give the FCA at least one month's advance notice of its management of the fund and will need to apply to the FCA for approval to market the fund in the UK, in a similar manner to an AIFMD marketing passport notification. For a UK AIF managed by a Small authorised UK AIFM or Small registered UK AIFM, the AIFM will only need to give the FCA at least one month's advance notice of its management of the fund.

(2) The unregulated collective investment scheme (UCIS) promotion restriction: For a UK AIF that is a collective investment scheme (other than an FCA authorised NURS or QIS), its promotion in the UK will be subject to FSMA's restriction on the promotion of UCIS by authorised firms, and can only be promoted to categories of persons exempted under either the Financial Services and Markets Act 2000 (Promotion of Collective Investment Schemes) (Exemptions) Order 2001 (the **PCIS Order**) or the rules in Section 4.12 of the FCA's Conduct of Business Sourcebook (**COBS 4.12**). Once the AIF is qualified for marketing under the AIFMD marketing restriction, its marketing to professional investors (defined to include professional clients under MiFID) will qualify for exemption under the UCIS promotion restriction. Marketing to retail investors will generally require an investor-specific analysis of the exemptions. A particular PCIS Order exemption for promotions to certain 'high net worth' businesses can be useful for smaller businesses not qualifying as professional clients and covers promotions to:

    - a corporation which (1) has called-up share capital or net assets of at least £5 million or (2) is a member of a group in which includes a company with called-up share capital or net assets of at least £5 million. However, where the corporation has more than 20 shareholders or it is a subsidiary of a company with more than 20 shareholders, the £5 million share capital/net assets requirement is reduced to £500,000;
    - a partnership or unincorporated association with net assets of at least £5 million;
    - a trust which has had gross assets (ie total assets held before deduction of any liabilities) of at least £10 million at any time within the year preceding the promotion.

For natural person retail investors, the exemptions in COBS 4.12 will tend to be more useful and include the following exempt categories:

- certified high net worth investors: This applies to an individual who has signed within the last 12 months a statement in a prescribed form to the effect that the individual had during previous year annual income of at least £100,000 or net assets of at least £250,000 (excluding the individual's primary residence and certain pension and insurance assets);
- self-certified sophisticated investors: This applies to an individual who has signed within the last 12 months a statement in a prescribed form to the effect that the individual has been a member of a network or syndicate of business angels for at least the last six months, has more than one investment in an unlisted company in the last two years, is working or has in the last two years worked in a professional capacity in the private equity sector or in the provision of finance for small and medium enterprises or is currently or has in the last two years been a director of a company with an annual turnover of at least £1 million;
- solicited advice: amongst other things, this requires that the individual has not previously received a financial promotion or any other communication from the firm (or from a person connected to the firm) which is intended to influence the client in relation to the fund.

Moreover, the FCA rules will require for the promotion of any UCIS to a retail investor that the firm's compliance officer make a record of the promotion, specifying the particular category of exemption being relied on.

(3) The approved prospectus requirement: For a UK AIF that is not a collective investment scheme – this will mainly comprise closed-ended investment companies, including listed investment trusts – it will either be necessary for any initial offer of securities to be on the basis of a prospectus approved by the UKLA or to comply with one of the exemptions in Part VI of FSMA, which implements the EU Prospectus Directive. These exemptions include:

- the offer is made to or directed only at 'qualified investors', which include professional clients and eligible counterparties as defined in MiFID;
- the offer is made to or directed at fewer than 150 persons other than qualified investors, per EEA State;
- the minimum investment in the fund's securities is at least €100,000;
- the fund's securities are denominated in amounts of at least €100,000.

SETTING UP A LOCAL MANAGEMENT COMPANY/INVESTMENT MANAGER

16.76 FCA authorised funds will require a UCITS management company (for a UCITS Scheme) or AIFM (for a NURS or QIS) that is either authorised by the

FCA with appropriate permissions or an appropriately regulated EEA firm which has exercised its passporting rights.

16.77 Authorisation as a UCITS management company may be combined with authorisation as a Full-scope UK AIFM, but neither a UCITS management company nor a Full-scope UK AIFM may also be authorised under MiFID. Notwithstanding this, both UCITS management companies and Full-scope UK AIFMs can be permitted to provide certain additional services within the scope of MiFID, including portfolio management.

16.78 MiFID investment firms may act as sub-manager to a UCITS management company or AIFM and they may also be permitted to act as a Small authorised UK AIFM.

16.79 The FCA permissions of a UK AIFM to an FCA authorised fund must include 'managing an authorised AIF', whereas the permissions to manage any other type of AIF, including an AIF authorised in another EEA member state, would include 'managing an unauthorised AIF'.

16.80 An FCA authorised firm must have its head office in the UK, which the FCA considers to be the location of its central management and control. FCA authorised firms are generally established either as UK private limited companies or limited liability partnerships.

16.81 An FCA authorisation application is made using an application pack tailored to the type of authorisation sought. The principal parts of this include:

(1) Checklist: This specifies the documents comprised in the application and requires certain undertakings as to the accuracy of the information provided.

(2) Sector supplements: One or more will be required depending upon the type of authorisation sought. In general, they request basic information covering the applicant's corporate structure, business details, information on financial resources, detailed information to describe the nature of business requiring authorisation, a list comprising the specific FCA permissions sought, information on the staff to be registered as approved persons and information on proposed compliance arrangements.

(3) IT Self-Assessment form: This requires very basic information on the firm's proposed use of IT systems with a view to determining whether more detailed IT forms are required.

(4) Fees and Levies Supplement: This requests certain estimates.

(5) Controllers Forms: One such form is required for each of the applicant's controllers. In general, the controllers will include, each parent company of the applicant and each person who owns 10% or more (or 20% in the case of a Full-scope UK AIFM) of the applicant or any of its parents. The forms request basic information on the controller and confirmation of various matters and events to assist the FCA in determining whether the controller is fit and proper.

(6) Individual Registration Forms (Form A): One such form is required for each of the applicant's proposed approved persons. They request basic information on the individual and his background and experience, including his employment history, and confirmation of various matters and events to assist the FCA in determining whether the individual is fit and proper.

16.82 These forms are submitted to the FCA together with a variety of supporting documentation, such as a compliance monitoring programme, group and internal management structure charts, capital resources projections, evidence of capitalisation, etc. Other documents will need to be prepared and be ready to be inspected by the FCA on request, but would not need to be attached to the application, including in particular compliance procedures.

16.83 The FCA's filing fee would currently be £5,000 for an application to be a Full-scope UK AIFM, UCITS management company or MiFID investment firm.

16.84 The FCA's statutory time limit for processing the application of a Full-scope UK AIFM is three months plus a further three months if the FCA considers it necessary due to the specific circumstances of the application and notifies the applicant accordingly. For other applications, the FCA's statutory time limit is six months from receipt of a complete application or 12 months from receipt of an incomplete application.

OTHER KEY SERVICE PROVIDERS

16.85 A wide range of fund service providers operate in the UK.

16.86 For FCA authorised funds, there are a number of providers prepared to act as a UCITS management company or Full-scope UK AIFM to an FCA authorised fund and to delegate investment management to their client investment manager.

16.87 FCA authorised funds require the appointment of an appropriately authorised and regulated depositary. They do not require the appointment of an administrator or a transfer agent, but many funds do so.

16.88 Because ICVCs may not be self-managed, the focus of the FCA rules is on the appointment of the ACD. There is no requirement for an ICVC to appoint any individual directors and the vast majority of ICVCs do not do so.

TAX REGIME

Taxation of UK Funds – General

16.89 A common criticism of the UK tax regime for UK funds is that it is overly complex, particularly when compared to the simpler regimes in place in other popular fund jurisdictions such as Ireland and Luxembourg. While it is true that the UK regime is relatively complex, particularly in not offering outright tax exemptions, the net effect is generally competitive due to the ability to deduct management expenses in determining taxable profits and the UK's wide tax treaty network. As such, while the UK tax regime can act as a disincentive to establishing a UK fund, this is frequently due to a lack of familiarity with the UK rules and additional administrative complexity rather than increased overall tax leakage.

OEICs (a/k/a ICVCs)

Income

16.90 OEICs are generally subject to corporation tax on income at the basic rate of 20%. Special rules apply to OEICs that have more than 60% of their investments (by market value) in qualifying investments. Qualifying investments are, broadly, interest bearing assets such as debt instruments, cash and cash equivalents. Such OEICs are typically referred to as 'bond funds'".

16.91 Bond funds are subject to corporation tax on income received (in effect, interest) but are entitled to a corresponding tax deduction when that income is distributed to investors by way of interest distribution. The net effect is that bond funds are typically not subject to tax on interest income.

16.92 OEICs generally benefit from the UK dividend exemption meaning that they are not subject to corporation tax on dividends received (whether UK or non-UK dividends).

Gains

16.93 OEICs are exempt from tax on chargeable gains provided that the gains do not represent profit on trading transactions. Provided an OEIC meets a genuine diversity of ownership test, most (if not all) typical transactions carried out by an OEIC will be treated as non-trading transactions, such that an OEIC usually pays no tax on gains realised on disposals of underlying assets.

Double Tax Treaties

16.94 Because they are taxable at the basic rate of income tax, OEICs are 'subject to tax' for double tax treaty purposes. As such, unlike many non-taxable funds established outside the UK, they can benefit from the UK's extensive network of double tax treaties which can help reduce withholding taxes in other jurisdictions and assist in claiming credit for foreign taxes incurred on foreign sources of income. However, see the section below regarding the availability of double tax relief for dividend income in relation to OEICs which have elected for Tax Elected Fund (**TEF**) status.

Taxation of UK Investors on Distributions from an OEIC

16.95 OEICs may make dividend distributions or interest distributions. Interest distributions can only be made by a bond fund.

Interest Distributions

16.96 Interest distributions from an OEIC bond fund are treated and taxed like yearly interest, meaning they are subject to income tax for individual investors and corporation tax for corporate investors. Bond funds are required to withhold tax at 20% from interest distributions unless an exemption applies. For example, interest distributions may be paid free of withholding tax to UK companies and non-residents.

16.97 Interest distributions paid to UK resident individuals will be subject to 20% withholding tax. Higher and additional rate income taxpayers must account for additional tax through their self-assessment returns.

Dividend Distributions

16.98 Dividend distributions from an OEIC are taxed like dividends from a UK company. UK resident individuals currently benefit from a £5,000 tax-free dividend allowance, though that is expected to reduce in forthcoming legislation (possibly to £2,000). Any excess over such allowance will be subject to income tax at 7.5% (for basic rate taxpayers), 32.5% (for higher rate taxpayers) or 38.1% (for additional rate taxpayers). Any additional tax must be paid through the investor's self-assessment tax return.

Application to Equity Funds, Debt Funds, Property Funds and Mixed Funds

Debt Funds

16.99 An OEIC which invests solely in debt instruments will be a bond fund. As a bond fund, it should suffer no material corporation tax since its interest income will be distributed to investors as tax deductible interest distributions and any gains should be exempt. Investors in an OEIC bond fund will receive interest distributions which will be taxed as yearly interest.

Equity Funds

16.100 An OEIC which invests solely in equities should suffer no material corporation tax since its dividend income should benefit from the dividend tax exemptions and any gains should be exempt. Investors in an OEIC equity fund will receive dividend distributions which will be taxed as dividends.

Property Funds

16.101 An OEIC which invests directly in real estate will suffer corporation tax at 20% on any property income received, after deducting any allowable management expenses incurred by the fund. Any gains should be tax exempt. Investors in an OEIC property fund will receive dividend distributions which will be taxed as dividends.

16.102 Any corporation tax paid by the OEIC is not creditable for investors. The Property Authorised Investment Fund (**PAIF**) regime exists to counter this tax leakage. A PAIF is a special kind of OEIC which achieves tax neutrality at the fund level by moving the point of taxation on property income from the OEIC to its investors.

Mixed Funds and TEFs

16.103 An OEIC which invests in a mix of equity and debt instruments but is not a bond fund will be subject to corporation tax at 20% on its interest income, after deducting any allowable management expenses incurred by the fund. Whether any corporation tax will be payable therefore depends on the level of interest income and deductible management expenses. A mixed fund will not be subject to tax on its dividend income or capital gains. Investors in such a fund will receive dividend distributions which will be taxed as dividends.

16.104 Any corporation tax paid by an OEIC is not creditable for investors. The Tax Elected Fund (**TEF**) regime exists to counter this tax leakage. A TEF is an OEIC which has elected to participate in a special tax regime, the effect of which is to exempt the OEIC from tax on specified categories of income and to tax investors as if they held the underlying assets of the TEF directly. It achieves this in a broadly similar way to a bond fund, by paying tax deductible interest distributions in respect of interest income (though without the need to satisfy the more than 60% qualifying investments test).

16.105 The position is complicated in the case of a mixed fund which also invests directly in real estate. Such a fund would be subject to corporation tax at 20% on its interest income and property business income, after deducting allowable management expenses. However, since TEFs are not permitted to generate property business income, such a fund cannot elect to be a TEF. A TEF which generates property business income will be excluded from the TEF regime by HM Revenue and Customs (**HMRC**).

16.106 TEFs are not subject to tax on dividends for the purposes of double tax treaties. As such, in respect of the small number of tax treaties which require the claimant to be 'subject to tax', a TEF may not be able to claim treaty relief in respect of any withholding applied to dividends.

Investment Trusts

16.107 Like OEICs, investment trusts are subject to tax on income but exempt from tax on capital gains. Investment trusts can elect to stream interest income, the effect of which is to move the tax point on interest from the investment trust to its investors, and should also generally be exempt from tax on dividends. Unlike OEICs, investment trusts can stream interest income even if they do not qualify as bond funds. As a result, for a fund following a bond fund strategy, an investment trust and an OEIC should be largely tax neutral. For a fund which does not follow a bond fund strategy, an investment trust could potentially offer a tax advantage as a result of its ability to stream interest income (though the degree of advantage will depend on the level of deductible management expenses in the fund).

ACS

16.108 An ACS (whether established as a co-ownership or limited partnership scheme) is transparent for income tax purposes. This means no tax should be incurred at the level of the fund.

16.109 Unlike a limited partnership ACS, a co-ownership ACS is not transparent for capital gains tax purposes. Consequently, investors in a co-ownership ACS can 'roll-up' underlying capital gains and only pay tax upon the ultimate disposal of their interests in the ACS. In contrast, investors in a limited partnership ACS will be subject to tax in respect of any gains arising on underlying disposals.

16.110 As a transparent vehicle is not subject to tax, an ACS should also be attractive for other investors investing directly into the relevant fund. It should allow certain such investors (such as pension funds) to benefit from any more favourable double tax treaty rates available to such investors. It would, however, involve an additional layer of tax treaty administration in that fund and investors would be required to submit their own applications for treaty relief in respect of any withholding suffered on the fund's underlying investments.

Limited Partnerships

16.111 A UK limited partnership (whether registered in England and Wales, Scotland or Northern Ireland) is transparent for UK tax purposes and therefore no tax should be incurred at the level of the partnership. Partners in the partnership would generally be treated as receiving their share of the profits that are recognised or distributed by the limited partnership or that are allocated to them under the limited partnership agreement and their tax liabilities would depend on their own particular circumstances.

Scottish Limited Partnership

16.112 Despite its separate legal personality, a Scottish limited partnership is transparent for UK tax purposes in the same way as an English limited partnership as set out above, and is not subject to taxation itself (unlike a company).

Private Fund Limited Partnership

16.113 The tax treatment of the new PFLP (see **16.65** et seq above) is no different to any other UK limited partnership.

LOCAL STOCK EXCHANGE

16.114 UK listed investment funds include ETFs (see **16.51** above) and listed investment trusts (see **16.69** et seq above).

CONFIDENTIALITY LAWS

16.115 For an FCA authorised fund, the register of unitholders of is required to be kept at an address in the UK and made available for inspection by other unitholders. An ICVC must also make directors' service contracts also available for inspection, which will generally mean the ACD's contract of appointment.

16.116 UK listed investment trusts will be established as PLCs and will be subject to inspection rights, including inspection of the register and of directors' service contracts.

ANTI-MONEY LAUNDERING LAWS

16.117 In June 2017, the UK implemented the EU Fourth Money Laundering Directive in The Money Laundering, Terrorist Financing and Transfer of Funds (Information on the Payer) Regulations 2017 (the **Money Laundering Regulations**). The UK is also a member of the Financial Action Task Force (**FATF**).

16.118 The Money Laundering Regulations include requirements for customer due diligence on persons with whom an FCA authorised firm proposes to establish a business relationship. In general, this will include identification of the customer, of any individuals who beneficially own 25% or more of the customer, the source of funds and information on the purpose of the transaction. Enhanced due diligence is required in certain circumstances, including where the customer is a politically exposed person (**PEP**).

16.119 The application of these requirements can be complex, and the UK financial services industry benefits from a set of detailed 'Guidance for the UK Financial Sector' on the Money Laundering Regulations published by the Joint Money Laundering Steering Group.

CONCLUDING REMARKS: WHAT ARE THE JURISDICTION'S UNIQUE SELLING POINTS?

16.120 The UK is one of the leading countries in the world for managers and investment advisers of private funds, largely due to London's position as one of the global capital markets and financial services hubs, its historically benign taxation regime for investment managers, access to Europe, and time zone. It retains deep pools of fund investment talent and professional services providers including accountants, lawyers, corporate finance advisers, placement agents and administrators.

16.121 The UK limited partnership has been widely used as a fund vehicle by UK and non-UK fund sponsors of private funds, and has been the base structure that has been replicated by other jurisdictions' unregulated fund vehicles. However, the increasing sophistication of other jurisdictions' regulators and private funds regimes, their more benign tax regimes, and Brexit have resulted in fewer funds being established in the UK and an outflow to other European countries (particularly Ireland and Luxembourg), though the fund adviser or manager may remain in the UK.

16.122 From a regulatory perspective, other than regulated retail funds such as UCITS Schemes and NURS targeted at a domestic UK investor base, the establishment of UK funds has been discouraged by the restricted scope of the FCA authorised fund structures available, the limited scope of non-FCA authorised fund structures able to access favourable fund level taxation regimes, the permissive rules for marketing non-UK based retail and private fund structures in the UK, and the development of management and administration operations by UK-based service providers in other countries, including Ireland and Luxembourg.

16.123 Brexit presents the UK with an opportunity to reverse this trend. There are some early signs from the UK government and regulators of a growing awareness of the importance of a competitive regulatory, legal and taxation regime for investment funds, their management entities and investment professionals.

CHAPTER 17

THE UNITED STATES OF AMERICA — DELAWARE

GENERAL DESCRIPTION OF THE JURISDICTION

17.01 The United States of America (US) is a federal republic in which power is divided between a central governing authority and the individual states. Federal and state law comprise both common law and statutory law. The system of law in the US results in investment advisers and investment funds being subject to both federal and state law. Federal law predominates in the areas of securities regulation and tax, while state law governs advisers and funds as business organisations (whether corporations, partnerships, limited partnerships (LPs), limited liability partnerships (LLPs), limited liability companies (LLCs), etc).

17.02 Among US states, Delaware is preferred as a state of incorporation because of the extensiveness, stability and relative predictability of its corporate law. Accordingly, information about Delaware and its laws is provided below, where state-specific information is relevant to the discussion.

17.03 The state of Delaware is located on the eastern seaboard of the US, and Dover is the state's capital and financial centre. Its time zone is GMT minus five hours. The principal language used throughout the US, including Delaware, is English. The currency is the US dollar; there are no exchange controls.

The US benefits from Organisation for Economic Cooperation and Development (**OECD**) membership, which may have marketing advantages, and it is one of the G7 countries (the most industrialised countries in the world).

KEY MANDATORY REQUIREMENTS

Federal requirements

17.04

- Investment advisers offering services in the US are generally required to register as an investment adviser with the US Securities and Exchange Commission (SEC), unless specifically excluded or exempted by the Advisers Act.
- US funds that offer securities publicly in the US must register with the SEC.

- Unregistered US funds offering securities in the US must do so on a private basis.
- To avoid the adverse tax consequences of being classified as a publicly-traded partnership, unregistered US funds should: (i) limit investors to 100; (ii) ensure that at least 90% of the fund's annual gross income consists of passive investment-type income; or (iii) restrict liquidity to avoid risk of providing investors with the substantial equivalent of a secondary market (eg, a closed-end fund).
- Unregistered US funds that are established as LPs or LLCs must file annual information returns with the US Internal Revenue Service, together with a Schedule K-1 for each investor.
- The acceptance of subscription monies from prospective investors into a fund is subject to 'know your client' regulations.

Delaware requirements

17.05

- A fund and/or adviser organised as an LLC must file a certificate of formation with the Delaware Secretary of State.
- A fund and/or adviser organised as an LP must file a certificate of limited partnership with the Delaware Secretary of State.
- If organised as an LLC or LP, a fund and/or adviser must have a registered agent and a registered office within Delaware.

SETTING UP A FUND

17.06 The Investment Company Act requires 'investment companies' to register with the SEC and regulates their activities. Certain funds are excluded from the definition of 'investment company'. For example, Section 3(c)(1) of the Investment Company Act generally excludes funds that are: (i) not publicly offered; and (ii) owned by 100 or fewer US persons. In addition, Section 3(c)(7) of the Investment Company Act generally excludes funds that are: (i) not publicly offered; and (ii) owned exclusively by 'qualified purchasers' (eg, natural persons with US$5 million or more in investments or entities with US$25 million or more in investments). The foregoing calculations exclude certain employees and affiliates of the adviser. These 'private' funds do not have to register with the SEC and are exempt from almost all Investment Company Act provisions. Accordingly, private funds established in the US may make good hedge fund and other alternative fund vehicles.

17.07 The discussion below generally applies only to funds that are not required to register under the Investment Company Act pursuant to Section 3(c)(1) or 3(c)(7) thereunder.

Organisation

17.08 Generally, the discussion about Delaware LLCs and/or LPs under this section, applies equally to investment funds as well as investment advisers. In addition, when considering organising a fund as a Delaware LLC or LP, it should be noted that:

- overall, the time it takes to set up a fund in Delaware generally is comparable to the time taken to do so in other jurisdictions; and
- umbrella funds, open-ended funds, closed-ended funds, multi-class funds and funds of funds are among the fund structures permitted.

Marketing fund interests

17.09 Private funds organised as LPs and LLCs under US state law generally are marketed only to US investors because non-US investors in such funds may be subject to unfavourable US tax laws. In addition, the offer or sale of private fund interests must not involve a public offering to avoid registration requirements under US federal securities laws.

17.10 Private placements of fund interests to US investors generally are made in accordance with the exemption from registration pursuant to Section 4(a)(2) of the US Securities Act of 1933, as amended (Securities Act) and Rule 506 of Regulation D thereunder. Section 4(a)(2) of the Securities Act exempts from registration under the Securities Act any offer or sale of a security by an issuer that does not involve a public offering. The SEC has adopted Rule 506 of Regulation D as a 'safe harbour' under Section 4(a)(2) of the Securities Act. This means that an offering made in accordance with the provisions of Rule 506 is deemed to have complied with Section 4(a)(2). Specifically, Rule 506(b) generally provides that an offering is deemed to comply with Section 4(a)(2) if (i) sales are made only to 'accredited investors'; (ii) there is no general solicitation or advertising involved with the offering; and (iii) the accredited investors buy the securities for investment and not for resale. Rule 506(b) also permits sales of securities to up to 35 sophisticated, but non-accredited investors, subject to heightened disclosure standards. Under Rule 506(c), there is no restriction on general solicitation and general advertising, provided the issuer takes reasonable steps to verify that all purchasers are accredited investors based on the particular fact and circumstances of the offering (eg, verification of income or net worth through additional due diligence requests). The foregoing safe harbours are non-exclusive.

17.11 Additionally, any private placement relying on Rule 506 will be disqualified to the extent it involves the participation of certain 'felons' and other 'bad actors'. Such covered persons include the investment manager of the issuer, certain of its affiliates and any 20% beneficial owner of the issuer's outstanding voting equity securities.

INVESTMENT RESTRICTIONS

17.12 The Investment Company Act imposes certain limits on the amount of shares that a private fund can purchase from, and sell to, an SEC-registered fund (eg, Section 12(d)(1)(A) of the Investment Company Act imposes a 3% ownership cap on the outstanding voting shares of an SEC-registered fund).

17.13 In addition, a fund that purchases 'new issues' securities or engages in exchange-traded futures or options on futures transactions as well as most transactions in the over the counter market is subject to the following rules and regulations. Participation in the profits and losses of investments in 'new issues' securities is subject to significant restrictions under rules of the US Financial Industry Regulatory Authority (**FINRA**). 'New issues' are, generally, equity securities that are part of an initial public offering (sometimes referred to as IPOs). Rule 5130 imposes restrictions on the purchase of new issues by broker-dealers, employees of broker-dealers, portfolio managers and certain other people, as well as accounts (such as private funds) in which such 'restricted persons' invest. Rule 5131 supplements Rule 5130 by generally prohibiting quid pro quo allocation and 'spinning' of new issues to favoured customers, such as certain executive officers and directors of potential investment banking clients, in exchange for investment banking business. Although the new issues rules only apply to FINRA member firms, it affects private funds and managers when FINRA members ask for representations and additional information regarding a private fund and its investors in order to ensure compliance with such rules. Generally, a private fund's application form contains a questionnaire designed for this purpose. Certain exemptions and exceptions are available that permit the allocation of new issues to persons otherwise restricted under the new issues rules.

17.14 Under the US Commodity Exchange Act of 1936 (**CEA**), and rules and regulations of the US Commodity Futures Trading Commission (**CFTC**), an investment fund is considered to be a 'commodity pool' subject to CFTC regulation if the fund transacts in commodity interests (ie, futures contracts or options on futures contracts or commodities and most types of OTC derivatives) to any extent. Thus, unless an exemption is available, prior to engaging in such transactions the operator or marketer of a commodity pool must register as a commodity pool operator (**CPO**), and one who manages a fund that trades in futures or who gives advice about futures trading must register as a commodity trading advisor (**CTA**).

17.15 A commonly used exemption from CPO registration that many fund operators rely on is found under CFTC Rule 4.13(a)(3) (the de minimis activity exemption), which is based upon a requirement, among other things, that the commodity pool engage in transactions in commodity interests only to a very limited extent (eg, solely for occasional hedging purposes) and does not market the commodity pool as a commodity fund. A CPO that is unable to qualify for an exemption from registration must (among other things): (i) register with the CFTC through the US National Futures Association (**NFA**); (ii) become a member of the NFA; (iii) include specified disclosures (including but not limited to risks, conflicts, fees and costs, and performance) in its pool offering documentation; (iv) comply with certain advertising and promotional material requirements; (v) distribute periodic account statements and reports; (vi) distribute audited annual financial reports; (vii) implement prescribed policies and procedures; and (viii) maintain and make accessible prescribed books and records. Registered CPOs can seek some relief from the disclosure, reporting and recordkeeping requirements by applying for an exemption under CFTC Rule 4.7.

17.16 A commonly used exemption from CTA registration is found under CFTC Rule 4.14(a)(10), which exempts persons who, during the preceding 12 months, have not furnished commodity trading advice to more than 15 'persons' and who do not hold themselves out generally to the public as a CTA. The CTA registration exemption permits non-US CTAs to exclude its non-US clients for purposes of the foregoing calculation.

OTHER KEY SERVICE PROVIDERS

17.17 There is a wide array of service providers, including administrators, attorneys, auditors and banks. Generally, there are no specific requirements regarding a fund's arrangements with its service providers (but see 'Custody requirements' below). However, as noted above, an LLC/LP is required to have a registered agent within Delaware.

TAX REGIME

17.18 Investment companies maintaining and managing intangible investments, and collecting and distributing income from such investments or from tangible property outside Delaware, are exempt from Delaware corporate income tax.

17.19 Investment companies that are not registered under the Investment Company Act typically are organised to be classified as partnerships for US federal income tax purposes. US law currently provides a largely elective regime for determining partnership status. Nonetheless, investment companies classified as partnerships must be structured to avoid 'publicly-traded partnership' status, which would cause them to be taxable as corporations. The primary methods of avoiding publicly-traded partnership status are:

- limiting the number of investors to 100;
- assuring that at least 90% of the partnership's annual gross income consists of passive investment-type income; or
- limiting liquidity (through transfer and withdrawal restrictions) so as to avoid creating the substantial equivalent of a secondary market.

17.20 With partnership classification, an investment company is not itself subject to US taxes; rather, its partners or other beneficial owners individually take into account their allocable share of the company's items of income, gains, losses, deductions and tax credits, whether or not distributed. Thus, the character of the income earned by the company (for example, ordinary income or capital gains) passes through to the beneficial owners. This is beneficial to both US and non-US investors, to the extent that the company generates capital gains. Long-term capital gains are taxable to non-corporate US investors at favourable rates relative to ordinary income and short-term capital gains. Non-US investors escape US tax with respect to capital gains (both long- and short-term), unless the gains are effectively connected with a US trade or business, as described below.

17.21 Non-registered investment companies that seek to attract non-US investors generally attempt to avoid being deemed to be engaged in a trade or business within the US. US trade or business status would cause all of a non-US investor's share of the company's earnings that are effectively connected with the US trade or business (including capital gains) to be taxable at the rates applicable to US investors. The company would withhold tax from such earnings on a quarterly basis. Such withheld taxes would be credited against the non-US investor's US federal income tax liability. Non-US corporate taxpayers also would be subject to a 30% branch profits tax. In addition, non-US investors would be required to report their earnings on US income tax returns.

17.22 Non-registered investment companies generally can avoid US trade or business status by complying with a safe harbour that limits the activities of such entities to trading in stocks and securities, certain commodities and related derivative instruments for their own account. Non-US investors will then only be taxable in the US on their share of US source dividends and certain limited types of US source interest income. This tax is generally withheld at source by the company at a rate of 30%. Thus, a company that generates non-US source income, capital gains or interest income generally is much more attractive to non-US investors than one that generates US-source dividend income, as the former generally is a US tax-free vehicle for non-US investors. Regardless of whether a non-registered US investment company is engaged in a US trade or business, it must file annual information returns with the US Internal Revenue Service, together with, for each investor (whether US or non-US), a Schedule K-1 that reports tax and financial data for that investor. In addition, each investor (whether US or non-US) must obtain and provide the company with a US taxpayer identification number.

17.23 Income tax treaties between the US and various countries may improve the tax treatment described above. For example, many such treaties reduce the withholding tax rate on US-source dividends to 15% and exempt interest income from the tax. Also, with respect to a company that is engaged in a US trade or business, permanent establishment clauses may limit the scope of taxable effectively connected income, as well as reduce or eliminate the branch profits tax.

ERISA

17.24 The Employee Retirement Income Security Act of 1974 (**ERISA**) is the comprehensive US statute that governs the operation and administration of most private US pension and welfare benefit plans. ERISA imposes special (and often materially onerous) duties on, and prohibits certain transactions by, persons who are defined to be 'fiduciaries' with respect to such plans.

17.25 Whether an investment adviser is managing 'plan assets' when it is managing a pooled investment vehicle depends on whether assets of that pooled fund are deemed to include 'plan assets.' A US Department of Labor regulation provides that when ERISA plans invest in a pooled fund, that fund's assets will not be deemed to include plan assets if underlying investors subject to ERISA do not own 25% or more of the value of any class of equity interests in the fund.

CONFIDENTIALITY LAWS

17.26 Interest holders or management of a Delaware LLC/LP is generally confidential. A Delaware LLC/LP is not required to disclose its members or limited partners, respectively, to the public.

ANTI-MONEY LAUNDERING LAWS

17.27 The US has anti-money laundering laws. Historically, the US has been an active participant in the Financial Action Task Force (**FATF**). Overall, the US anti-money laundering system meets the FATF 40 Recommendations in most respects. New regulations have been, and continue to be, proposed and adopted.

OTHER FILINGS AND FILING FEES

State law

17.28 Many US states require notice filings and fees when securities are offered within their borders. Most of these are one-time fees, paid when the securities are first sold within each state; a few, however, are annual fees. To the extent the fund and/or adviser conducts business in a US state that is different from its state of organisation, it may be required to separately qualify to do business in such state by making the necessary filings and payments.

Federal law

17.29 All funds making an offering of securities in reliance on an exemption under Regulation D must file a notice with the SEC on Form D, but there is no federal filing fee.

STOCK EXCHANGE

17.30 There is no local stock exchange. The US stock exchanges have various financial, corporate governance and other requirements for listing securities that generally preclude the listing of private fund interests.

SETTING UP A LOCAL MANAGEMENT COMPANY/INVESTMENT MANAGER

17.31 As discussed more fully below, any person (or entity) who is engaged in the business of providing advice regarding securities to US clients for compensation generally must register with the SEC as an investment adviser. A non-US person (or entity) may register with the SEC as an investment adviser. It is not necessary to organise a US entity to do so, although there may be business or tax reasons for taking that approach.

Organisation

17.32 An investment adviser may be organised under Delaware law as, inter alia, a corporation, a partnership, an LP, an LLP or an LLC. Advisers to private funds typically are organised as LPs or LLCs for, among other reasons, the attractive treatment of such entities under US tax law. For purposes of the following discussion, we assume that the adviser elects to organise as an LLC.

Competitive advantages

17.33 An LLC can be viewed as a partnership whose partners have limited liability. LLCs have all of the best features of partnerships with none of their rigidity. As with a partnership, the relationships among the LLC 'members' and among the members and the company, are determined by an agreement. In an LLC, that agreement typically is called an 'operating agreement'. The Delaware Limited Liability Company Act (Delaware LLC Act) is considered to be the most modern and flexible in the US; it places almost no restrictions on the creativity of business persons and attorneys in drafting operating agreements. Although an operating agreement may be either written or oral, it is not advisable to have an oral operating agreement. If no operating agreement is adopted, the Delaware LLC Act serves as the default agreement.

17.34 An LLC generally is managed by some or all of its members, although it may be managed by a third party appointed by the LLC. Each person who manages the LLC is called a managing member (or a non-member manager, as applicable). Managing members are similar to directors and officers of corporations and may have titles such as president, vice president, etc.

Establishing and maintaining an LLC

17.35 Establishing an LLC is a quick and straightforward process. An LLC may be established under Delaware law by preparing and filing the proper documents with the Secretary of State. The documentation is simple and brief, and approval from the Delaware Secretary of State can be received in as little as one or two hours. Delaware LLCs generally must have a registered agent and a registered office in the state. There is no minimum authorised or share capital for an LLC.

17.36 An LLC is managed by its managing members in accordance with the provisions of its operating agreement. There are no specific requirements under Delaware law with respect to meetings of the managing members of a Delaware LLC. Therefore, managing members of a Delaware LLC may meet within or outside Delaware. A Delaware LLC is not required to hold an annual members' meeting and, in fact, an operating agreement may provide that any member or class or group of members has no voting rights.

FEES

17.37 The filing' fee for a Delaware LLC ranges from US$50 for a standard 24-hour filing, to US$1,000 if one-hour expedited processing is requested.

ACCOUNTS/AUDITS REQUIREMENTS

17.38 LLCs generally do not have to make accounts available to the public and there are no legal requirements on accounting dates or the length of accounting periods. There is no requirement that a Delaware LLC must have an annual audit or appoint an auditor, although there may be business or regulatory reasons for doing so.

Supervision

17.39 The federal supervisory authority is the SEC, a member of the International Organisation of Securities Commissions. In Delaware, the state supervisory authority is the Delaware Securities Division.

17.40 In addition, the SEC has exclusive regulatory jurisdiction over advisers whose principal place of business is in a country outside the US. Advisers who do not meet the federal eligibility requirements generally must register at the state level. Even SEC-registered advisers, however, generally must satisfy certain state notice filing and fee requirements.

Registration

Federal Level

17.41 The SEC regulates investment advisers pursuant to the Investment Advisers Act of 1940, as amended (**Advisers Act**) and the rules thereunder. The Advisers Act defines the term 'investment adviser' generally to include any person (or entity) who for compensation is engaged in the business of providing advice to others or issuing reports or analyses regarding securities. In general, investment advisers with discretionary authority over at least US$100 million in regulatory assets under management (**RAUM**) must register under the Advisers Act, unless specifically excluded or exempted, or subject to primary regulation by state authorities.

17.42 An adviser who must register with the SEC must submit its application electronically through the Investment Advisers Registration Depository (**IARD**) using Form ADV. The IARD permits investment advisers to satisfy their filing obligations under state and federal law with a single electronic filing made over the Internet. Form ADV has two parts: Part 1 discloses specific information about a registered investment adviser that is important to regulators, such as its name, the number of employees, the form of the organisation and the nature of the business; Part 2 requires the creation of a narrative brochure, which acts as a disclosure document for clients of the business and includes information, such as services provided, fees levied, and whether the investment adviser acts as a broker-dealer. The Advisers Act provides that, within 45 days after a person files an application for registration with the SEC, the SEC must either grant registration or institute a proceeding to determine whether registration should be denied.

17.43 Three of the more common exemptions from registration used by investment advisers are (i) the foreign private adviser exemption, (ii) the private fund adviser exemption and (iii) the relying adviser exemption.

17.44 A foreign private adviser is any investment adviser that:

- has no place of business in the US;
- has, in total, fewer than 15 US clients and investors in the US in private funds advised by the investment adviser;
- has aggregate RAUM attributable to (i) clients in the US (including US-domiciled private funds) and (ii) US investors in private funds advised by the adviser of less than $25 million; and
- neither (i) holds itself out generally to the public in the US as an investment adviser nor (ii) advises registered investment companies or registered business development companies.

17.45 A private fund adviser is any investment adviser that solely advises private funds with less than $150 million in aggregate RAUM. Generally, a non-US adviser only needs to include assets managed at a place of business in the US for purposes of the foregoing calculation. An adviser relying on the 'private fund adviser exemption' is also referred to as an 'exempt reporting adviser' (**ERAs**).

ERAs are required to submit to the SEC, and update at least annually, certain (but not all) reports on Part 1 of Form ADV. Although exempt from registration, ERAs are still subject to ongoing compliance obligations, such as the anti-fraud provisions of the Advisers Act, supervisory requirements to prevent violations of securities laws, and the SEC's 'pay to play' rules. While the SEC has indicated that it does not anticipate that it will conduct compliance examinations of exempt reporting advisers regularly, it has the authority to do so and may examine the records of exempt reporting advisers.

17.46 The 'relying adviser exemption' permits umbrella registration if a group of related advisers is operating a single advisory business where each of the relying advisers is controlled by or under common control with the filing adviser, provided:

- all advisers advise only private funds and separately managed accounts for qualified clients who are eligible to invest in those private funds, and whose accounts pursue substantially similar investment objectives and strategies as those private funds;
- the principal office and place of business of the filing adviser is in the US;
- each relying adviser, its employees and those acting on the relying adviser's behalf are 'persons associated with' the filing adviser, and thus under the supervision and control of the filing adviser;
- the relying advisers' advisory activities are governed by the Advisers Act and relying advisers are subject to examination by the SEC; and
- all advisers operate under a single code of ethics, single set of written policies and procedures, and have the same CCO.

State Level

17.47 A US-based investment adviser that is not federally registered with the SEC generally must register with the state in which it is conducting its business, unless otherwise exempted at the state level. In fact, investment advisers with less than US$25 million in RAUM are prohibited from registration with the SEC, and investment advisers with between US$25 million and US$100 million in RAUM generally must first look to register with the state in which it has its principal office and place of business (excluding New York).

17.48 Each individual state generally provides for statutory exemptions or exclusions from registration as an investment adviser. For example, the relevant New York statutes exclude from the definition of 'investment adviser' any investment adviser with under six New York clients.

Form PF

17.49 Certain registered investment advisers may also be required to file Form PF with the SEC in order to provide the Financial Stability Oversight Council with information necessary to monitor the systemic risk created by private funds and determine whether particular entities should be designated as significant financial institutions.

Regulation

17.50 This is a brief summary of some of the more important provisions of US federal investment adviser regulation that are applicable to SEC-registered advisers. In some instances, these regulations also apply to advisers excluded from the definition of 'investment adviser' or otherwise are exempt from SEC registration.

Anti-fraud provisions

17.51 Section 206 of the Advisers Act prohibits misstatements or misleading omissions of material facts and other fraudulent acts and practices in connection with the conduct of an investment advisory business. As a fiduciary, an adviser owes its clients its undivided loyalty and may not engage in activity that conflicts with a client's interests without the client's consent. Advisers have an affirmative obligation of utmost good faith and full and fair disclosure of all material facts to its clients, as well as a duty to avoid misleading them. Both registered and unregistered investment advisers to pooled investment vehicles, including private funds, are prohibited from making false or misleading statements or otherwise defrauding investors or prospective investors in those pooled investment vehicles.

Disclosure obligations

17.52 Advisers generally are required to deliver to each prospective advisory client a written disclosure statement or 'brochure' as required by Part 2 of the Form ADV describing the adviser's business practices and educational and business background. Advisers that have custody of client funds or securities also must disclose to clients any financial conditions that may impair the adviser's ability to meet its contractual commitments to clients. Advisers that exercise investment discretion over large amounts of assets may also be required to make periodic filings with the SEC regarding the holdings that it manages.

Performance fees

17.53 The Advisers Act generally prohibits advisers from receiving any type of advisory fee calculated as a percentage of capital gains or appreciation in the client's account (a performance fee). The Advisers Act contains exceptions from this prohibition for investment advisory contracts with, among others: (i) clients that are not US residents; and (ii) private investment funds that rely on the exemption from registration as an investment company provided by Section 3(c)(7) of the US Investment Company Act of 1940, as amended (Investment

Company Act). (For a further discussion of Section 3(c)(7) funds, see **17.06** above.)

17.54 In addition, a performance fee may be charged to 'qualified clients'. Pursuant to Rule 205-3 under the Advisers Act, the term 'qualified client' generally includes, among others:

- any natural person who has at least US$1 million under the management of the adviser;
- any natural person or company with a net worth of at least US$2.1 million;
- any 'qualified purchaser' as defined in the Investment Company Act; and
- certain affiliates and employees of the adviser.

17.55 Each investor in a private investment fund that is relying on the exemption from registration as an investment company provided by Section 3(c)(1) of the Investment Company Act, is deemed to be a client of the adviser for purposes of the performance fee restriction. (For a further discussion of Section 3(c)(1) funds, see **17.06**.) Therefore, each investor in such a fund generally must separately meet the definition of a 'qualified client' in order for the adviser to charge the fund a performance fee.

Books and records to be retained

17.56 Pursuant to Section 204 of the Advisers Act and SEC Rule 204-2, an adviser must maintain and preserve true, complete and current specified books and records and make them available to SEC examiners for inspection. These books and records generally fall within three categories: (i) business records of the adviser; (ii) records of the adviser that relate to the adviser's clients and the advisory activities of the adviser; and (iii) records relating to the adviser's compliance program.

Prohibition on assignments of advisory contracts

17.57 Pursuant to Section 205(a) of the Advisers Act, an advisory contract generally must provide that it may not be 'assigned' without the client's consent. An 'assignment' generally includes any direct or indirect transfer of a contract by an adviser or any transfer of a controlling block of the adviser's outstanding voting securities.

Advertising restrictions

17.58 Advisers are prohibited from using any advertisement that contains any untrue statement of material fact or that is otherwise misleading. The term 'advertisement' is broadly defined to include any notice, circular, letter or other written communication addressed to more than one person, or any notice or other announcement in any publication or by radio or television that offers any investment advisory service. In practice, the advertising rules place limitations on the presentation of investment performance and related data, which must be fairly presented (eg, no cherry-picking of favourable time periods or investments) and adequately supported by reputable back-up data. Additionally, certain practices such as the presentation of testimonials or endorsements are generally viewed by the SEC as inherently misleading and thus subject to greater scrutiny. For example, the SEC generally restricts the publication of any testimonials posted on an investment adviser's own social media site.

Other fiduciary duties

17.59 As fiduciaries, advisers owe their clients a duty to provide only suitable investment advice. In addition, advisers have a duty to seek to obtain 'best execution' of client transactions (ie, advisers must execute securities transactions for clients in such a matter that the clients' total cost or proceeds in each transaction is the most favourable under the circumstances).

Custody requirements

17.60 Advisers with custody of client funds and securities must comply with the custody rule under the Advisers Act. An adviser is deemed to have custody if it holds client funds or securities, has any authority to obtain possession of them, or has the ability to appropriate them. The custody rule details how client funds and securities in the custody of the adviser must be held, and requires an SEC-registered adviser with custody to provide specified information to clients.

17.61 A commonly used exception to the custody rule is the 'private fund audit exception', which generally requires (i) use of a qualified custodian for the fund's custodied assets; (ii) an annual audit of the fund by a qualified independent public accountant; and (iii) delivery of audited financial statements to the fund's investors within 120 days of the fiscal year-end.

Payment of referral fees and related considerations

17.62 Advisers generally are prohibited from paying a cash fee to a third party (solicitor) for referring clients to the adviser, unless the arrangement complies with a number of conditions, such as:

- there must be a written agreement between the adviser and the solicitor detailing the arrangement;
- the solicitor must provide a written disclosure document describing the arrangement to the client; and
- the adviser must receive a written acknowledgement from the client that the client received the adviser's brochure and the solicitor's disclosure document.

17.63 Such prohibition does not apply to private funds. However, separate broker-dealer registration considerations may be necessary when the adviser or an affiliate conducts related broker-dealer activity, which may include finding potential investors or otherwise soliciting securities transactions for compensation. Section 15(a) of the Securities Exchange Act of 1934 requires any person that satisfies the definition of 'broker' or 'dealer' to register with the SEC if it makes use of the US mail or any means or instrumentality of interstate to effect any transactions in, or to induce the purchase or sale of, any security. Generally, the SEC views any affirmative effort by a broker or dealer that is intended to induce transactional business for the broker-dealer as the solicitation of a securities transaction.

Aggregation of client orders

17.64 In directing orders for the purchase and sale of securities to a broker-dealer for execution, an adviser may aggregate or 'bunch' those orders on behalf of two or more of its accounts in accordance with written procedures, so long it is done for purposes of achieving best execution and no client is systematically advantaged or disadvantaged thereby.

Principal transactions and agency cross transactions

17.65 Under Section 206 of the Advisers Act, Advisers may not, as principals, sell securities to or purchase securities from a client without notifying the client and obtaining the client's prior consent to each such transaction. An adviser may act as a broker for both its client and the party on the other side of a brokerage transaction (agency cross transaction) without obtaining the client's prior consent to each such transaction, provided that the adviser obtains a prior consent for these types of transactions from the client and complies with other specified conditions.

Insider trading procedures and duty of supervision

17.66 Advisers must establish, maintain and enforce written policies and procedures designed to prevent the misuse of material, non-public information by the adviser or any of its associated persons. Advisers also have a duty to supervise persons associated with the adviser, with respect to activities performed on the adviser's behalf.

Proxy voting policies and procedures

17.67 Advisers that exercise voting authority over client proxies must:

- adopt policies and procedures reasonably designed to ensure that the adviser votes proxies in the best interests of clients;
- disclose to clients information about those policies and procedures; and

- disclose to clients how they may obtain information on how the adviser has voted their proxies.

17.68 Advisers must also maintain certain records relating to proxy voting.

Code of ethics

17.69 Advisers must adopt a code of ethics that sets forth standards of conduct and require compliance with federal securities laws. Codes of ethics must also address personal trading and require advisers' personnel to report their personal securities holdings and transactions, including those in affiliated mutual funds, and must require personnel to obtain pre-approval of certain investments.

Compliance programme

17.70 Advisers must adopt and implement written policies and procedures reasonably designed to prevent violation of the Advisers Act by the adviser or any of its supervised persons. Advisers must consider their fiduciary and regulatory obligations under the Advisers Act and formalise policies and procedures to address them.

CONCLUDING REMARKS: WHAT ARE THE JURISDICTION'S UNIQUE SELLING POINTS?

17.71 The United States, and the State of Delaware in particular, is a desired domicile for the establishment of private funds because of the extensiveness, stability and relative predictability of its corporate law, which is a perceived benefit for both fund sponsors and investors. Additionally, the State of Delaware offers a suite of tax-efficient vehicles for US investors and relatively simple processes for organising and subsequently re-organising or otherwise amending an entity and/or its terms.

At-a-glance Comparative Table

	Bermuda	BVI	Cayman Islands	France	Germany	Guernsey	Hong Kong	Ireland
Time zone	GMT –4 EST +1	GMT –4 EST +5	GMT –5 EST +4 or +5	GMT +1	GMT +1	GMT EST +5	GMT +8	GMT.
Local currency	BD$	US $	Cayman Islands Dollar (pegged to US Dollar)	Euro	Euro	Sterling	HK$	Euro.
Language	English	English	English	French Fund documentation may be provided in a language other than French usually used in business, if investors targeted are deemed to work with this language	German	English	Chinese/ English	English and Irish
Local stock exchange	The Bermuda Stock Exchange (BSX)	N/A	The Cayman Islands Stock Exchange (CSX)	Euronext Paris	Frankfurt stock exchange and others	The International Securities Exchange (TISE)	Hong Kong Stock Exchange (HKEx)	Irish Stock Exchange
Local service provider required?	A local service provider is required to set up a registered office in Bermuda.	A BVI registered agent, office and authorised representative is required.	No requirements for Cayman based directors or officers, managers, administrators or custodians.	No requirement to appoint a local service provider. For French funds, accountant, custodian and auditor shall be located in France.	A Kapital-verwaltung-gesellschaft must be appointed unless the fund is internally managed. A depositary must be appointed.	Local manager/ administrator. Trustee/custodian usually also required for open-ended funds, but concessions are available for certain types of fund. Closed-ended funds must have at least a local administrator.	Private funds are rarely established in Hong Kong – requirements on service provider depend upon the jurisdiction in which the fund is established. If unit trust is established, there should be at a minimum a trustee and a manager.	Depositary, administrator (if AIFM is not performing administration function itself) and external auditor.

Italy	Jersey	Luxembourg	Malta	Singapore	UAE	UK	USA (Delaware)
GMT + 1 EST +6	GMT	GMT + 1 EST +6	GMT +1. EST +6.	GMT+8	GMT +3	GMT	GMT –5
Euro	Sterling	Euro	Euro	SG$	AED	Sterling	US$
Italian	English	Luxembourgish. French, German and English are commonly spoken	English, Maltese	English	English	English	English
Borsa Italiana S.p.A. (London Stock Exchange Group)	The International Securities Exchange, headquartered in Guernsey, has Jersey offices	Luxembourg Stock Exchange	Malta Stock Exchange (MSE)	Singapore Exchange	NASDAQ Dubai	London Stock Exchange	There is no local stock exchange
Italian funds must have: (i) a manager (SGR or EU asset manager and/ or EU AIFM) and (ii) a custodian authorised in the country of origin of the UCI to undertake mandate as custodian.	Local manager/ administrator. Trustee/custodian usually also required for open-ended funds, but concessions are available for certain types of fund. Closed-ended funds must have at least a local administrator (which will fulfil a 'designated service provider' for certain types of fund).	Depositary with its registered office in Luxembourg, or established in Luxembourg if its registered office is in another EU Member State (except for unregulated funds out of scope of the AIFM Law). The central administration of any UCI or SICAR must be located in Luxembourg.	None for professional investor funds (local representative required for liaison with regulator and compliance).	Yes, the fund is typically managed by a separate fund management entity. Independent custody as well as independent valuation/ reporting of fund assets is also generally required.	Custodian – must be licensed in DIFC, rest of UAE, a DFSA-recognised jurisdiction or a Zone 1 country (see main text for list). Exemption available in case of real estate funds and private equity funds (subject to satisfaction of certain CIR requirements) Auditor – must be registered with the DFSA.	FCA authorised funds and unauthorised funds managed by a full-scope AIFM must have a depositary.	No specific requirements but LLC/LP is required to have a registered agent within Delaware.

	Bermuda	BVI	Cayman Islands	France	Germany	Guernsey	Hong Kong	Ireland
Types of vehicle	Company Limited by shares LLC Partnership Unit Trust	Business company, limited partnership and, for public, private and professional funds, a unit trust.	A wide variety of different types of company, including companies limited by guarantee, unlimited companies, limited duration companies and segregated portfolio companies. In addition, other types of vehicle are available, including partnerships, limited partnerships, unit trusts and trusts.	A wide variety of different types of company, corporate vehicle, contractual funds, and limited partnerships.	Sondervermögen; Spezial-Sondervermögen; Investment stock corporation with fixed or variable capital; Limited investment partnership (Investment-kommanditgesell-schaft).	Unit Trust Company Limited Partnership	Unit trust	Irish Collective Asset-management vehicle (ICAV) Variable capital company (VCC) Unit Trust Investment Limited Partnership (ILP) Common Contractual Fund (CCF) 1907 Act Limited Partnership

Italy	Jersey	Luxembourg	Malta	Singapore	UAE	UK	USA (Delaware)
S.p.A. (ie joint stock company) for management company (SGR), where the fund is not a legal separate entity. Where the fund is a legal separate entity: 'variable capital investment company' (SICAV): open-ended UCI fomed as a joint stock company with variable capital with registered office and general management in Italy with the exclusive purpose of the collective investment of the assets obtained by the offer of its own shares; 'fixed capital investment company' (SICAF): closed-ended UCI constituted in the form of a joint stock company with fixed capital with registered office and general management in Italy with the exclusive purpose of the collective investment of the assets obtained by the offer of its own shares and other financial instruments of equity held by the same.	Unit Trust Company Limited Partnership	'Regulated' private funds may be established using the following three main types of legal structure: SICAV: open-ended or closed-ended investment company whose capital is variable. SICAF: an investment company where the capital is not adjusted automatically to match the net worth of the fund. A SICAV or SICAF may be established under different corporate forms, but also as a limited partnership. FCP: similar to an open or closed-ended unit trust. An FCP does not have a separate legal identity. Limited partnerships. Different types of partnerships exist, including one having no legal personality.	LP Unit Trust SICAV INVCO Private/Public Limited Company	Unit trusts (in almost all cases).	Investment company (limited by shares) Investment partnership (limited partnership) Investment trust (express trust) Protected cell company	FCA authorised vehicles are: Investment Company with Variable Capital (ICVC) (a/k/a Open-Ended Investment Company (OEIC)). Authorised Unit Trust (AUT) and Authorised Contractual Scheme (ACS), the latter being either a Co-ownership Scheme or a Limited Partnership Scheme. Non-FCA authorised are not restricted as to vehicle type but are typically limited partnerships.	An investment vehicle may be organised under Delaware law as, inter alia, a corporation, a general partnership, an LP, an LLP or an LLC.

	Bermuda	BVI	Cayman Islands	France	Germany	Guernsey	Hong Kong	Ireland
Investment restrictions	Typically no restrictions on investment objectives or strategies unless contained in fund documents.	No investment restrictions imposed.	No investment restrictions imposed.	Depending on type of fund and investments undertaken. No restriction for SLP and FPS.	Depends on type of fund. See the KAGB.	Closed-ended: only those imposed by fund's constitution. Open-ended: Class A: detailed rule book applying rules similar to UK-authorised schemes. Classes B and Q: only those imposed by fund's constitution, but subject to the overriding requirement to invest with the aim of spreading risk. Private investment funds (PIFs): only those imposed by fund's constitution (if any).	Private funds are rarely established in Hong Kong – requirements on service provider depend upon the jurisdiction in which the fund is established.	Limited. QIAIFs may not originate loans unless authorised as a Loan Originating QIAIF. QIAIFs are not permitted to acquire securities carrying voting rights which would enable them to exercise significant influence over the management of issuing bodies. This restriction does not apply to holdings in underlying funds or to QIAIFs established as private equity, venture capital or development capital funds. Certain restrictions apply with respect to investment in other funds.

Italy	Jersey	Luxembourg	Malta	Singapore	UAE	UK	USA (Delaware)
UCI's which intend to invest in the following assets must be set up in the form of a close-ended AIF: – unlisted financial instruments (the 20% threshold does not apply); – real estate property, real estate rights, including those derived from leasing real estate contracts with translatable nature and from concessionary relationships, and shareholdings in real estate companies, units/shares of other real estate AIFs, including foreign real-estate AIFs; – receivables and debt securities, including engaging in direct lending activities towards commercial borrowers; – other goods for which there is a market, having a value which may be determined with a periodicity of at least six months.	Closed-ended: only those imposed by fund's constitution, other than for retail funds.	No restrictions in terms of eligible assets for Part II Funds, SIFs and RAIFs. General investment restrictions applicable to Part II Funds are set in CSSF circulars. Additionally, Part II Funds may not invest, in principle, more than 20% of their assets in one single issuer. SIFs may not invest in principle more than 30% of their assets in securities of the same kind issued by the same issuer. The CSSF may grant derogations or, depending on the specific investment policy of the SIF, impose additional investment restrictions. RAIFs must be managed in compliance with the principle of risk spreading. SICARs are not required to operate under the principle of risk-spreading, but are limited in terms of eligible assets.	No regulatory investment restrictions on PIFs unless the PIF is available solely to experienced investors, in which case, certain restrictions on leverage and risk spreading may apply.	Specified in the Code on Collective Investment Schemes. Varies depending on the type of fund, the fund structure and the investments undertaken.	Generally none, unless falling within a specialist class (ie, Islamic Fund, Fund of Funds Feeder Fund Master Fund Private Equity Fund Property Fund REIT Hedge Fund Umbrella Fund Money Market Fund).	For FCA authorised, varies by type of fund.	The Investment Company Act imposes certain limits on the amount of shares that a private fund can purchase from, and sell to, a SEC-registered fund. A fund that purchases 'new issues' securities is subject to significant restrictions under rules of the US Financial Industry Regulatory Authority (FINRA). A fund that transacts in commodity interests (ie, futures contracts or options on futures contracts or commodities and most types of OTC derivatives) to any extent is subject to rules and regulations of the US Commodity Futures Trading Commission (CFTC).

	Bermuda	BVI	Cayman Islands	France	Germany	Guernsey	Hong Kong	Ireland
OECD membership	Yes	Yes, associate member	Yes, associate member	Yes	Yes	Yes	Yes	Yes
Anti-money laundering	Committed to implementing a compliance legal framework and effective compliant instructions from the 2012 revised FATF's 40 Recommendations. Member of CFATF.	BVI has some of the strictest and most stringent AML laws in the world.	Complies with FATF recommendations and other international AML standards. Member of CFATF.	EU fourth anti-money laundering directive. FATF member.	Germany has implemented the Fourth EU Anti-Money Laundering Directive. FATF member.	Member of CFATF. Commitment to implement FATF's 40 Recommendations.	FATF member.	The Criminal Justice (Money Laundering and Terrorist Financing) Act 2010, as amended by Part 2 of the Criminal Justice Act 2013 transposes the Third Money Laundering Directive (2005/60/EC) and its Implementing Directive (2006/70/EC) into Irish law. The European Union (Anti-Money Laundering: Beneficial Ownership and Corporate Entities) Regulations 2016 implements Article 30 of the Fourth Anti-Money Laundering Directive (EU 2015/849). FATF member.

Italy	Jersey	Luxembourg	Malta	Singapore	UAE	UK	USA (Delaware)
Yes	Rated 'largely compliant' with OECD standards.	Yes, associate member	No	No. But Singapore is participating in the OECD initiative on Base Erosion and Profit Sharing.	Non-member, but UAE is a participant in the DAC and party to an IGA on CRS.	Yes	Yes
Except for financial institutions, investors' data to be registered; periodical reporting of amounts greater than €12,500. FATF member.	Complies with FATF recommendations and other international AML standards.	Stringent rules apply and the acceptance of subscription monies from prospective investors is subject to KYC. Luxembourg is currently in the process of implementing the provisions of the Fourth AML Directive 2015/849. FATF member.	Local legislation in line with EU Directive and FATF Recommendations.	FATF member, and of the Asia-Pacific Group on Money Laundering.	Member of MENAFATF.	Complies with EU Fourth Money Laundering Directive. FATF member.	The US has anti-money laundering laws. Historically, the US has been an active participant in the Financial Action Task Force (FATF). Overall, the US anti-money laundering system meets the FATF 40 Recommendations in most respects. New regulations have been, and continue to be, proposed and adopted.

	Bermuda	BVI	Cayman Islands	France	Germany	Guernsey	Hong Kong	Ireland
Tax	'Tax Neutral' jurisdiction. No corporation, profit, withholding, capital gains, or income taxes applicable to an investment fund, share or unit holders, or partners not resident Bermuda. May apply for assurance that should such taxes be implemented, they will not apply for a fixed period (currently 2035).	No income tax, corporation tax, capital gains tax, inheritance tax, gift tax, wealth tax or any other form of direct taxation or withholding. No currency exchange controls.	No income tax, corporation tax, capital gains tax, inheritance tax, gift tax, wealth tax or any other form of direct taxation or withholding. There are no currency exchange controls.	No registration taxes. No stamp tax on subscription, redemption, or sale of fund's shares. FCP: tax transparent; SICAV: tax exempt. Transparency principle: taxation is managed at the level of the investor, depending on the nature of incomes distributed by the fund to such investor. Foreign investors: no tax on capital gain; dividend originated by French assets may be subject to a withholding tax, with a credit tax if treaties are applicable.	Pursuant to the new rules as of 2018, two different tax regimes will apply, one to 'investment funds' and another to 'special investment funds' (which are eligible only for institutional investors). The regime that will be applicable to 'special investment funds' will be similar to the former transparent taxation regime whereas the regime that will be applicable to 'investment funds' will provide for a new opaque taxation of the funds and its German investors. These funds will be subject to corporate tax (15%) at fund level on domestic dividends, income from real estate and other domestic sources (eg interests from bonds and other financial instruments and a lump sum taxation at investor level of 70% of the German basic interest rate will apply.	No profits, income or corporation tax. May apply for assurance that should such taxes be implemented, they will not apply until 2016. US/Bermuda mutual assistance in tax matters.	In relation to an offshore private fund, none of the offshore fund profits tax exemption applies.	Irish authorised and regulated funds are not subject to any taxes on their income (profits) or gains arising on their underlying investments. Non-Irish resident investors are not subject to any Irish withholding taxes in respect of the distribution of payments or on redemption, cancellation or transfer of shares.

Italy	Jersey	Luxembourg	Malta	Singapore	UAE	UK	USA (Delaware)
26% final withholding tax, plus additional exemptions/ derogations.	Standard zero per cent rate of corporate tax for Jersey tax resident companies (subject to limited exceptions not relevant to this area). No withholding tax, capital gains tax, inheritance tax, gift tax, or wealth tax. No currency exchange controls in Jersey.	Regulated funds (except RAIFs investing only in securities representing risk capital) are exempt from corporate income taxes and net wealth tax but are subject to an annual subscription tax. No withholding tax is levied on payments by such Luxembourg private funds to their investors. Subscription tax is an annual tax, payable quarterly and assessed on the total net asset value on the last valuation day of each quarter. An AIF adopting the form of an SCS/ SCSp acting as an investment vehicle remains fully transparent without being subject to municipal business tax as long as its general partner does not hold more than 5% of the partnership interest, without the SCS/SCSp carrying out commercial activities.	CIS: exempt. Non-Maltese Investors: no CGT or income tax.	Single tier corporate tax.	No corporate or income tax; no exchange controls on the remittance of profits or repatriation of capital.	Tax regime relatively complex. Application depends on type of fund.	Investment companies maintaining and managing intangible investments, and collecting and distributing income from such investments or from tangible property outside Delaware, are exempt from Delaware corporate income tax. Investment companies that are not registered under the Investment Company Act are typically organised to be classified as partnerships for US federal income tax purposes. With partnership classification, an investment company is not itself subject to US taxes; rather, its partners or other beneficial owners individually take into account their allocable share of the company's items of income, gains, losses, deductions and tax credits, whether or not distributed. Long-term capital gains are taxable to non-corporate US investors at favourable rates relative to ordinary income and short-term capital gains. Non-US investors escape US tax with respect to capital gains (both long- and short-term), unless the gains are effectively connected with a US trade or business.

Acknowledgements and Contacts

Dechert LLP would like to thank Tonesan Amissah, Matthew Ebbs-Brewer and Gary Harris (Appleby (Bermuda) Limited), Rachael McDonald (Mourant Ozannes, British Virgin Islands), Robert Duggan (Mourant Ozannes, Cayman Islands), Sabina Comis and Antoine Sarailler (Dechert LLP, France), Angelo Lercara (Dechert LLP, Germany), Darren Bacon (Mourant Ozannes, Guernsey), Michael Wong (Dechert, Hong Kong), Jeff Mackey and Lindsay Trapp (Dechert, Ireland), Francesco di Carlo and Camilla Fornasaro (Craca Di Carlo Guffanti Pisapia Tatozzi & Associati, Italy), Tim Morgan and Eleanor Mulligan (Mourant Ozannes, Jersey), Marc Seimetz, Johan Terblanche and Jean-Baptiste Juvin (Dechert LLP, Luxembourg), André Zerafa (GANADO Advocates, Malta), Eric Chan (Shook Lin & Bok LLP, Singapore), Phillip Sacks and Edward Brown (Dechert LLP, United Arab Emirates), Richard Heffner, Ed Kingsbury, Daniel Hawthorne and Nicolas Kokkinos (Dechert LLP, United Kingdom) and Adrienne Baker and Timothy Spangler (Dechert LLP, United States) for their kind assistance in preparing this book.

Tonesan Amissah
Partner, Appleby (Bermuda) Limited
Canon's Court
22 Victoria Street
PO Box HM 1179
Hamilton
HM EX
Bermuda
Tel: +1 441 298 3201
tamissah@applebyglobal.com

Rachael McDonald
Partner, Mourant Ozannes
Palm Grove House
PO Box 4857
Road Town
Tortola
British Virgin Islands
Tel: +1 284 852 1722
rachael.mcdonald@mourantozannes.com

Robert Duggan
Partner, Mourant Ozannes
6th Floor, 125 Old Broad Street
London
EC2N 1AR
United Kingdom
Tel: +44 20 7796 7622
robert.duggan@mourantozannes.com

Sabina Comis
Partner, Dechert LLP
32 rue de Monceau
75008 Paris
France
Tel: +33 1 57 57 81 66
sabina.comis@dechert.com

Antoine Sarailler
Partner, Dechert LLP
32 rue de Monceau
75008 Paris
France
Tel: +33 1 57 57 80 16
antoine.sarailler@dechert.com

Angelo Lercara
Partner, Dechert LLP
Skygarden
Erika-Mann-Straße 5
Munich 80636
Germany
Tel: +49 89 21 21 63 22
angelo.lercara@dechert.com

Darren Bacon
Partner, Mourant Ozannes
PO Box 186
1 Le Marchant Street
St Peter Port
Guernsey
GY1 4HP
Channel Islands
Tel: +44 1481 731 503
darren.bacon@mourantozannes.com

Michael Wong
Partner, Dechert
31/F Jardine House
One Connaught Place
Central
Hong Kong
Tel: +852 3518 4738
michael.wong@dechert.com

Jeff Mackey
Partner, Dechert
3 George's Dock
IFSC
Dublin D01 X5X0
Ireland
Tel: +353 1 436 8521
jeff.mackey@dechert.com

Francesco di Carlo
Partner, Craca Di Carlo Guffanti Pisapia Tatozzi & Associati
Via degli Omenoni 2 20121 Milano Italy
Tel: +39 02 3041 331
f.dicarlo@5lex.it

Tim Morgan
Partner, Mourant Ozannes
22 Grenville Street
St Helier
Jersey
JE4 8PX
Channel Islands
Tel: +44 1534 676 817
tim.morgan@mourantozannes.com

Marc Seimetz
Partner, Dechert (Luxembourg) LLP
1 Allée Scheffer
B.P. 709
Luxembourg L-2017
Tel: +352 45 62 62 23
marc.seimetz@dechert.com

André Zerafa
Partner, GANADO Advocates
59 Strait Street
Valletta
VLT 1434
Malta
Tel: +356 2123 5406
azerafa@ganadoadvocates.com

Eric Chan
Partner, Shook Lin & Bok LLP
1 Robinson Road
#18-00 AIA Tower
Singapore 048542
Tel: +65 6439 788
eric.chan@shooklin.com

Phillip Sacks
Partner, Dechert LLP
Unit 501, Level 5
Precinct Building 2
Dubai International Financial Centre
PO Box 506675
Dubai
Tel: +971 4 425 6340
phillip.sacks@dechert.com

Richard Heffner
Partner, Dechert LLP
160 Queen Victoria Street
London
EC4V 4QQ
United Kingdom
Tel: +44 207 184 7665
richard.heffner@dechert.com

Adrienne Baker
Partner, Dechert LLP
One International Place
40th Floor, 100 Oliver Street
Boston
MA 02110-2605
United States
Tel: +1 617 728 7151
adrienne.baker@dechert.com

Timothy Spangler
Partner, Dechert LLP
Orange County
650 Town Center Drive
Suite 700
Costa Mesa
CA 92626-1905
United States
Tel: +1 949 442 6044

Silicon Valley
2440 W. El Camino Real
Suite 700, Mountain View
CA 94040-1499
United States
Tel: +1 650 813 4803
timothy.spangler@dechert.com

Index

[All references are to paragraph number]